EASY LIVING

EASY LIVING

The Rise of the Home Office

ELIZABETH A. PATTON

RUTGERS UNIVERSITY PRESS
New Brunswick, Camden, and Newark, New Jersey, and London

Library of Congress Cataloging-in-Publication Data

Names: Patton, Elizabeth, 1975- author.
Title: Easy living : the rise of the home office / Elizabeth A. Patton.
Description: New Brunswick : Rutgers University Press, 2020. | Includes bibliographical references and index.
Identifiers: LCCN 2019045293 | ISBN 9781978802223 (Paperback) | ISBN 9781978802230 (Hardback) | ISBN 9781978802261 (PDF) | ISBN 9781978802247 (epub) | ISBN 9781978802254 (Mobi)
Subjects: LCSH: Home offices—Social aspects—United States—History—20th century.
Classification: LCC HD62.38 .P38 2020 | DDC 306.3—dc23
LC record available at https://lccn.loc.gov/2019045293

A British Cataloging-in-Publication record for this book is available from the British Library.

∞ The paper used in this publication meets the requirements of the American National Standard for Information Sciences—Permanence of Paper for Printed Library Materials, ANSI Z39.48-1992.

www.rutgersuniversitypress.org

Manufactured in the United States of America

CONTENTS

EASY LIVING

INTRODUCTION

> As a general rule, in this private space one rarely works, except at that indispensable work of nourishment, of cleaning, and of conviviality that gives a human form to the succession of days and to the presence of others. . . . Here one invites one's family and neighbors and avoids one's enemies or boss, as long as the society's power respects the fragile symbolic barrier between public and private. —Michel de Certeau

> The home is evolving in step with the demands we place upon it.
> —Avi Friedman and David Krawitz

On July 11, 2015, the HGTV *House Hunters Renovations* episode "A Newlywed Buffalo Couple Tackles Their First Renovation" (S6:E11) was aired, featuring a young professional couple who want to find their first home in one of the hot gentrifying neighborhoods in Buffalo, New York. Like most millennials, their budget is limited, but they want a home that will accommodate a home office, a large kitchen, and enough bedrooms for future children. For Spencer, an attorney, a house without a finished attic or an extra bedroom for a home office is a deal breaker. He proclaims that he needs a quiet space to work every day, away from his wife and their dogs. He insists on spending $6,000 to finish the attic, even though the cost is beyond their budget. Kanika, an English teacher, insists that their agent find a home with a big, open kitchen that she can renovate. Kanika explains that she loves to create gourmet meals and that a kitchen that meets her standards is necessary because she does all of the cooking. She also needs a space to work but settles for a desk in the guest bedroom. After watching just a few hours of *House Hunters Renovations,* one gets the impression that middle-class professionals are preoccupied with work and recognize the necessity to incorporate their work life into their private life by finding housing that allows for a home office or reduces their commute to work.

Since 2008 I have noted ubiquitous references to home offices and middle-class consumers' desire for extra bedrooms (to use as home offices / guest rooms) in mass media narratives and on popular lifestyle channels such as HGTV. In fact, observations about the merging of the public and private spheres are prominent themes in contemporary mass media.[1] Sociologist Dalton Conley argues in *Elsewhere, U.S.A.* that the breakdown of the boundaries between work and leisure—what he refers to as "weisure"—in everyday life since the end of the twentieth century is especially problematic, as this transformation has subsequently affected social identity for the middle class and consequently for the broader society.[2] As Conley puts it, "Technological gadgets structure family life."[3] Despite public concern about work-life balance, there is also ambivalence within public discourse about the role of technology and work in the private sphere. This is evidenced by the increasing use of new communication technologies in the form of smartphones; the emergence of smart home technologies such as Amazon Echo, which combines consumption, entertainment, security, and utility within the home; and the growth of residential Wi-Fi to make work, consumption, and entertainment increasingly accessible within the private sphere.[4]

The quest for work-life balance is a prominent theme in contemporary mass media, especially for professional women. Consider the support for and criticism of Sheryl Sandberg's *Lean In: Women, Work, and the Will to Lead* (2015) and Anne-Marie Slaughter's *Why Women Still Can't Have It All* (2015) in public and academic discourse. Today, advocates frame the decision to work at home as a holistic one to achieve work-life balance or, more accurately, work-life integration in a capitalist system that demands longer hours and increased productivity from its workers. Home offices have become "utopian solutions to tensions felt in everyday life."[5] In public discourse, working at home as a form of work-life integration is framed as a means of agency in managing the shifting boundaries between work and personal life. Communication technology such as smartphones and video chat services, and the growth of residential Wi-Fi, have created innovative ways for employees to creatively pursue professional goals and be flexible and productive workers by, for example, telecommuting and collaborating with co-workers and clients within the private sphere. However, there is mounting public discourse about the negative effects of professionals increasingly working at home outside of traditional work hours and the potential breakdown of long-standing social and family ties. Still, many people in the United States feel compelled to work from home. Where does this expectation come from? If we are always working, does the distinction between working at home or in the office really matter? And if so, for whom? Was there ever a time in modern history when the home was used only as a space for reproduction and leisure?

Raymond Williams's term "mobile privatization" explains this contradiction: simultaneous desires for increased mobilization and increased privatization.[6] Williams employed this term to explain increased privatization exemplified by the domestic sphere and spatial mobility because of technologies of transportation and communication, and traces this contradiction to the late nineteenth-century emphasis on the private sphere. Since its conception, the public/private distinction has persisted, despite evidence to the contrary. In fact, the terms "private" and "public" are slippery to deploy theoretically and difficult to untangle in practice, even though the dichotomy persists in Western culture. Feminist scholar Nancy Fraser claims that many scholars, especially feminists, have used the concept of the public sphere to "refer to everything that is outside the domestic or familial sphere."[7] This use in turn conflates what she identifies as three distinct concepts: (1) the spaces of public discourse, (2) the state, and (3) the "official economy of paid employment."[8] Therefore, the private sphere is constructed through conceptions of the public sphere and has inherited similar conflations (e.g., work in the home and mass media as domesticated spaces of public discourse). Despite the continual use of the terms "public" and "private" and the persistent narrative of the home as the material space of the private sphere, the distinction between private and public spheres is difficult to preserve and therefore often contradictory.

This book examines how the idea of working within the home was constructed and disseminated in popular culture by the communication and real estate industries through U.S. mass media during the twentieth century. How did people in the United States come to believe that working at home is possible, desirable, and productive, and something that could potentially help a family achieve work-life balance within the context of a historically novel public/private binary that emerged with the Industrial Revolution? I argue that even though industrial capitalism introduced the public and private spheres as a principle of the political economy (wage labor vs. reproductive labor), the emergence of the home office demonstrates that the dichotomy collapsed in practice due to social and economic forces. Home-based work practices and communication technologies transformed social and labor relations within and outside the home by disrupting ideological spatial divisions between the sites of leisure (formerly coded as unproductive by disregarding unpaid labor) and sites of market labor.

This book looks at the politics of media practices in relation to work and leisure, the politics of gendered space, and the politics of media representations of class and race through its primary object of study: the home office. I use the term "home-based work" in this book to draw attention to all forms of work that are practiced in the home and ultimately contribute to the market (public sphere). A historical examination of different forms of labor in the home reveals how cultural perceptions of what counts as work have changed, even though rhetorical distinctions persist in public discourse. This becomes evident if you consider the types of work that are done in the home, whether paid or unpaid. In this book I examine four forms of home-based work: (1) compensated market work, that is, work historically identified with professional men and the public sphere that was conducted in the study or home office; (2) paid part-time market work that was conducted in the home by women; (3) uncompensated household management, categorized as "women's work," to maintain the home; and (4) children's educational homework or chores in exchange for an allowance.

I demonstrate how the typewriter, telephone, computer, and real estate industries, along with cultural producers and critics, embraced the ideology of separate spheres to support the existing economic order and also started to break down this symbolic dichotomy to promote consumerism. For example, during the 1950s most advertisers of domestic laborsaving technologies operated under the belief that female audiences were primarily working at home as homemakers. However, typewriter companies marketed the use of portable typewriters for wage-earning opportunities in the home to the same homemakers. Ultimately, these actions supported the development of the new emerging economic order—the knowledge economy—associated with no-collar workers and the merging of work and leisure.[9] Overall, the notion of the home as a space that exists solely in the private sphere is a myth because the social meaning of the home and its market value in relation to the public sphere are intricately linked. An examination of the U.S. home, specifically the home office as a politicized workspace, reveals that the growth of U.S. consumerism necessitated the expansion of market labor in the home. Therefore, this book problematizes the ideological narrative of the ideal home and the historical narrative of the private sphere as a space of exclusion from wage-based labor. It reveals that the current discourse on the ever-present status of work in the home has a longer history and argues that people in the United States were encouraged through public discourse to believe that by working at home they could achieve work-life balance. However, this book is also an attempt to remind readers that work is work—even if you love your job and consider it a part of your identity, and it can be done from the comfort of your bedroom.

A complete history of the home and all the representations and notions that define it is well beyond the scope of a single book. Therefore, it is necessary to be clear about the limitations of this study and to define its parameters. I draw evidence from national magazines and newspapers, television and film, housing floor plans, and marketing and advertising materials from the housing, telecommunications, and office technology industries. I chose this approach to demonstrate that public discourse reflected changing concepts over time about what it means to work in the home. In other words, my aim is to historicize contemporary discourse about the role of work within the home. Therefore, I have predominantly used interpretive methods grounded in archival research in order to understand the social, cultural, and historical contexts of the emergence of the home office and the mediated practices within.

This book is organized around the technological, political-economic, and social forces that have shaped shifting public discourse on working at home in the twentieth century. These historical frames determined how persuasive actors such as telephone companies, home design advocates, cultural critics, and others shaped public discourse on home and work, but also explain how our attitudes about the role of work within the home are mediated. Part 1, "Where Does Work Belong? Toward a New Conception of Home," considers the technological and economic forces that influenced the emergence of the private/public dichotomy and the corresponding changes in domestic architecture and the meaning of work at home during the Second Industrial Revolution (c. 1875–1930) in the United States. These forces include the rise of industrial capitalism, unprecedented urbanization, and the invention of the telephone and typewriter. I have followed three primary paths of inquiry in this examination of the home as a space of work: the emergence of the home office, the role of gender and class in home-based work practices, and the impact of communication technology use in the home.

Chapters 1 and 2 delineate the socioeconomic legacy of nineteenth-century concepts of the home and the historical evolution of the bedroom-study as a designated space for privacy within the middle-class home. I approached my examination of the private sphere considering Roger Silverstone and Eric Hirsch's claim that the private sphere must be understood in relation to the public sphere.[10] Since the Industrial Revolution, bolstering the private sphere has been proposed as a safeguard against the perceived threat of new technology and the alienating force of the market economy. Therefore, I started my examination of the domestic sphere in relation to the emergence of the public sphere and the market economy. I look at floor plans of typical homes of the professional class (e.g., business owners, doctors, writers, etc.) to illustrate how the home became a fundamental part of bourgeois identity formation instead of just a place for sleep and reproduction. I trace the evolution of the generically named "chamber" room in floor plans into the "library," "gentlemen's parlor," "study," or "den" to explain how it became a space of masculinity and consequently a workspace for the male head of the household.

I consider the ideological history of the domestic sphere in relation to the family economy to examine how the ideal middle-class family household no longer functioned as an economic unit but became the focus of private life during the Second Industrial Revolution in the United States. I demonstrate that the home has always been a space of work despite ideological constructions to the contrary. To make this argument, I examine how middle-class social reformers writing for newspapers and popular magazines in the early twentieth century framed household labor practices of the working class. Specifically, I examine market-based work within the home as a violation of the values of the idealized family, where women and children were encouraged to divorce themselves from the world of work that was transforming the public sphere.

In chapters 3 and 4, I look at early marketing of the telephone and the typewriter for residential use to understand the origins of contemporary attitudes about the gendered role of market labor within the home. The introduction of the telephone and the typewriter into the home played a crucial role in making possible the merger of the public and private spheres, as these were the first modern communication technologies to penetrate the private zones (i.e., bedrooms) of the house. Although initially most telephones appear to have been installed in the public spaces of the home, there is visual evidence that the telephone migrated into the bedroom as early as the turn of the twentieth century. Telephone and typewriter companies marketed their products as necessary tools to help women successfully manage the home and as an opportunity to participate in the official market economy within the ideological confines of domesticity through home-based work. The presence of market-based work in the home and the advancement of such work by career experts and companies such as Remington and Bell Telephone reveal the cultural and economic shifts that contradicted gendered notions of the role of the private sphere. Consequently, the presence of the official economy and communication technology practices in the bedroom-study transformed the home both physically and conceptually by employing the terms "public sphere" and "private sphere" not in binary opposition but as nested in one another and consequently influencing each other.

In part 2, "The Consumption of Office Practices and Communication Technology in the Postwar Middle-Class Home," I examine the postwar period, when the home became a fertile ground for consumer practices traditionally associated with work life. I focus on suburban bedroom communities in the United States between 1946 and 1968. The social and political-economic forces that shaped public discourse on home-based work include rapid economic expansion and the emergence of consumer culture, the growth of the suburbs and the expansion of the middle class, and the re-emergence of the "cult of domesticity." I draw evidence from popular culture, mass media, and marketing and advertising materials to demonstrate that postwar suburban consumers received conflicting messages about the public/private dichotomy.

In chapter 5, I focus on public discourse on the role of the suburban home in promoting the concept of togetherness, which represented the re-emergence of the cult of domesticity and the primacy of family life over work during the postwar period. The home was represented as a space of leisure, divorced from market labor. However, advertisements for residential use of telephones and typewriters and representations of work within the home on postwar television and in films often contradicted this message. As evidence, I present efforts by the housing, telecommunications, and office technology industries to promote wage-based labor within the suburban home to expand their consumer markets.

In chapter 6, I look at public discourse in national newspapers regarding the relationship between home-based labor practices and middle-class homemakers and representations of gendered work within the home on postwar television and film. Working at home was framed by communication technology companies and popular culture as fitting into the life pattern of white middle-class homemakers who worked in the public sphere before marriage and left the labor force after having children.

Chapters 7 and 8 analyze subthemes that emerge from my analysis of the home as a space of work. These include the enculturation of the work ethic in middle-class childhood spaces and representations of domestic spaces for fathers in popular culture. An examination of the postwar U.S. home, specifically the study/home office as a technologized workspace, reveals that the growth of U.S. consumerism advanced the expansion of market labor in the home. In the quest to expand their markets, communication technology companies did not see the private sphere as out of bounds despite public discourse to the contrary. These chapters examine how the importance of homework for children and for men to have an office away from their office in the city was constructed and disseminated by business industries via mass media during the postwar period. I demonstrate how this discourse relates to broader social and economic forces (e.g., the rise of the knowledge worker and the no-collar worker in the postindustrial economy) and to the public discourse on work-life balance and flexibility in the workplace that has emerged today. Collectively, these chapters demonstrate that because of growing consumerism, the private sphere became another space to extract use value within the system of capitalism.

Part 3, "The Birth of the Live-Work Lifestyle," considers the relationship between second-wave feminism and the sexual revolution in the United States (c. 1958–1970) and representations of urban homes as a space of work and leisure. These social and political forces propelled the emergence of the knowledge-cultural professional in the 1990s and new ideas about what it means to live the good life in relation to work and leisure practices within middle- and upper-middle-class homes in the city. In this part, I primarily look at national publications such as *Cosmopolitan* and *Playboy,* as well as popular television shows and films that featured single professionals living the good life in the city. I historicize the growing importance of class status in relation to lifestyle. This includes the types of occupations and the homes that were celebrated in popular culture during the 1960s. Ultimately, these representations reflected the paradigm shift to the knowledge economy and foretold the prominent visibility of the knowledge-cultural class in today's economy.

Chapter 9 looks at representations of the bachelor pad in popular culture, which centered masculinity in the space of the city. I argue that the relationship between cities and representations of masculinity during the 1960s should be understood within the context of work, leisure, and the home. For example,

Playboy promoted an image of the urban apartment as a place for young and primarily white, single professional men to experience domesticity and sexual freedom and to increase career opportunities. Chapter 10 focuses on the counterpart of the "playboy" bachelor, the "single girl." Helen Gurley Brown's *Sex and the Single Girl* (1962) and *Cosmopolitan* magazine, as well as popular bedroom comedy films like *Pillow Talk* (1959), contributed to gendered definitions of the good life in public discourse and constructed the—albeit brief—possibility of sexual freedom and career fulfillment for single white women before marriage and eventual life in the suburbs. This chapter also looks at representations of the telephone in undoing the spatial divisions between domestic sites of leisure, reproduction (sex/pleasure), and wage-based labor for women during the 1960s and 1970s. Chapter 11 focuses on shifts in the construction of domestic space and the promotion of communication technologies in the home that occurred in relation to the ideal space of the bachelor pad in the 1960s. I look at media representations of ideal urban domesticity that actively incorporated aspects of the public sphere—work life and entertainment—to understand how "Do what you love" has become the motto of our time. Popular culture laid the groundwork for contemporary definitions of work-life balance by redefining the good life to include the possibility of combining work and leisure within the city apartment. Collectively, these chapters argue that representations of urban domesticity and the influx of communication technologies into the home were indicative of wide-ranging social changes in the arrangement of market-based work in relation to the domestic sphere.

Part 4, "Neoliberal Domestic Workspaces," builds on the discussion of the emerging knowledge-cultural class in chapter 11 to examine how neoliberalism shaped public discourse on the relationship between home and work. As evidence, I look at popular discourse in national magazines and newspapers, popular films and television shows, and floor plans, as well as marketing and advertising materials from computer companies such as Apple and IBM that feature home offices. This part examines changes in the labor market caused by the shift from an industry-based economy to the information economy to trace the emergence of the knowledge-cultural class that is at the center of public discourse on work-life balance today. It covers the social, political-economic, and technological forces that define the transition to the postindustrial period (c. 1972–1995). These include increasing economic inequality, significant changes to family structure, the shift to the postindustrial economy, and the emergence of personal computing.

In chapter 12, I focus on the adoption of personal computers in middle-class homes during the 1980s. I look at the marketing of personal computers to professionals as a way to achieve work-life balance and promote educational goals for children, and as a form of family leisure to explain how the home office became a natural space to locate these new instruments of work and leisure. Chapter 13 examines the rise of the new middle class in the knowledge economy and the role of the home office in facilitating new ideas about work-life balance. I look at representations of professional families in popular culture, newspapers, and national magazines that validated women's decision to work outside the home by allowing men to both support their families financially and adopt a central role in the domestic sphere. I argue that the issue of access to work-life balance for middle-class families is directly related to socioeconomic status and is obscured by changing conceptions of work driven by neoliberalism that ultimately are detrimental to feminism and worker solidarity in the postindustrial knowledge economy. Finally, in chapter 14, I consider the loft, the material embodiment of work life within the domestic sphere. In the loft, public and private spaces collapse—the bedroom and workspace become interchangeable space in the home. I examine advertisements, newspapers, and popular representations of loft spaces and gentrification in New York City starting in the 1970s to determine the changes in the relationship between labor and leisure in the knowledge economy and the ascendancy of the knowledge-cultural class.

Overall, this book historicizes contemporary discourse about the role of work within the private sphere for middle-class professionals. Feminist scholarship has repeatedly demonstrated that boundaries between public and private are not rigid.[11] As Lynn Spigel argues, "Instead of a total collapse of private and public spheres, we are faced with a much more contradictory environment where different models of domesticity exist in emergent, residual, and dominant forms."[12] Perhaps it is necessary to follow Susan Gal and Gail Kligman's recommendation that the private/public binary is "best understood as a distinction that can be used to characterize, categorize, organize and contrast spaces, institutions, groups, identities, discourses, activities, interactions, relations. Where one draws the line between public and private is generally a political contest."[13] Therefore, critically examining the private sphere by looking at the presence of market employment or the incorporation of the "official economy" in the home reveals the ideological determinants that socially construct domestic space in relation to the public sphere. The following chapters focus on the presence of the official economy and the role of communication technology in transforming the home both physically and conceptually by employing "public sphere" and "private sphere" not in terms of a dichotomous relationship, in opposition to each other, but as nested in one another and consequently influencing each other, thereby challenging existing understandings of work, leisure, and domestic spaces.

PART 1

WHERE DOES WORK BELONG?

Toward a New Conception of Home

1 • THE HOME AND ITS FUNCTION

The American home is the material realization of ideals. The contemporary belief that true happiness, intimacy, and fulfillment are primarily located within the private institution of the family (embodied by the home) has its roots in the late nineteenth century, but it did not fully emerge until the twentieth century. New technologies in transportation, communication, and labor-saving devices, as well as urban services and amenities, facilitated the design and management of the new middle-class home. Furthermore, the household labor practices of the working class, the introduction of the telephone, the devaluation of middle-class women's household labor, and the continued presence of productive labor in the study / home office of the businessman problematizes the notion of the eradication of productive labor in the private sphere. In reality, the American home remained a space of work.

PRE-INDUSTRIAL HOMES

To demonstrate how the home in actuality is a space of work, I begin with an examination of the family economy in preindustrial America, when a family's public and private activities (reproduction and production) were conducted in the household in the great hall or other large multipurpose rooms.[1] In 1775, during the American War of Independence, Abigail Adams wrote to her husband, John, describing the difficulties she encountered as home manager. The letter is very revealing about women's lives and work during that period, as well as the function of the home. In the following excerpt from her letter dated July 16, Abigail tells John about her difficulty in accommodating boarders:

> Mr. Trot I have accommodated by removeing the office into my own chamber, and after being very angry and sometimes persuaideding I obtaind the mighty concession of the Bedroom, but I am now so crouded as not to have a Lodging for a Friend that calls to see me. I must beg you would give them warning to seek

> a place before Winter. Had that house been empty I could have had an 100 a year for it. Many [persons] had applied before Mr. Trot, but I wanted some part of it myself, and the other part it seems I have no command of.[2]

To accommodate Mr. Trot, a boarder, Abigail consolidates the office, presumably John's space of business, into her own chamber. Eventually, the house became so crowded accommodating boarders that she had to give up her bedroom and forego entertaining friends.

In preindustrial America, a family's public and private activities were conducted in the household. All members of the household pitched in to support the family's livelihood during this pre-wage period, which is in stark contrast to an economy based on wages that removed men's paid labor from the home and devalued women and children's economic contributions to the household. Contrary to the persistent myth that the majority of preindustrial families lived with extended families, households generally consisted of the nuclear family and unrelated individuals who reflected the social station or economic activities of the family.[3] Nonfamily members lived and often slept in the same rooms as and worked alongside family members in conducting domestic-based business in the household.[4] There was no expectation of privacy, as rooms served multiple functions, with family members and sometimes strangers coming and going at will.[5] In seventeenth-century America, there were no bedrooms, only multipurpose family rooms where all members of the family slept on makeshift beds.[6] In colonial America, the majority of colonists lived in one- or two-room homes.[7] The bedroom itself did not emerge until the latter half of the eighteenth century. Because there were no rooms dedicated exclusively to sleeping and sexual activity, consequently there was little expectation of privacy for most of the population. The house represented more than a dwelling for domestic activities and was understood as a "site of production, as a welfare agency and correctional institution, as an educational institution, and as a place for religious worship."[8]

A space for productive work was considered in representations of ideal home design. Author and designer John Claudius Loudon, who influenced the Cottage Movement in the United States and Britain, argued that housing design should be practical and espouse democratic ideals. He believed that architects should design homes based on "theory formed on nature . . . and on the changing conditions of society, rather than on . . . the rules of former ages."[9] In *An Encyclopedia of Cottage, Farm, and Villa Architecture and Furniture,* Loudon describes and illustrates in detail houses that he believed were functional and aesthetically pleasing, houses that ultimately "improve[d] the dwellings of the great mass of society."[10] These houses often featured public rooms, such as offices or workrooms, within the dwelling. One such house is the "English Cottage Dwelling of Two Stories for a Man and His Wife and with Servant and Two or Three Children, with a Cow-House and Pigsty." The house is a modest, middle-class dwelling that Loudon designates as in a style suitable for a typical bailiff in Britain or a small proprietor in America.

This floor plan contains an office or tool-house, and a courtyard with a cow- and henhouse (see figure 1.1). Upon entering the house, a visitor would immediately encounter spaces that were then considered public work spaces and private/public service spaces instead of family spaces, such as the living room or parlor of modern and contemporary houses. The rooms visible from the entrance lobby are the kitchen and office, with the parlor accessible through the kitchen. The bedrooms, the private zone of the house, occupy the entirety of the second floor,

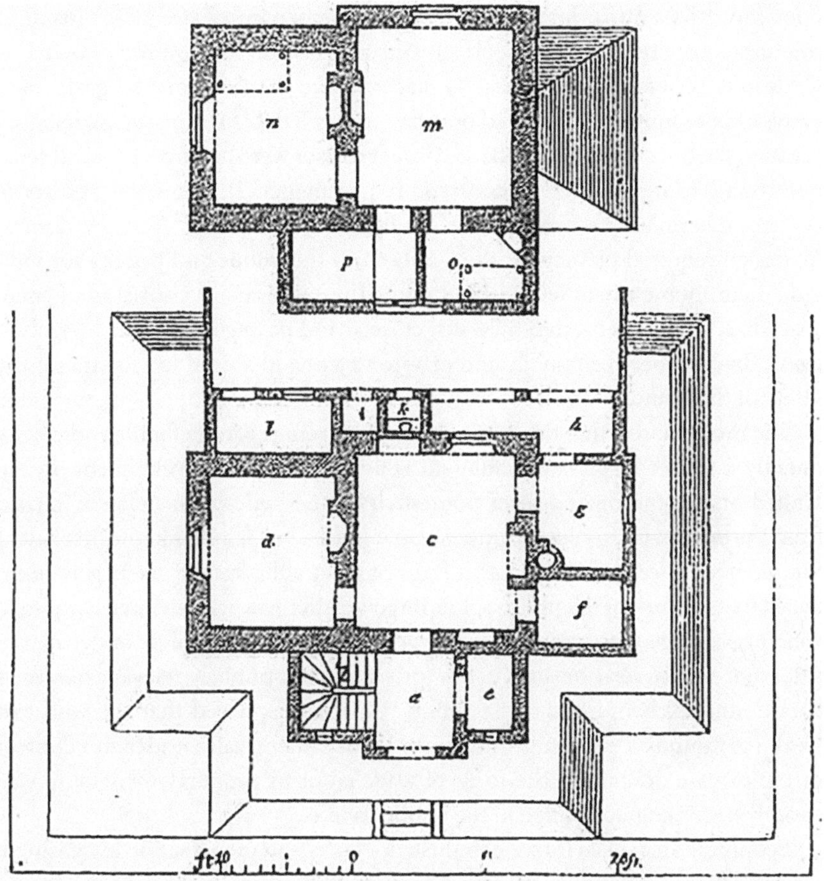

FIGURE 1.1 Floor plan for English cottage dwelling of two stories. Ground floor: *a*—an entrance lobby; *b*—staircase; *c*—kitchen; *d*—parlour; *e*—tool-house or office for paying men; *f*—pantry and dairy; *g*—back kitchen; *h*—shed for wood and fuel; *i*—dusthole; *k*—privy; and *l*—cow-house, with hen-house over. Bedroom floor: *m*—best bed-room; *n*—second bed-room; *o*—third bed-room; and *p*—a stair. (*Source*: John Claudius Loudon [1834], in *The Encyclopedia of Cottage, Farm, Villa Architecture.*)

which is typical of houses after the late seventeenth century. The toilet is located in the courtyard, accessible through the back of the house. It is not until later in the nineteenth century when domestic technologies such as plumbing are invented that the bathroom migrates to the private zones of the house.

THE PRIVATE SPHERE

As Sharon Zukin observes, the homes that the middle class build reflect "new ideas about space, and what it represents, in each time period."[11] During the nineteenth century, the typical American house in towns and cities transformed again. For example, the layout of homes changed as rooms were arranged to open into a hall, mirroring a house arranged to open into a street. The inside of the home now reflected the social organization of the community. Michel de Certeau described private spaces as places where the fundamental gestures of "ways of operating" are deployed on a day-to-day basis.[12] During the nineteenth century, the houses of the middle and upper classes were organized around separate rooms to meet different domestic requirements. The function of a room could be determined by its name (e.g., dining room, bedroom).[13] This new domestic design required privacy for the family from the public and privacy for individual family members within the home. The ideal layout consisted of small specialized rooms separated by walls, closets, and passageways, which symbolized a division between public and private spaces and a need to retreat into the safety of the home.[14]

The modern idea that the home should be a refuge for the family and consequently a source of private fulfillment is a relatively new development. In the United States, the new ideal of domesticity—the concept of home as retreat from the public sphere—fully emerged in middle-class families in the first half of the nineteenth century. Understandings of the public sphere are largely influenced by the work of the philosopher Jürgen Habermas, who defined the public sphere as a place where private persons came together as a public to debate the rules that govern relationships in the "privatized but publicly relevant sphere of commodity exchange and social labor."[15] Habermas noted that the world of work (commodity exchange and social labor) historically under the control of the private domain in the form of wage labor or property ownership was steadily becoming objectified in the public sphere.

Economic and social forces of industrialization and urbanization increasingly removed formal labor from the home. Consequently, the household ceased to be the center of the family economy. Writing about the nineteenth century, Walter Benjamin succinctly stated, "For the private individual, the place of dwelling is for the first time opposed to the place of work."[16] The official economy was in opposition to the space of domesticity, establishing the conditions for the public/private dichotomy. Representing human activity in spatial terms, the public sphere was the location for productive labor, while the private sphere became the space for rejuvenation, reproduction, and consumption. The ideal home in the nineteenth century became a space for entertainment, such as listening to music, reading, and spending time with the family.[17] The house was constructed as an exclusive space that protected the privacy of individuals by separating family members from outsiders and public space from private space. Therefore, the single-family home represented the ideal home.

As historian Jeanne Boydston asserts, "Middle-class families went to great lengths to attempt to make their homes refuges from the rest of society" by separating spaces of business from spaces of dwelling and removing household members typically seen in the preindustrial economy (e.g., apprentices, boarders and journeymen) from the home.[18] The home came to be thought of as a safe haven from the social pressures of the outside world and symbolized family values and morality. The "cult of domesticity" or "cult of true womanhood" established the Victorian middle-class home as the separate, proper sphere for women and for men, a refuge from the hostility, violence, contamination, and strangeness associated with the city and modern life.[19] This new ideology could be found in advice books, women's magazines, literature, and newspapers.[20]

In the United States, the nineteenth century witnessed a boom in the fortunes of the middle and upper classes. The home became a key institution of industrial capitalism. Houses of the rich generally increased in size and, for the bourgeoisie, separate rooms for distinct domestic functions became important. Three zones of domestic activity emerged in the typical home during the mid-nineteenth century: the social, private, and service zones. The areas open to the public became the social zone of the house. The service zone included the kitchen and laundry areas. Finally, the sleeping and personal hygiene areas emerged as the private zones of the house. The master bedroom and older children's bedrooms moved to the private zone, often on the upper floors of the home. The staircase to the second floor was moved to the side of the house instead of occupying a central position in relation to the entrance hall.[21] Guest and servant bedrooms were moved to the back of the first floor or to attic levels, preserving the privacy of the family and consequently separating the private zone from the social and service zones.[22]

The modern domestic organization of space served the specific activities of individual family members. For example, homes were designed with sitting or sewing rooms for women, nurseries for children, and libraries or study rooms for men (see figure 1.2). Note that the billiard room takes up the majority of the space compared to the girl's room. This is a manifestation of what Richard Sennett claims is "the private realm [seeking] order and clarity through applying the division of labor to the emotional realm of the family, partitioning its experience into rooms."[23] However, as Clifford Clark recognizes, there is a difference between what happened in practice and what social reformers during the period

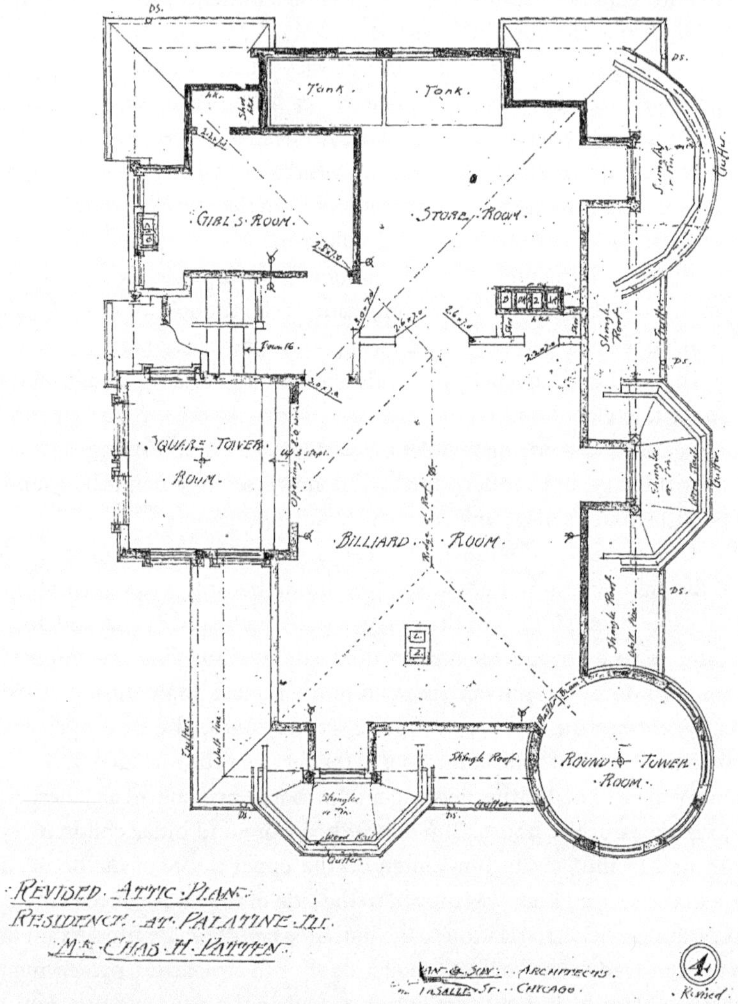

FIGURE 1.2 Floor plan for the attic of the Charles H. Patten House located in Palatine, Illinois, built in 1898 by Julius F. Wegman. (*Source*: National Register of Historic Places, Charles H. Patten House, Palatine, Cook County, Illinois, National Register #06001018.)

advocated. If the ideal home was designed to shelter the family from the negative influences of modernization and urbanism through the promotion of family unity, in actuality the specialization and rationalization of house design seemed to promote the formation of a disparate group of individuals who came together only for family rituals such as entertaining guests or at mealtimes.[24]

By the second half of the nineteenth century, the home had become a fundamental part of middle-class identity formation instead of a place to sleep and work. As historian Candace Volz argues, the American middle-class home "was viewed by contemporary prescriptive literature as a retreat from the demands of the workplace and as a moral haven for the proper nurturing of children and the transmission of traditional cultural values."[25] A good example of such a space within the home that emerged from the generically named "chamber" room on floor plans on the first or second floors of middle-class houses is the library, sometimes referred to as the gentlemen's parlor, the study, or the den. The library or study was understood to be a masculine room and decorated as such.[26] Although it was primarily the domain of the father, women did use the space in educating the children of the household. Families started educating children at home after residential libraries became available to the middle-class homes. This practice emerged after the development of printing technology in the early nineteenth century allowed for the production of man-made paper and reduced the price of books. Publishers began to print series referred to as "libraries" that brought a wide range of books to middle-class households.[27] American middle-class families in the latter half of the nineteenth century were able to ensure that middle-class values were transmitted to their children through home education. Middle-class men also had a dedicated space in the home to indulge in scholarly pursuits, entertain male friends, or conduct business at home. The library/study was a productive space and a place to develop character.

However, by the early twentieth century, to factor in the increased economic costs of technology such as heating and plumbing, the square footage of new middle-class homes was substantially reduced. Middle-class homes could now accommodate permanent bathtubs, flush toilets, and porcelain sinks. In addition, with the growth of the consumer economy and the subsequent decline in home-based production, additional space to store items such as extra material for homemade clothes and linen or canned or dried food at home became unnecessary. Housewives wanted the modern amenities but had to adjust to smaller dwellings.[28] Rooms such as libraries, music rooms, sewing rooms, and extra bedrooms that only served a single purpose had all but disappeared by 1930 in typical middle-class homes. Therefore, by the 1940s moderately priced homes usually consisted of six rooms and a bathroom (see figure 1.3). The living room, dining room, and kitchen took up the entire first floor, and three bedrooms, which were exclusively used for sleeping and privacy, were located on the second floor. Extra rooms for servants, guests, or children's activities were costly and were no longer considered necessary. In comparison, the homes of professionals and business owners in established suburban neighborhoods often had additional spaces such a den or library and private spaces for each family member (i.e., four or more bedrooms on the second floor; see figure 1.4).

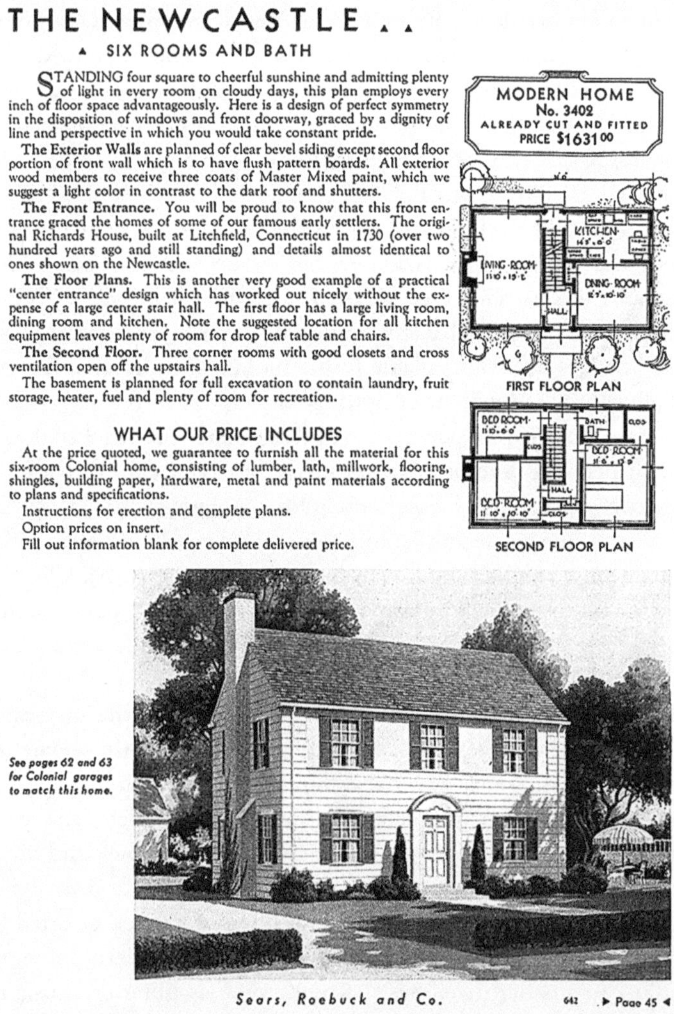

THE NEWCASTLE . .

▲ SIX ROOMS AND BATH

STANDING four square to cheerful sunshine and admitting plenty of light in every room on cloudy days, this plan employs every inch of floor space advantageously. Here is a design of perfect symmetry in the disposition of windows and front doorway, graced by a dignity of line and perspective in which you would take constant pride.

The Exterior Walls are planned of clear bevel siding except second floor portion of front wall which is to have flush pattern boards. All exterior wood members to receive three coats of Master Mixed paint, which we suggest a light color in contrast to the dark roof and shutters.

The Front Entrance. You will be proud to know that this front entrance graced the homes of some of our famous early settlers. The original Richards House, built at Litchfield, Connecticut in 1730 (over two hundred years ago and still standing) and details almost identical to ones shown on the Newcastle.

The Floor Plans. This is another very good example of a practical "center entrance" design which has worked out nicely without the expense of a large center stair hall. The first floor has a large living room, dining room and kitchen. Note the suggested location for all kitchen equipment leaves plenty of room for drop leaf table and chairs.

The Second Floor. Three corner rooms with good closets and cross ventilation open off the upstairs hall.

The basement is planned for full excavation to contain laundry, fruit storage, heater, fuel and plenty of room for recreation.

WHAT OUR PRICE INCLUDES

At the price quoted, we guarantee to furnish all the material for this six-room Colonial home, consisting of lumber, lath, millwork, flooring, shingles, building paper, hardware, metal and paint materials according to plans and specifications.

Instructions for erection and complete plans.

Option prices on insert.

Fill out information blank for complete delivered price.

MODERN HOME
No. 3402
ALREADY CUT AND FITTED
PRICE $1631.00

FIRST FLOOR PLAN

SECOND FLOOR PLAN

See pages 62 and 63 for Colonial garages to match this home.

Sears, Roebuck and Co. 642 ▸ Page 45 ◂

FIGURE 1.3 Floor plan for the Newcastle Colonial, Model No. 3402, 1936. (*Source*: *Modern Homes Catalog*, Sears, Roebuck and Co., Searsachives.com.)

Historically, the ability to hire servants conferred middle-class status on a family as the wife gained valuable time to entertain guests and pursue hobbies. By the latter half of the nineteenth century, maintaining servants became even more important due to the formality of social life and the wife's greater responsibility for the management of the home, as she no longer worked alongside the domestic staff.[29] The new model of the middle-class household was not only a

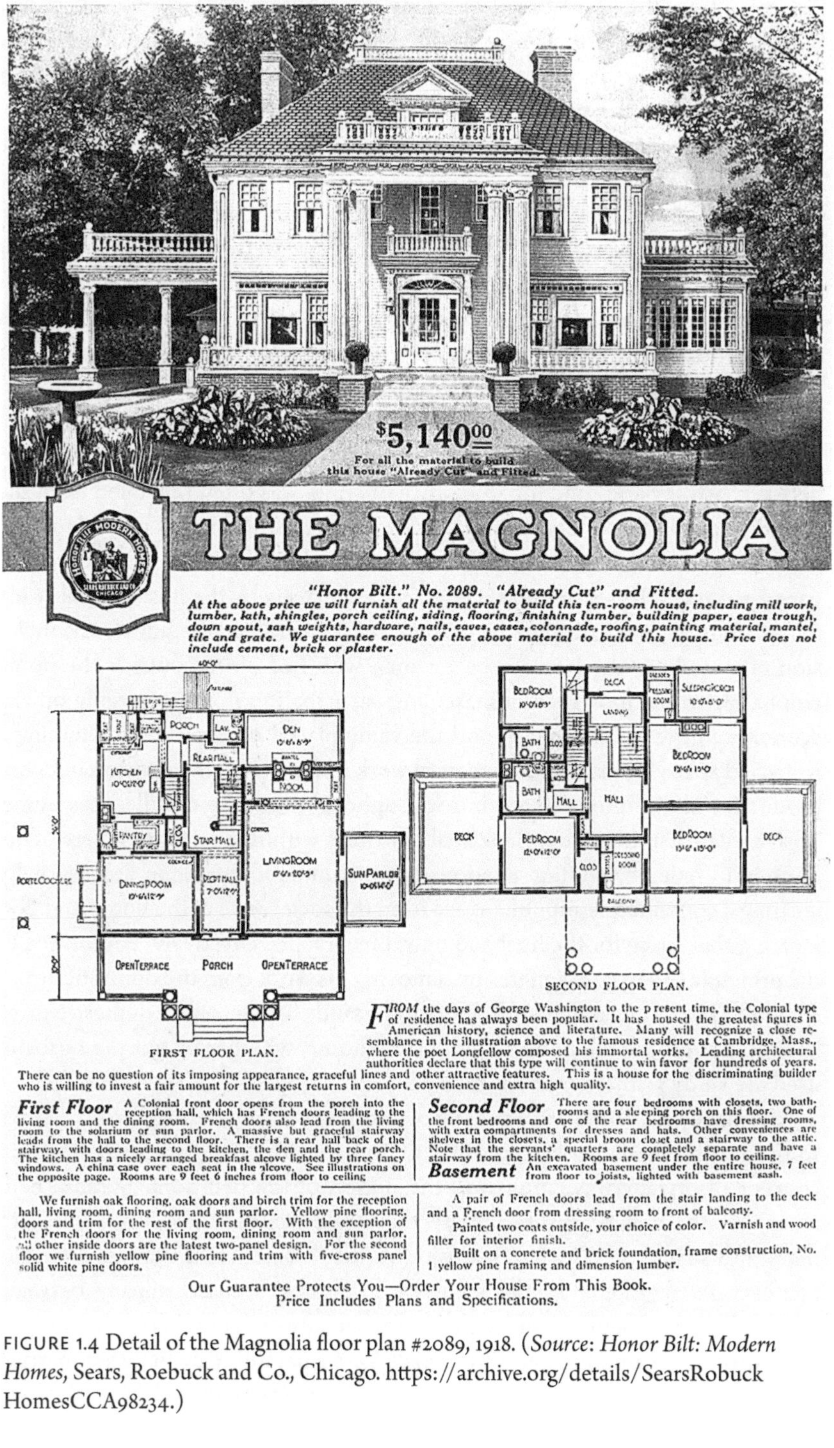

$5,140.00

For all the material to build this house "Already Cut" and Fitted.

THE MAGNOLIA

"Honor Bilt." No. 2089. "Already Cut" and Fitted.

At the above price we will furnish all the material to build this ten-room house, including mill work, lumber, lath, shingles, porch ceiling, siding, flooring, finishing lumber, building paper, eaves trough, down spout, sash weights, hardware, nails, eaves, cases, colonnade, roofing, painting material, mantel, tile and grate. We guarantee enough of the above material to build this house. Price does not include cement, brick or plaster.

FIRST FLOOR PLAN.

SECOND FLOOR PLAN.

FROM the days of George Washington to the present time, the Colonial type of residence has always been popular. It has housed the greatest figures in American history, science and literature. Many will recognize a close resemblance in the illustration above to the famous residence at Cambridge, Mass., where the poet Longfellow composed his immortal works. Leading architectural authorities declare that this type will continue to win favor for hundreds of years. There can be no question of its imposing appearance, graceful lines and other attractive features. This is a house for the discriminating builder who is willing to invest a fair amount for the largest returns in comfort, convenience and extra high quality.

First Floor A Colonial front door opens from the porch into the reception hall, which has French doors leading to the living room and the dining room. French doors also lead from the living room to the solarium or sun parlor. A massive but graceful stairway leads from the hall to the second floor. There is a rear hall back of the stairway, with doors leading to the kitchen, the den and the rear porch. The kitchen has a nicely arranged breakfast alcove lighted by three fancy windows. A china case over each seat in the alcove. See illustrations on the opposite page. Rooms are 9 feet 6 inches from floor to ceiling

Second Floor There are four bedrooms with closets, two bathrooms and a sleeping porch on this floor. One of the front bedrooms and one of the rear bedrooms have dressing rooms, with extra compartments for dresses and hats. Other conveniences are shelves in the closets, a special broom closet and a stairway to the attic. Note that the servants' quarters are completely separate and have a stairway from the kitchen. Rooms are 9 feet from floor to ceiling.

Basement An excavated basement under the entire house, 7 feet from floor to joists, lighted with basement sash.

We furnish oak flooring, oak doors and birch trim for the reception hall, living room, dining room and sun parlor. Yellow pine flooring, doors and trim for the rest of the first floor. With the exception of the French doors for the living room, dining room and sun parlor, all other inside doors are the latest two-panel design. For the second floor we furnish yellow pine flooring and trim with five-cross panel solid white pine doors.

A pair of French doors lead from the stair landing to the deck and a French door from dressing room to front of balcony.

Painted two coats outside, your choice of color. Varnish and wood filler for interior finish.

Built on a concrete and brick foundation, frame construction, No. 1 yellow pine framing and dimension lumber.

Our Guarantee Protects You—Order Your House From This Book.
Price Includes Plans and Specifications.

FIGURE 1.4 Detail of the Magnolia floor plan #2089, 1918. (*Source*: *Honor Bilt: Modern Homes*, Sears, Roebuck and Co., Chicago. https://archive.org/details/SearsRobuckHomesCCA98234.)

departure from the home-based economy in the elimination of apprentices and lodgers; there were also changes to the number of servants living in the home and the spatial separation of their living quarters from the family's. In wealthier homes, the servants were accommodated far away from the family bedrooms; often their rooms were next to the kitchen and pantry in the work zone of the home or in the attic.

By the mid-nineteenth century, middle-class homes were being designed to reflect Victorian ideas about privacy and function. Because most middle-class houses no longer supported family-based industries, rooms used solely for commercial business, such as workshops, offices, and cellars were eliminated, with the exception of the study for some professional men. Especially for what John Tosh defined as independent professional men, such as clergy and doctors, having a study or an interview room was necessary, as their work was more likely to be conducted at home.[30] Because of the importance placed on the relationship between privacy and function, the office or study was often separated from the private zones of the house, placed as close to the front door as possible in the social zone, limiting the ability of household members to intrude upon the occupant's privacy.[31] This space was often used exclusively by the husband, allowing him to focus on work despite the presence of the family in the house. The inclusion of a study in the home even for men who had offices outside the home emphasizes the importance of masculine participation in the emerging official economy in the public sphere, and the value placed on capital. By retaining a restricted space for professional men to work in the home, the division between productive and unproductive labor was upheld within the middle-class home. Tosh argues that this change in spatial dynamics within the private sphere of the household reflected shifting relations between men and women in society. By creating a contained semipublic space from the social zone of the house and designating that space for the husband only, this practice effectively "conformed to the principle of separate spheres by removing his work from the domestic atmosphere."[32] By the late nineteenth century, the study had become a domestic space in which to escape the feminization of the home, whether or not the husband used the study primarily for business.

The master bedroom was a key site of meaning in this new middle-class home. In the United States, it was not until the nineteenth century that the modern concept of privacy was coupled to the notion of the bedroom. Because bedrooms are the sites of private activity, they are commonly associated with intimacy and sexuality. With the seclusion of the "master" bedroom in domestic architecture beginning in the eighteenth century, sexual intimacy between couples became doubly privatized within an already private sphere, and the master bedroom became the permitted space for sexual intimacy between married couples to take place.[33] As Mark Wigley argues in *Sexuality and Space*, the bedroom became a sacred space in the private life of the heterosexual white married couple. The idea of family came to be based on the physical privatization of sexuality behind closed doors.[34] By 1924, the *Oxford English Dictionary*'s extended definition of "bedroom" included "implying sexual relationship; sexy." Privacy became a condition for intimacy to be possible and the foundation for our contemporary belief that intimacy and privacy go together. The household became an emotional center, a sanctuary or retreat, a place for the expression of intimacy between husband and wife and where children became the focus of attention. The sphere of work, which necessitates competitive relationships based on rationality and professionalism, had no place in the intimate space of the home.

As the household ceased to be the primary site of labor and economic relations, the distinction between personal, political, and economic relationships became more notable. In *The Invention of Heterosexuality*, Jonathan Katz argues that by the turn of the nineteenth century romantic love, dating, marriage, and children were legally and socially located in the territory of family life, the private domain.[35] Men supported this arrangement in the public domain. By the late nineteenth century, the economically stable middle class was firmly entrenched in American culture, and this "freed it to publicly affirm, in the name of nature, its own 'heterosexuality.' The making of the middle class and the invention of heterosexuality went hand in hand."[36] The heterosexual relationship came to be defined by the division of labor and an emphasis on romance within the institution of marriage, which was embodied by the home. The home became the space of marriage and family, where heterosexual men and women practiced and developed love, support, and companionship. Even though this representation of the home became the dominant narrative, in reality domestic practices still included work, which will be examined in the next chapter.

2 • INDUSTRY STAY OUT

The nineteenth-century American home mirrored shifts in gender relations in the public and private spheres. However, as Jeanne Boydston argues, "The language of the ideology of spheres was the language of gender, but its essential dualism was less precisely the opposition of 'female' and 'male' than it was the opposition of 'home' and 'work,' an opposition founded on the gendering of the concept of labor."[1] The concept of labor, which had been associated with the family economy in the first half of the nineteenth century, became increasingly coupled to the notion of wages rather than products within the public sphere by the end of the century. The growth of factory-based industries created a system of labor that was more inflexible in terms of gender division; it shifted the location where work was performed and altered the relationship between production and the market. In response to changes in the structure of the economy, middle-class families assigned men to the market and women and children to the household, in contrast to working-class families, which had to put as many of their members as possible into the growing public-based market regardless of age, marital status, or gender. Consequently, because middle-class women and children were discouraged from working to produce goods and provide domestic services beyond the household, home-based production by the middle class dramatically decreased over the nineteenth century.[2]

The discourse on the private sphere removed middle-class women from the pecuniary aspect of the family economy and framed their roles as being supportive and uplifting for men, the sole breadwinners. For example, an editorial in *Godey's Lady's Book* sought to draw readers' attention to

> one curious fact, which those who are aiming to place women in the workshop, to compete with men, should consider: namely, that none, or very few specimens of female ingenuity or industry will be found in the world's great show-shop. . . . We trust this will prove of importance in settling the question of what woman's province really is, and where her station should be in the onward march of civilization. It is not mechanical, but moral power which is now needed. . . . There is no need that she should help him in his task of subduing the world.[3]

In the case of white middle-class women and children, housework was divorced from the concept of labor. Only immigrant and minority women's domestic employment (which although paid was devalued by cheap wages) and men's employment in the public sphere were considered labor.[4] Nineteenth-century ideologies of the home imagined the public sphere as the space of production, conceptualizing housework as unproductive. Consequently, most forms of work in the middle-class home were understood as supporting the reproductive goals of the family and conflated with concepts of morality and leisure.

In both rural and urban working-class households in the second half of the nineteenth century, the home continued to serve a variety of functions connected to survival. As had been the case in middle-class homes before the Industrial Revolution, in many working-class homes private and public life overlapped, as work in the home represented a viable way to earn additional income to pay down debts and avoid poverty, and enabled women and elderly people to remain independent. In urban centers, women and children performed "homework" in makeshift sweatshops, manufacturing garments and cigars in crowded conditions. For example, Jacob Riis (1849–1914) in *How the Other Half Lives* (1890) described and documented through photography the live-work conditions of tenement house cigar-making factories.[5] Riis described how families worked seven days a week under crowded conditions and were charged unreasonably high rent. If working-class families rebelled and complained, they faced not only eviction but also the loss of their livelihood. Riis documented how one family slept in the same bedroom in which they stored moist tobacco leaves and did not seem to be bothered by the overwhelming smell. He drew attention to the poor quality of the accommodations, specifically the sleeping areas he grudgingly referred to as bedrooms, with their dark interiors and lack of windows.

Although historically the family economy was based in the home, by the early twentieth century wage-based labor in the domestic sphere was unacceptable to social reformers. Economic conditions left working-class women few options to support their families. This was especially problematic for married women, as more of the household labor performed in the past by other family members fell to the lot of the wife. Like their middle-class counterparts, many married working-class women wanted to stay home and raise their children.[6] For married immigrant women in cities such as New York, working at home (often in makeshift "factory" bedrooms and kitchens) was more practical than factory work, as public workspaces did not accommodate mothers' schedules, obligations to the family, and childrearing responsibilities. In Eileen Boris's words, "The work that reformers judged a demoralizing element of domestic life, immigrant families embraced as a strategy for household survival."[7] Despite these economic and social challenges, middle-class reformers worked to shape public opinion against homework and to ban its unionization.

In order to survive, children of working-class families also had to contribute to the family economy by participating in the labor force. Consequently, working-class and poor children spent less time in school at the turn of the twentieth century than middle-class children.[8] To protect children from greedy employers and from parents they considered selfish, middle-class reformers publicly pushed for "the separation of the house from work, private from public."[9] In 1922, Emma Duke, a U.S. Children's Bureau agent, submitted a report to the Department of Labor detailing her conclusions from a study of homework and child labor in Rhode Island. Duke argued that the practice of homework had caused "the disorganization of the home" over the past century and stated that "elimination rather than regulation is necessary for the protection of the children and the public health."[10] Social reformers, once nostalgic about family-based production, became increasingly fired up about the poor living conditions in urban tenements and critical of young children working full time at home, blaming immigrants for introducing the practice of child labor. Working-class women earning income at home violated the values of the idealized American family, and women and children were encouraged by reformers to divorce themselves from the world of work. The U.S. government also argued that the practice of homework was a societal problem because it was undermining factory wage rates; nearly 50 percent of homeworkers were receiving public assistance because they were not paid a living wage by their employers.[11]

In order to continue receiving government benefits such as the mothers' pension and to maximize the income potential of the home, working-class families, particularly those headed by women, also provided childcare for "infant boarders"[12] of parents who worked outside the home. Judging by the abundance of sensational newspaper articles, boarding infants for money, termed "baby farming," was a widespread practice in the United States and other Western countries and was considered very controversial. The claim that childcare for working- and lower-class women was linked to infant murder was promulgated by the medical community in statements published in major U.S. newspapers.[13] For example, one physician wrote to the New York Board of Health in 1874 stating that a deceased infant was "victim to baby-farming which prevails so extensively in our city. I frequently find illegitimate children placed with careless and ignorant women for the apparent purpose of causing their death."[14]

The practices of baby farming and home manufacturing reveal contradictions in public discourse about the sanctity of the home and motherhood. Women were expected to put their family first by being present in the home to take care of them. Therefore, working-class women who engaged in home manufacturing or ran baby farms to earn income upheld middle-class ideals by not leaving the domestic sphere. Home manufacturers, taking advantage of public sentiment about the role of the mother, argued that if home-based labor were made illegal, women would leave their children unattended to work in factories. However, by the early twentieth century, a growing number of public health officials, doctors, and social advocates started to argue that home-based childcare was beneficial to working-class women and their children. Dr. Annie S. Daniel, director of the New York Infirmary for Women and Children, contended that home manufacturing was the real problem. She elaborated:

> It would be better, both for [the mother] and her children . . . [if the mother] went to a factory and paid 5 cents a day for each of the children at a day nursery. I find that a good many tenement-house women have day nurseries of their own. They take eight or ten children whose mothers go out to work, care for them in their own rooms, and keep them till the mothers come home at night. They get 5 cents apiece for the children, and it seems to work very well.[15]

The practice of boarding infants allowed some mothers, both single and married, to continue working outside the home and others to utilize their home as a source of income. Although the public fear and outcry were directed at poor, African American, and immigrant women, the obsession with the perceived evils of baby farming and home manufacturing reflected a greater concern about women in general and middle-class notions about the sanctity of the home.

Through photographic exhibitions and expositions, middle-class reformers used graphic representations to expose the social evils of mothers and children participating in home-based labor. Organizations such as the National Child Labor Committee (NCLC) wanted to awaken middle-class audiences to the realities of everyday life in the tenements and galvanize political support to end undesirable labor practices.[16] Lewis Hine, a pioneer of documentary photography, worked as an investigative photographer for the NCLC to record working and living conditions of children and mothers in the early twentieth century.[17] He documented homework in working-class homes for the 1912 New York State Factory Investigating Commission.[18] To further its agenda, the NCLC created posters that utilized Hine's compelling images of unkempt children and mothers in unsanitary living conditions working in the home for wages. The posters provided visual proof of the argument that homework for wages ruined family life by keeping children out of school, preventing mothers from taking proper care of the home, and encouraging fathers to "shirk responsibilities" as breadwinners.

One poster juxtaposes a photo of a middle-class bedroom with one of a multipurpose bedroom used for sleeping and labor in a tenement apartment (see figures 2.1 and 2.2). The photograph of the middle-class bedroom depicts a girl sitting on her mother's lap next to a bed with clean white linens. White garments emphasize their purity and exclusion from physical labor. In contrast, the other image features a working-class mother, Mrs. Guadina, finishing pants for low wages in a dirty bedroom with her three small children. The room appears exceptionally untidy. Her children are unkempt, inferring that they are uncared for. The poster

FIGURE 2.1 Exhibition poster for the National Child Labor Committee, c. 1913. (*Source*: Lewis Wickes Hine [1874–1940] Photographic Collection, Library of Congress Prints and Photographs Division, Washington, DC.)

FIGURE 2.2 Mrs. Guadina, living in a rear house at 231 Mulberry Street, New York, c. 1913. (*Source*: Lewis Wickes Hine (1874–1940) Photographic Collection, Library of Congress Prints and Photographs Division, Washington, DC.)

directly addresses an imagined audience of working-class mothers, advising them to embrace middle-class values regarding motherhood and the sanctity of the home and shaming them by representing their poor living conditions. It constructs the act of working at home as a choice, not as a necessity for survival. Ironically, Hines documented working-class mothers and children finishing linens similar to the ones used to dress the bed in the middle-class bedroom (see figure 2.3). The abundance of crisp white linens in the middle-class bedroom in contrast to the dinginess of the working-class bedroom compels the middle-class audience to confront the relationship between consumption and exploited labor in the homework system of production that the reformers railed against. The photographs reveal contradictions in the notion of the home constructed as a private space, because manufacturing was understood to belong in the public sphere. This example demonstrates that, in reality, this was not the case because capitalism and the private sphere cannot be separated, as they are mutually dependent on each other.

Eileen Boris makes an interesting observation in examining the history of the homework system: "Labor supply may have influenced spatial organization."[19] In the case of nineteenth-century working-class dwellings, the home as "factory annex" justified employers' self-interest in reducing costs in the form of low wages and reduced rents because the practice of home-based labor coincided with immigrant women's need to stay at home to satisfy their obligations to their families.[20]

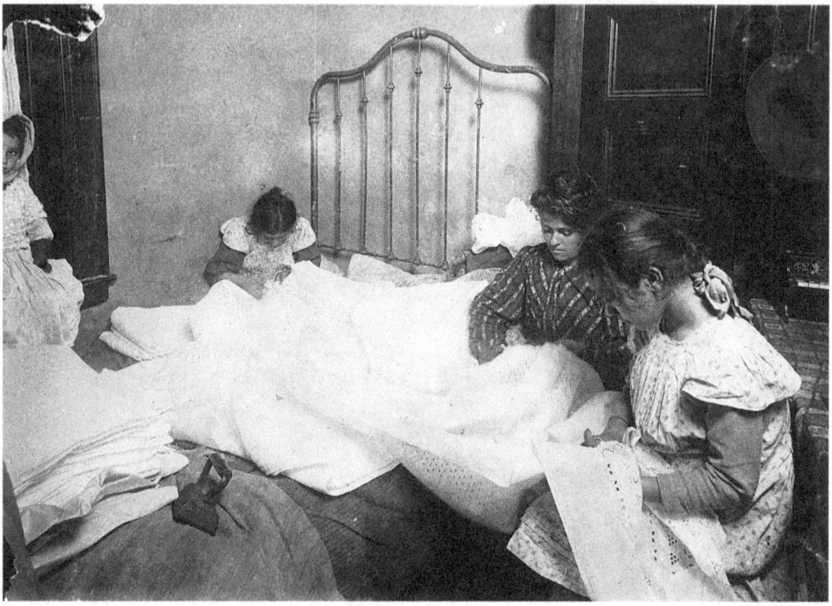

FIGURE 2.3 Family doing cut embroidery in a tiny, crowded bedroom in New York City, November 1912. (*Source*: Lewis Wickes Hine (1874–1940) Photographic Collection, Library of Congress Prints and Photographs Division, Washington, DC.)

Even middle-class reformers who benefited economically from the rapid development of industrial capitalism while simultaneously recognizing the negative impact on poor and working-class families understood the irony of the homework system.

Writing in 1914 for the NCLC, Hine questioned the relationship between work and home in examining the tenement homework system: "'Be it ever so humble, there's no place like home' for what? It is the best place for the family—therefore there is no better place for industry—Q.E.D. Then, why be selfish and try to reserve the home for the family? It has other, broader uses."[21] Families had historically participated in the household economy, and although the wage-based system emerged in the public sphere, systematically reorganizing the relationship between home, family, and work within the household, why not bring the work to the location of the working-class family if every member must participate in the family economy? Hines ironically states that the "master minds of industry" were disturbed to find out that millions of mothers' and children's economic potential was not harnessed, as they were "spending whole days at housework, children at play, neighbors visiting with each other." Homework was the social solution to idle hands that led to juvenile delinquency and starvation, because children and mothers working increased the family income. After lambasting industry's exploitation of the working class, Hine concluded, "The home is for the family. Industry Stay Out."[22]

3 • THE TELEPHONE AND BETTER LIVING

Initially, after making its debut at the 1876 centennial exhibition in Philadelphia, the telephone was referred to as a "scientific toy."[1] However, as use of the telephone became routine in business and industry, public anxiety developed about the impact of the telephone on family and the home. In entering the private space of the home, the telephone transformed the relationship between individual and family and the public sphere. A news article published on March 15, 1903 in the *Washington Post* clearly illustrates the telephone's impact on notions of privacy. An older woman, referred to as a "Grandmother of Society," complained about the "long distance intimacies and the informal swiftness" influenced by telephones placed in the bedroom, altering ideas of privacy in the generation coming of age in the early twentieth century.[2] The grandmother emphatically believes the telephone belongs in the public spaces (work zones) of the home "where a servant or some one fully clothed can answer the calls."[3] Instead she complains that the common practice is for the younger generation to install telephones in their bedrooms for convenience. Scandalized, the society grandmother is forced to observe her granddaughter answering the phone in her bed clothes without a trace of modesty, sleepily discussing her state of dress with a young man also speaking from his bedroom. For the grandmother, the most disturbing aspect of this scene is the ease and informality of this discussion "as though they had met on the street and stopped for a chat."[4]

The grandmother's reaction to the inclusion of the telephone in the bedroom represents three aspects of modernity: (1) shifting notions of what constitutes privacy; (2) the public-private dichotomy in relation to space; and (3) the emerging sense of immediacy. The story encapsulates the tension between premodernity/modernity and private/public with the inclusion of the telephone within private areas of the home. Social norms and experiences were changing rapidly for people of the grandmother's generation. For her, the bedroom represented the last space of privacy and connection to premodern social practices, as discussed in chapter 1. The introduction of the telephone into the bedroom was the final affront, foreshadowing the use of webcams in late twentieth-century homes. The grandmother prayed that she would never live to see the day when "X-rays will be connected with the telephone, as doubtless it [*sic*] will be before many years go by."[5]

The grandmother's use of the phrase "informal swiftness" is significant considering the location of the telephone within the home. Installing a telephone in the bedroom was convenient because it both promoted and assuaged a desire for immediacy in the user. For the grandmother, this created new forms of intimacy and understandings of privacy that had previously developed over long periods of time and transitioned through distinct spaces. This example illuminates Anthony Giddens's claim that "the advent of modernity increasingly tears space away from place by fostering relations between 'absent' others, locationally distant from any given situation of face-to-face interaction. In conditions of modernity, place becomes increasingly phantasmagoric: that is to say, locales are thoroughly penetrated by and shaped in terms of social influences quite distant from them."[6] Early accounts described the telephone as "phantasmagoric." Unlike the telegraph, it added a new layer to long-distance communication: the human voice. For one early user of the telephone the experience of hearing someone on the other line "was like a voice from another world. Here I was speaking to a person far away from me whom I could hear as though he was at my side and yet I could not see him."[7]

In 1875, the ability of most Americans to communicate frequently across large distances was limited, as messages by telegraph were generally restricted to use by businesses and for emergencies. By 1925, an increasing number of Americans could quickly communicate by telephone with others in the same town or city, or across the country.[8] As historian Claude Fischer notes, "The possibilities of personal communication expanded vastly."[9] The telephone fostered new forms of relating and social influence between "absent" others in the public sphere, but also between and within the space of the home. The American Telephone and Telegraph Company (which became the parent company of the Bell System in 1899) promoted telephone use based on notions of sociability, communication, and national identity.[10] A widely circulated Bell advertisement titled "The Telephone Unites the Nation" features a U.S. map with two telephones flanking the West and East coasts.[11] To illustrate the role of the telephone in joining the nation, the states' outlines are composed of wire linking the two phones. Bell told its imagined audience that the telephone, along with the telegraph and the railroad, made Americans a "homogeneous people" and "facilitated communication and intervisiting, bringing us closer together, giving us a better understanding and promoting more intimate relations."[12] The ad visually and rhetorically links the expanding U.S. railroad network with the communications network as modern technologies that transformed social relations and separated space from place. However, as Fischer argues, "The telephone captures most cleanly the magnification of social contact, without the complications of freight hauling or commuting involved in, say, the automobile or railroad."[13]

Examining early efforts by the Bell System to promote residential telephone use reveals how the integration of communication technology in the home contributed to changes in the conception of work and the family in relation to private life in the United States. In addition to masculine and feminine transgressions of separate spheres and the practice of home-based wage labor by the working class discussed in chapters 1 and 2, the telephone played a critical role by making possible the merger of the public and private spheres as one of the first modern technologies to penetrate the private zones of the home. Although most phones appear to have been installed in the public spaces of the home, there is visual evidence that the telephone migrated into the most private space of the home, the bedroom, as early as the turn of the twentieth century.

For example, an Ivory Soap advertisement marketed in medical journals during the 1940s shows a doctor taking an emergency call late at night from his bedroom at the turn of the century (see figure 3.1). The economic and domestic lives of middle-class professional men such as doctors were still primarily conducted in the home. However, the economic lives of most businessmen and laborers were increasingly conducted in the public sphere because of the process of industrialization. Consequently, the private sphere became the space for family. I will argue in later chapters that communication technology continually fostered and fueled the reintroduction of workspaces (often starting with an extra "chamber"[14] or spare bedroom) in the middle-class home throughout the twentieth century.

The association of the public sphere as the space of work and masculinity, and the private sphere as the space of domesticity and femininity, contributes to binary constructions of gender. Brian Ott and Robert Mack identify one such binary: logic/emotion. Examining media, they argue that texts have traditionally constructed emotion as a feminine trait and logic as a masculine one: "The masculine public sphere is related to politics and decision-making, so masculinity is marked in turn by the kinds of rational thinking associated with these processes. The private sphere is concerned with family and nurturance, and femininity is defined by irrational or emotional impulse as a result."[15] Ott and Mack's observation can be applied to understand the marketing, use, and accompanying discourse on communication technologies in the home and the problematic presence of work within the home. The association of technology with masculinity and work has far-reaching implications that become evident in examining communication practices within the domestic sphere.

Although there are late nineteenth-century advertisements marketing telephones to residences and businesses, Bell System did not acquire adequate data to break down actual telephone use by residential or business customers. Although the telephone would later be primarily marketed to women, in the 1890s telephone

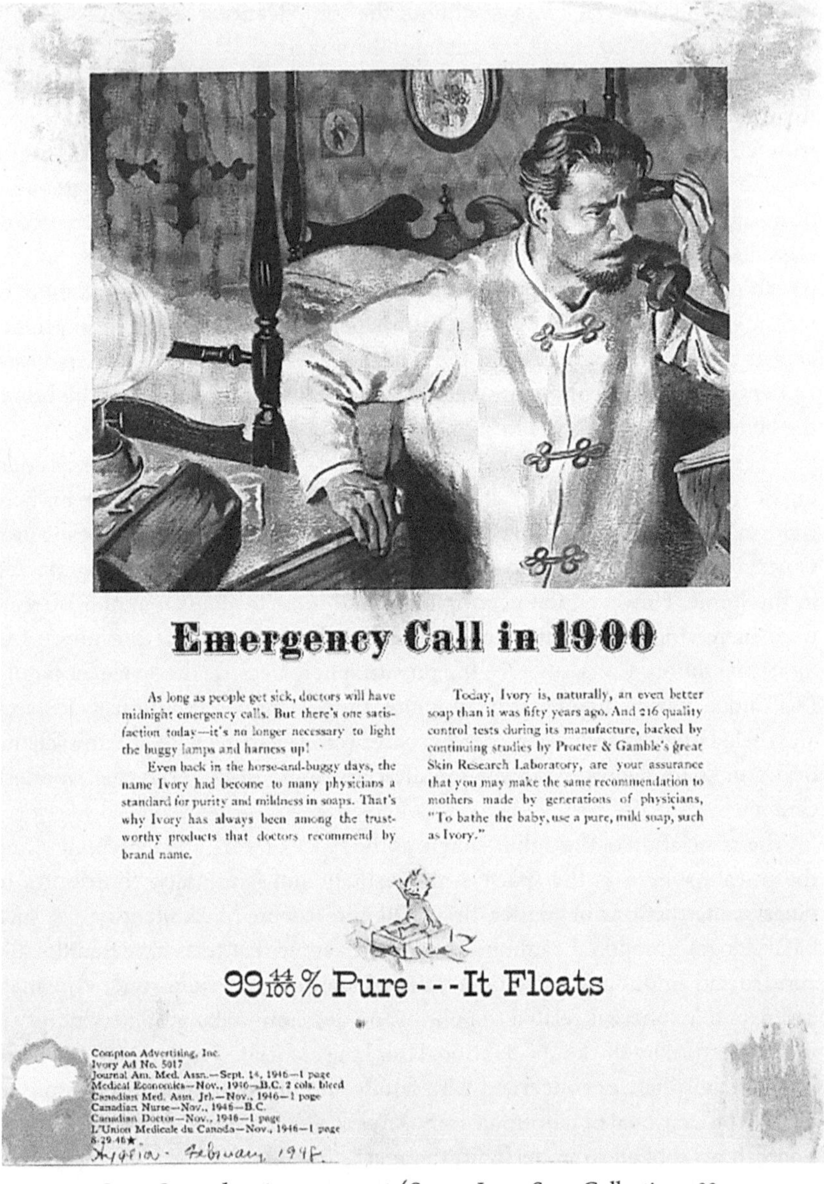

FIGURE 3.1 Ivory Soap advertisement, 1946. (*Source*: Ivory Soap Collection, 1883–1990, Archives Center, National Museum of American History. Gift of Procter & Gamble.)

entrepreneurs were not interested in telephone use by women or rural populations.[16] The telephone was understood as a tool for businessmen. For enterprising telephone capitalists, the telephone was a means to assist business activity. As Michele Martin argues, "At first, the telephone was intended to be used as a means of circulation of capital."[17] In 1882, a residential phone cost as much as

$150 per year in New York and $100 in Boston.[18] Ultimately, the high cost of telephone service excluded use by the average laborer and working-class families. Consequently, early residential use of the telephone was largely by wealthy men.

Businessmen were the dominant users of the telephone during its first thirty years. They could afford the high rates and already utilized the existing telegraph network. Consequently, telephone companies marketed directly to them. Sidney Aronson's research makes clear the extent to which business monopolized the telephone. He notes that businessmen made up the vast majority of subscribers in telephone directories. For example, in 1879 Pittsburgh's telephone directory listed three hundred subscribers. Of these, only six had telephones installed in their residences, and all were businessmen who wanted a direct connection to their office from their home.[19] Consequently, newspaper accounts of early telephone adopters were about men using the telephone for business activities, to link offices to factories, and, germane to this research, to contact the office from the comfort of home. What was known as a "private line" typically connected a businessman's home and office (see figure 3.2).

The early telephone exchanges connected two or more businessmen's households and offices. For example, one of the earliest adopters of the telephone was a banker in Wisconsin named Alfred Galpin. He believed that the "scientific toy" had practical use and in 1877 ran a line connecting his residence to his bank.[20] Similarly, in the Boston area that same year, James Emery Jr., a businessman, installed a private line over the existing telegraph line between his residence and his brother's for commercial purposes.[21] Furthermore, to encourage men to move to developing suburbs outside of cities like Washington, D.C., real estate articles touted new homes equipped with telephones in a den or study to ensure that businessmen could stay in "closer touch" with any business or residence through instant communication with commercial, banking, and mercantile businesses at a reasonable rate. In addition to modern rapid transit, developing communication technology brought the city to the countryside for business or professional men and their families.

During the early years of the telephone, however, businessmen like these were the exception. Telephone entrepreneurs staged numerous demonstrations around the country to persuade skeptical businessmen of the benefits of the telephone. Some visionary men in the professions (especially doctors and bankers) and industrialists caught on and realized the potential of the telephone as a system of communication. After connecting the editorial and counting room to the business manager's residence in Lincoln, Nebraska, in 1879, the *State Journal* commented in an editorial that "the telephone is a big thing, and we can hardly understand how a well regulated business house can be without it."[22] Telephone use began to spread rapidly. The U.S. Special Census in 1902 reported 2,315,297 telephones in use. Fifteen years later, that number had increased more than fivefold to 11,716,520 and approximately 50 percent of households had a telephone.[23]

FIGURE 3.2 "In Touch with His World," c. 1910. (*Source*: Courtesy of AT&T Archives and History Center.)

As the *Boston Globe* declared, the telephone was "no longer a luxury but is an actual necessity in home and business circles."[24]

By the turn of the century, the telephone was understood as a device for saving time and labor, an instrument that created notions of immediacy by diminishing temporal barriers and spatial boundaries. Through the forces of industrialization, the concept of time was steadily associated with production—in other words, time equaled money.[25] The "captains of industry" understood this concept and began to utilize the telephone to accumulate capital. For example, George W. Perkins, of J. P. Morgan, developed the "Perkins plan of rapid transit telephony." The plan required preparation of a list of ten to thirty men to be phoned in rapid succession as quickly as the operator could connect them.[26] According to J. P. Morgan himself, Perkins was able to "raise twenty million in twenty minutes."[27] For the self-employed American farmer, the telephone became a business asset because of its ability to close the distance between the country and the city. From their homes, farmers could ascertain by telephone the market value of wheat, meat, or vegetables and obtain weather reports.[28] By 1915, a quarter of telephones in the Bell System were located in rural areas.[29] To increase the rural market, Bell produced a series of advertisements encouraging farmers to acquire a telephone not only to grow their business by accessing crucial market information in the city, but also to permit their wives to order supplies to maintain the household and call the doctor in case of an emergency.

Comparing the adoption of the telephone in the United States and Britain, the *Saturday Review* attributed the importance of the telephone system of communication in the former as central to the growth of "unhampered private enterprise" and ultimately the country's success.[30] The telephone was markedly an American institution. During the early decades of the twentieth century, New York City had more telephones than most major British cities combined, and more than Belgium, France, Switzerland, and Holland.[31] In European countries the telephone was still largely a luxury. For middle-class British society, the telephone was associated with the town—the public sphere. Many residents walked or drove to telephone offices in town. In comparison, Americans were quicker to recognize the practicality of installing a telephone at home to connect with businesses and the community, thereby linking technological advancement, capitalism, and the American ideology of superiority. As early as 1895, a Portland businessman reported using his bedroom telephone as an alarm clock. Each night before retiring to bed, he called the central office and requested an operator call him at a designated hour to determine if his phone "worked properly."[32] The convenience afforded by the telephone justified the annual expense of renting a phone line.

Early in the history of communication technology, the telephone linked work, leisure, and consumerism within the private sphere. For convenience and to save consumers time, the New York Central Railroad offered rail tickets at home through a telephone service.[33] The service was marketed primarily to businessmen but also to wealthy families. Customers could purchase tickets or Pullman accommodations from their home or hotel, avoiding a long wait at the ticket office. Communication technology facilitated leisure and consumer activities such as vacation travel and productive activities in the form of business travel. A 1904 Bell handbook for telephone salesmen provides talking points to convince residential customers to install a telephone: "It is always on duty, shops in all weather, corrects mistakes, and hastens deliveries. It saves letter writing, orders the dinner, invites the guests, reserves the tickets, and calls the carriage. It makes appointments, changes the time, cancels them altogether and renews them. It calls the expressman, calls the cab, and instructs the office. It invites one's friends, asks them to stay away, asks them to hurry and enables them to invite in return."[34] This advice for salesmen bolstered the narrative that telephone service saved time and labor, simplified consumption, and ultimately facilitated household management.

Because women's household labor was considered unproductive, telephone companies were not initially interested in women as a market, as noted above. If women did use the telephone, it was for limited amounts of time to make social arrangements or order supplies for the home. However, by the early twentieth century American Telephone and Telegraph Company (AT&T) started to market extension telephone lines by advertising in publications mostly targeted to married women. The advertisements appealed to women as busy household managers and equated the home with the office. For a few extra cents a week, married women were encouraged to consider getting extension lines for bedrooms, dens, and sewing rooms to increase the ease of telephone use through immediacy and increased access. Extra telephone lines saved housewives the exertion of climbing the stairs multiple times during the day and "time and bother." figure 3.3 shows a woman seated at a writing desk who appears to be handling family business. These representations conflate spaces of reproduction (bedrooms) and spaces of household-based production (dens and sewing rooms), and blur the line between the work and private zones of the home and what constitutes public and private space.

Early twentieth-century newspapers and publications that featured home design and decorating advice for middle- and upper-class women suggested that in addition to having extension telephones in the bedroom, households should include one in the library or study as a convenience for the husband. The ideal home at the turn of the century was still imagined as a private space to exclusively meet the needs of the family, not conduct the affairs of the public sphere. Therefore, the practice of placing telephones in the home for business use did receive some resistance. One editorial on the influence of modern technology on society put it thus: "Science, it must be owned, has done not a little to destroy the old conception of privacy. With the telephone to pursue business men into their libraries and 'ring them up' in the very bosom of their families . . . it cannot be pretended that this crowning menace of outside affairs has not been led up to by the insatiable pioneers of scientific invention."[35]

Housewives were particularly targeted for telephone shopping. Middle-class women were persuaded to telephone their orders to the butcher, druggist, and other consumer businesses from the comfort of their homes (see figure 3.4).

FIGURE 3.3 "How Many Steps to *Your* Telephone?" *The State,* February 21, 1915. (*Source*: Courtesy of AT&T Archives and History Center.)

Advertisements addressed female audiences by appealing to idealized representations of the home as clean, comfortable, and inviting compared to the noisy, crowded, and polluted cities. To convince women of the potential time and energy that could be saved by using the telephone to shop, AT&T framed shopping as a time-consuming activity. Instead of spending a half day shopping,

FIGURE 3.4 "Send Your Voice." New York Telephone Company advertisement, 1910. (*Source*: *Wall Street Journal*, August 29, 1910.)

women could purchase the same goods in ten minutes over the telephone. New York Telephone told their subscribers, "Send your voice to do errands," and simultaneously asked newspaper readers, "By the way, have you a telephone?"[36] Linking the public and private spheres, these advertisements used rhetorical strategies that not only promoted consumer consumption through the promise of saving time and effort, but also created new telephone subscribers.

It did not take long before AT&T developed business partnerships with newspapers such as the *North American* in Philadelphia to capitalize on telephone news services. Residential subscribers were now able to call any time during the day to hear news summaries by telephone operators.[37] In 1912 advertisements appeared for the Oregon Telephone Herald Company (an associate company of the United States Telephone Herald Company of New York), a combined telephone, newspaper, and entertainment vendor.[38] Promoting the telephone as a necessity for office and home, the company provided important daily happenings, market reports, and news hours ahead of newspapers. The businessman could work from home or get a head start on market conditions and business news from his study before heading to his office in the city. Again, convenience and immediacy are implied, as the service was available from early morning to late at night and broadcasted over the telephone wires "not from records" but in "clear and melodious tones."[39]

The service also broadcasted live music, vaudeville, opera, baseball reports, educational lessons, and children's stories for the family. An Oregon Telephone Herald Company advertisement features a family at home, the businessman at his desk, his wife, mother, and children actively listening to their individual phone extensions. They form a circle surrounded by a telephone wire linking them to various settings in the public sphere—the opera, ball game, church, and stock market. The family is the center of the world, enclosed in the circle, suggesting the domestic sphere and the safety and privacy the home affords. However, the telephone wires provide connections to the public sphere—linking production and reproduction, work and leisure, public and private. This convergence of the telephone, radio, and newspaper foreshadowed the twenty-first-century smartphone and is an early example of the integration of work and leisure in the private sphere.

Although our current interactions with communication technologies such as laptops and smartphones have given us a hypersense of immediacy in relation to space and time, it was the inclusion of old communication technology in the private sphere—not only changes in the public sphere—that transformed our modern experience of space and time. Modern technologies such as the telegraph and telephone promoted the modern separation of time from space and space from place theorized by Anthony Giddens. News of events happening in other parts of the world could be reported quickly by telegraph and reach American homes through the burgeoning newspaper industry. We often think about technology and its impact on public spaces, but this desire to develop technology that creates uniform and exchangeable spaces also applies to the private sphere and is evident in the evolution of the middle-class home. Thus the public-private space, which had evolved from a premodern multipurpose space into a designated space for privacy and family life, began to evolve again into an interchangeable space of work and leisure, which, as the following chapter will show, was driven by the introduction of the typewriter.

4 • PORTABLE TYPEWRITERS FOR HOME USE

Although domestic servants in the United States experienced an increase in wages during the latter half of the nineteenth century, their numbers decreased. By the 1930s, most homes were built without maid's rooms, and kitchens were designed for homemakers, not servants. This meant that the amount of household tasks and the level of competence required increased for the middle-class wife.[1] By the turn of the century, the wife had become a home manager, with the role of organizing and managing the new household inventions, urban services, and amenities in an efficient and frugal manner, as well as making the home a visually pleasing and supportive environment for the family.

Women at the turn of the century expressed concerns about balancing domestic responsibilities with leisure, similar to the contemporary discourse around work-life balance. In the opening of her book *The New Housekeeping: Efficiency Studies in Home Management* (1913), Christine Frederick states: "A moderate income, two babies, and constant demands on my time, was the situation that faced me several years ago. I liked housework, and was especially fond of cooking; but the deadening point of the whole situation was that I never seemed to finish my work, never seemed to 'get anywhere,' and that I never had any leisure time to myself."[2] To resolve this problem, home economists such as Frederick championed adoption of the "new science of work," or Taylorism, within the domestic sphere. Frederick W. Taylor, a mechanical engineer, developed a system to eliminate waste and inefficiency by creating a distinction between mental and manual labor and ultimately transferring control over work from labor workers to management.[3] In addition to adapting efficiency systems designed for factories, Christine Frederick applied office practices and technologies such as filing systems, binders, and typewriters to keep records and maintain price lists for shopping. Conflating the private and public spheres, she argued that housework, through scientific management, "can be the most glorious career open to any woman."[4] This equates homemakers with professionals in the public sphere and consequently recognizes that the home is a workplace.

Other widely circulated publications included the *Lippincott's Home Manuals* series and Clarence Wilbur Taber and S. Maria Elliott's *The Business of the Household* (1918). Written as a textbook for home economics students learning business practices that can be applied to household management, *The Business of the Household* positioned housework for women as a form of labor equivalent to office work in the public sphere.[5] The authors recognized that "the work of the home is a most complex industry, involving factors dealt with in the factory, the office and the store, and in nearly every branch of business."[6] This meant that proper financial management of the household required the use of common office supplies and equipment in the home. The textbook argued that every home manager should have a fully stocked desk solely dedicated to the business of the household. The authors describe the various clerical tasks required to maintain a "well-regulated family," such as paying bills, ordering food, and keeping an inventory of household items, arguing that it would be "absurd to provide no one place where such labor may be performed and no tools with which to work."[7] One office technology they considered indispensable was the typewriter, which they describe as a household asset because it can save time for busy homemakers and also be used for educational purposes. Recognizing the expense of owning a new typewriter, the authors provide suggestions on how to find affordable secondhand machines for $15 to $40. Another textbook, *Mechanical Devices in the Home,* aimed at senior high school and junior college students instructed potential homemakers on the use of mechanical devices found in the home.[8] The textbook focused on common mechanical technology in the home during the early 1920s, such as heating and cooking devices, lighting, laundry and cleaning equipment, and measuring instruments such as thermostats, with an entire section on typewriters.[9]

Remington Rand began marketing the Remington Portable, the first standard-keyboard portable typewriter, for personal use in the home in 1921.[10] Advertisements for the portable typewriter highlighted its time-saving features, compact size, and convenience as ideal for home use because "you can carry it anywhere or use it anywhere, on your lap as you wish."[11] Marketing brochures suggested that men use the portable typewriter to conduct business or carry on their profession at home, and encouraged women to use one to manage the home and maintain social activities. The advertised price for a new portable typewriter with case was $60 in 1921 (equivalent to approximately $862 in 2019 dollars), indicating that Remington Rand's original target market was professional middle-class households.[12] However, Remington Rand did not see a predetermined saturation point in the market and believed that portable typewriters for the home would make up the bulk of their sales.[13] Therefore, by the 1930s the company introduced less expensive basic models, the Remington Special and the Remington Junior Portable, for $19.75 and $39.50, respectively, to expand their market.[14]

The Royal Typewriter Company began advertising to women with children beginning in the late 1920s (see figure 4.1). Royal's marketing division drew on existing norms about what constituted middle-class women's work and status in the home. The education of children at home represented one form of work that women performed in the home. For $60, which included a carrying case, "modern mothers" could "realize that typing with the Royal Portable is the ideal method of home instruction for young children."[15] Remington Rand also marketed portable typewriters as an "agent of education" in the home.[16] To emphasize the importance of purchasing a portable typewriter for home use, marketing brochures used research by educators to argue that students who have access to typewriters at home make more progress in their studies compared with students without a typewriter.[17] Therefore, as early as the 1920s, American middle-class families were exposed to technology associated with business in the home and arguably introduced to contemporary middle-class work practices that extended to the private sphere.

TYPEWRITERS FOR PROFESSIONAL USE AT HOME

In a detailed instruction manual for salesmen, Remington Rand identified promising customers for home use, including businessmen and secretaries, but also doctors, writers, and farmers, who often conducted at least some of their work at home.[18] The manual also provided salesmen with targeted sales tactics to expand the market for portable typewriters. The following example of a suggested sales pitch is enlightening for understanding how Remington Rand promoted home use of typewriters by professionals:

> Mr. ______, it doesn't take much penetration on my part to see that you are a very busy man. I will also hazard the guess that, like many other busy men, *your labors are not confined to office hours.* You cannot always leave your business problems in the office. *You take them home with you,* and I will guarantee that some of your best and most constructive business thinking and planning is done in the undisturbed quiet of your own home. Has it ever occurred to you what a help it would be on such occasions to have right at your elbow a compact, handy and complete little writing machine, on which you could transcribe these thoughts to paper much faster and more easily than you possibly could with a pen? *The same is true of much of your private and personal correspondence,* which many busy men find it difficult to attend to during business hours.[19]

Remington Rand's sales and marketing department exploited the likelihood that professionals were increasingly working longer hours and sometimes taking their work home with them. The company used the promise of convenience and the appeal of working within the comfort of one's home to sell their

FIGURE 4.1 “The Lessons He Types To-day on His Royal Portable.” Royal Portable Typewriters advertisement, 1929. (*Source*: *Good Housekeeping*, January 1929.)

portable typewriters. The portable typewriter, a major advance in communication technology, promised greater flexibility and portability by integrating work and leisure—in the form of personal correspondence—thereby blurring the boundary between the public and private spheres.

Although the majority of the sales tactics were directed at professional men at this time, Remington Rand also indirectly marketed portable typewriters to working women using the following sales script:

> I have noticed Mr. ______, that you have a very competent secretary, also that your correspondence at times appears to be very heavy. Doesn't it occasionally happen that closing time comes with much unfinished work still on her books? I know that you must *dislike to ask her to work overtime,* no matter how willing she may be. However, I have a suggestion to make which I feel sure will solve that difficulty. Why don't you make her a present of a Remington Portable? . . . *If you would do this the overtime problem would be solved.* Whenever you have some extra work that you especially want done I am sure Miss ______ would do it gladly—for then she would be able to do it at home and on her own machine.[20]

This sales tactic is based on the assumption that women working in the public sphere are a temporary condition, perhaps even unnatural. The sales pitch assumes that a businessman or professional would be uncomfortable asking his secretary to stay at work after hours even if she wanted to. Giving an employee a portable typewriter for home use absolves the gift giver of any guilt and affords the receiver the ability to balance work obligations and personal life at home. The expectation is that women were needed at home. Interestingly, women's paid work at home is not equated with overtime. The sales script suggests that home-based work for the secretary can be divorced from market labor and is more connected with leisure. This is one of the earliest examples I have found that hints at the contradiction that working at home represented for women, something I discuss in more detail in chapter 5: What forms of labor are considered "work" if performed in the home? For women, spaces of work are often conflated with leisure and noncompensated labor, blurring the line between work and leisure. In this example, participation in market labor at home is clearly not dependent on access to a portable typewriter, but the introduction of a machine usually associated with the office arguably contributed to the growing acceptance of market forms of labor in the home, further transgressing the public/private boundary.

Historically, most clerical workers and private secretaries were men. However, as Margery Davies has noted, by 1930 most secretaries in the workplace were women, which represented a striking change in the clerical labor force.[21] This dramatic development was the result of economic and cultural shifts during the early twentieth century. As discussed in the introduction and earlier in this chapter, by the end of the nineteenth century industrial work had largely replaced home manufacturing and other forms of home-based labor that women historically participated in to support their families. Davies argues that this "decrease of productive work in the home," along with the introduction of the typewriter, facilitated the entrance of literate middle-class women into the workplace, although in a subservient position to their male employers.[22] Remington Rand embraced its perceived role in giving women opportunities to make a living by marketing portable typewriters directly to women engaged in business. For example, Remington Rand celebrated the sixtieth anniversary of the invention of the commercial typewriter in 1873 with its "Women Were Freed" advertising campaign, which emphasized the typewriter's role in giving "women their first real chance to enter business."[23]

For women who could not or did not want to work outside of the home, owning a typewriter appeared to provide opportunities to support themselves and their families. In Emmett Leroy Shannon's *Money for the Woman Who Wants It* (1920), readers are informed about the benefits of having a typewriter and advised how to rent or buy an affordable model.[24] Having a typewriter could enable women to find work as a reporter or a freelance writer. The book also lists types of clerical work that could be done at home on a typewriter, including typing bills, statements, and letters. Readers are also told how to canvass their geographic area to find potential customers, such as doctors and small storeowners, who could provide steady work. The book even provides organizational strategies and suggests furniture and equipment to manage workspace in the home.

Women increasingly became a target audience of publishers due to their growing presence in the workforce. Colleges and commercial publishers printed career guides to help women navigate the range of occupations newly open to them, even though public discourse revealed differing opinions about this cultural shift. For example, in the introduction to *Vocations Open to College Women,* the University of Minnesota acknowledged public debate about whether women entering business and the professions were advancing their own agenda instead of considering the greater good of society.[25] Nevertheless, the university believed that, like other institutions that educate women, it was necessary to inform its students of career opportunities as more women worked out of necessity or simply desired to do so. Another example is Catherine Filene's *Careers for Women,* which discussed not only careers in the public sphere, but also jobs that could be done at home.[26]

In *Money for the Woman Who Wants It,* Shannon enters the public debate about the merits of bourgeois women earning a respectable income avoiding the need to "toil in the factory."[27] He opens the book with the following assertion: "We find the business and industrial world full of women today who prefer to make an adequate income by means of regular employment, yet these same women who go out to take their part in the business life, carry with them the love of home and home-made things, and an increased respect for those factors which go to make up a real home. This very fact spells opportunity for the home-staying woman who wants to add to the family income by using her spare time."[28] Shannon appealed to modern women, arguing that ambitious and capable women should not have to apologize for their desire to make money in their spare time or to engage in regular employment to achieve economic freedom. However, it is also clear that the author wants to find the middle ground in the debate between women pursuing a career in the public sphere and staying at home to take their assumed place as homemakers in the domestic sphere. This framing of the benefits of home-based work for middle-class women re-emerged in public discourse during the postwar period and is prescient of the work-life balance arguments that did not fully develop until the 1980s. Overall, the presence of market-based work in the home and the promotion of such work by career experts and typewriter manufacturers reveal the cultural and economic shifts that contradicted traditional notions of the role of the private sphere. In reality, the American home remained a space of work despite middle-class rhetoric to the contrary.

PART 2

THE CONSUMPTION OF OFFICE PRACTICES AND COMMUNICATION TECHNOLOGY IN THE POSTWAR MIDDLE-CLASS HOME

5 • THE QUEST FOR EASY LIVIN' IN THE SUBURBAN HOME

Many scholars have written about the re-emergence of the nineteenth-century "cult of domesticity" during the postwar period in the United States.[1] The postwar period is depicted as the golden years for the American family—when home life was uncomplicated by the pressures of work, time, technology, and the outside world (despite the social and political problems of the time). As discussed in chapter 1, the cult of domesticity or the doctrine of separate spheres emerged in the nineteenth century as "one of the most profound effects of industrialization" through the "separation of 'work places' from 'home places.'"[2] The notion that the private sphere (embodied in the home) was necessary to shelter family members from the pressures of the public sphere of work also emerged at this time. However, this distinction did not exist in actuality.[3] As Carolyn Goldstein notes, "Historians of women have found so much evidence of men and women crossing these supposedly rigid boundaries that they have called into question the entire 'separate spheres' concept."[4] Although I agree with these historians, the concept did serve a purpose during the postwar period as businesses—through advertisements, editorials, and social commentary—both reinforced and dismantled the public/private dichotomy to serve their own economic purposes in expanding their markets within the domestic sphere. Therefore, an additional aspect of the postwar period that deserves re-examination is the presumed separation of home and office and work and leisure in the middle-class suburban home.

In 1954, Otis Wiese, the editor of the popular American women's magazine *McCall's*, revamped the periodical as part of its "Togetherness" campaign in an attempt to shift its readership to the entire family.[5] Through this magazine, the concept of togetherness was unequivocally connected to the suburbs in the form of home ownership.[6] In modern terms, married couples were expected to focus on parenthood in favor of the entire family in the middle-class pursuit of work-life balance, championing the importance of the private over the public sphere. Togetherness would allow couples to obtain fulfillment through the uniting of the family within the spaces of the home. In addition, togetherness was supposed to restore men's presence in the home after a prolonged absence due to the war.[7] However, togetherness failed to reconcile the dual expectations for fathers: success at work and maintaining the role of involved companion at home. Togetherness did not challenge traditional gender roles. Women were still expected to be the primary caregivers and men the sole breadwinners. Married men and women still lived separate lives. This tension between the ideal of family togetherness and the reality of separate roles also extended to the spatial organization of the home through the simultaneous promotion of the family/living room as a space of togetherness and the continued necessity of private spaces such as bedrooms and the home office/study. Despite the push for togetherness and the strict promotion of family life in the home, compensated work was not absent.[8]

As the term implies, "bedroom communities" are residential places for those (primarily fathers during the postwar period) who spend the majority of their waking lives working in and commuting to the city. Postwar bedroom communities provided affordable housing for white middle-class families and offered fathers relatively close proximity to major U.S. cities for work. Therefore, such communities were primarily perceived as a place to sleep during the week and to do local shopping during the weekend, as bedroom communities tended to have few economic opportunities in the immediate area. The explosion of bedroom communities in postwar America spatially supported the societal ideal of separating work (and associated technologies) and private life by creating maximum distance from the perceived ills of city life.[9] Consequently, this (re)segregated middle-class white men and women into gendered spaces: the suburban home as the feminine world of privacy and leisure, and the city as the masculine space of work.

Between 1929 and 1945, construction of new housing fell short of demand in the United States.[10] The housing shortage and inadequate government subsidies due to the war effort forced many families to take in boarders or extended family members, which was antithetical to the notion of both privacy and the ideal family promoted since the mid-nineteenth century.[11] Nonetheless, during the 1940s and early 1950s companies like Simmons Bedding Company, a major mattress manufacturer, took advantage of the housing shortage to promote products such as sofa beds to turn living rooms into bedrooms.[12] With the return of servicemen after the war, the baby boom, and postwar economic expansion, pent-up demand caused an upsurge in housing starts. New construction was the highest in 1955, when 1.65 million houses were built, with the remainder of the decade averaging 1.5 million per year.[13]

Homeownership rates in the United States increased from 55 percent in the 1940s to 62 percent in 1960. Population growth in the suburbs was the main cause, as the suburbs saw a 35 percent increase in the 1950s and 1960s compared to a 5 percent increase in major cities.[14] During the postwar period, 85 percent of homes built were located in the suburbs. This was primarily due to government measures such as mortgages backed by the Federal Housing Administration (FHA) and the Veterans Administration, which financed the production of ten million homes between 1946 and 1953. In addition, the GI Bill of 1944 ensured that "college-educated veterans, mostly male, were best prepared to undertake the high-earning, white-collar work of the new postwar economy."[15] Access to a college education and tuition stipends allowed many white heterosexual working-class families to become middle class.

The popular radio show *The Goldbergs* (1949–1956), a comedy about an urban working-class Jewish family, made its debut on television in 1949. By 1951, two new family comedies situated in urban settings—*I Love Lucy* (1951–1957), about the Ricardos, a middle-class couple (played by Lucille Ball and Desi Arnaz) and their friends, and *The Honeymooners* (1955–1956), featuring a working-class couple and their friends and neighbors—aired on television. By the late 1950s, the majority of domestic comedies on television were about the middle class and depicted married heterosexual couples with children living in the suburbs. In 1956, *The Honeymooners* aired its last episode, and the Ricardos moved to the suburbs. The Goldbergs moved to the fictional New York suburb of Haverville in 1956, but the show never rebounded after its transformation from a comedy about an urban working-class family to one about an upwardly mobile ethnic family in the suburbs, and was soon canceled. The televised upward mobility and exodus to the suburbs mirrored reality in postwar America.

The suburbanization of the United States supported the pro-family ideology of the postwar period. As one popular advice book, *The Woman's Guide to Better Living*, stated, "The family is the unit to which you most genuinely belong. . . . The family is the center of your living. If it isn't, you've gone far astray."[16] Magazine and newspaper editors, politicians, social commentators, and medical professionals promoted marriage and family as the key to personal happiness and the foundation for a strong and prosperous society. According to historian Stephanie Coontz, social trends of the twentieth century before the 1950s reversed, as the average marriage age fell substantially, the number of divorces declined, and women gave birth to more children in closer succession at a younger age. During the 1950s, the proportion of married people to nonmarried people increased significantly compared to the first half of the twentieth century. The great increase in the number of babies born and the focus on the family created a society centered on childrearing. Yet, what we have come to know as the "traditional" family, along with the values associated with it, was actually a "new phenomenon."[17] Even more than during the Victorian period, the ideology of the family focused on the good life within the boundaries of the nuclear family and ultimately within the space of the home. Newspapers and magazines across the country featured articles on "happy suburban homeowners" who left the city in search of privacy and "easy livin'."[18] Therefore, by the late 1940s white Americans, primarily those who were middle class, were encouraged to move from the cities to the suburbs in search of safety, more space, single-family houses, and the latest domestic technologies.

As Pamela Wojcik argues, the television shows and films (and, I would add, advertisements) of the time represented the suburbs as an idealized place where white middle-class Americans ended up after getting married and having children.[19] In the white middle-class life cycle, apartment living is for singles, couples without children, and, in some cases, gay men. Television and film of the 1950s positioned the middle class as the social stratum to be envied by placing the middle-class family at the forefront and the rich and the working-class at the flanks as a means of comparison.[20] The middle class is regarded as carefree, honorable, ethical, and happy compared to the stuffy, formal, and materialistic rich and the struggling laborers of the lower class. In terms of work-life balance and the culture of consumption, postwar television failed to realistically represent the increasing effort it took to attain and maintain middle-class status. Fictional TV households were depicted as one-income families, and the fathers never appeared to be overworked or struggling to maintain their standard of living. This was especially egregious considering the fact that most of the suburban families depicted on television were actually upper middle class and did not represent the average middle-class family living in developments like Levittown that benefited from the GI Bill, FHA loans, and other government programs that allowed them to enter the middle class.

In order to bolster nonurban lifestyles, films such as *Mr. Blandings Builds His Dream House* (1948) and *Please Don't Eat the Daisies* (1960) open with views of a crowded city, overrun with people, with the cinematography emphasizing the rapid pace of life in the city and its overwhelming architectural environment. Homemakers can only successfully manage their households with ample space, outside the distractions of the city. Fathers need a sanctuary, an escape from the demands and rapid pace of the public sphere, and the farther away, the better. For the middle-class father, home should be an escape from the competing pressure and expectations of the office. In *Please Don't Eat the Daisies*, drama critic Lawrence Mackay (David Niven) has a long commute to the city, making it difficult for him to see plays late at night and get home before the last train. It is their house's study, which his wife, Kate (Doris Day), remodels for Lawrence, that allows him to embrace his new home.[21] In reality, creative professionals were encouraged to build houses that provided spaces for work. An examination of home-buying guides and domestic interior design books of the postwar period shows that many featured floor plans of actual houses of creative professionals such as writers, architects, and broadcasters that included a study and/or workroom. In addition to a standard study, some houses had darkrooms, drafting rooms, and photography studios to enable the owner to work from home.[22]

IDEAL LIVABLE HOMES

The housing boom provided work and opportunities for architects to influence the design of both custom and ready-made houses, as reflected in the abundance of guidebooks written by architects and housing consultants during the postwar period. Consultants employed by organizations such as the Housing Research Foundation of the Southwest Research Institute carried out programs to educate the public on good housing design and construction by publishing examples of well-designed houses.[23] In addition, publications such as *Life* magazine published editorials advancing the need for "livable homes" with at least three bedrooms, two bathrooms, and an additional study-guest room for maximum privacy. The editorials also suggested that wise investors "buy to the limit" to get the best house affordable.[24] As a result, spending beyond a family's means was encouraged to avoid skimping on privacy.

The postwar economic boom and the mounting desire to purchase consumer goods after the economic austerity of the 1930s and early 1940s encouraged families to concentrate their consumption on the home. Films like *Mr. Blandings Builds His Dream House,* with its competing themes of the necessity of consumerism and the need to obtain a private space for the family, bolster this belief. Jim (Cary Grant) refuses to give up his study, and his wife, Muriel (Myrna Loy), will not do without her sewing room and private space for the girls. The original plans for their home represented the standard houses built during the postwar middle-class housing boom, which lacked additional spaces such as a den or study, pantries, or play/nursery rooms that were associated with upper-middle-class suburban homes. In actuality, the majority of homes built during the postwar period were not like Mr. Blandings's dream house or any of the suburban homes represented on popular postwar sitcoms such as *My Three Sons* (1960–1965 [ABC]; 1965–1972 [CBS]), *Leave It to Beaver* (1957–1963), or *The Donna Reed Show* (1958–1966). The majority of the homes were modeled after the four-room layout popularized by the building firm Levitt & Sons.[25] A standard floor plan for a starter home often featured four rooms on one level: a kitchen, living room, and two bedrooms within 900–1,000 square feet, small enough to fit on a 50-foot-wide suburban lot and leave space for a front lawn and a backyard.[26] (See figure 5.1.) Real estate advertisements implied privacy, picturing houses surrounded by abundant greenery that would buffer the family from the neighbors and the outside world. Unlike the homes of upper-middle-class professionals and small-business owners in established suburban neighborhoods,[27] the smaller houses built primarily for families entering the middle class typically lacked separate spaces for men (such as a den or a library) and extensive private spaces for family members, for example, three or four bedrooms on the second floor. (See figure 5.2.)

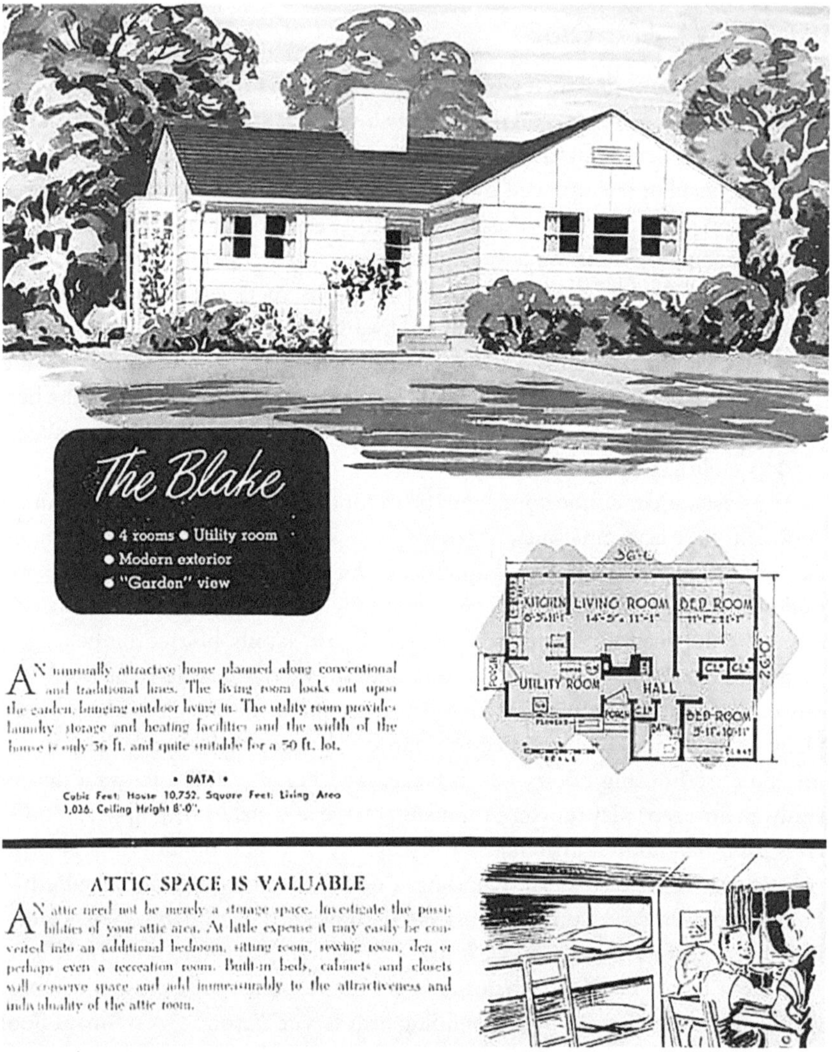

FIGURE 5.1 A standard mass-produced affordable postwar home. (*Source*: The Blake, *National Homes of Moderate Cost*, 1949, Antiquehome.org.)

In reality, although most of the new postwar homes in developing suburbs were small, real estate and lifestyle sections of national newspapers featured upper-middle-class homes that were tailored to meet the needs of each member of the family.[28] For example, architects used the concept of privacy to promote the purchase of houses that featured enough bedrooms so that each child would have a room of their own. In an interior design guide published in 1955, design and architectural consultants Katherine Morrow Ford and Thomas Creighton claimed that each child needed a private bedroom, as "the development of a

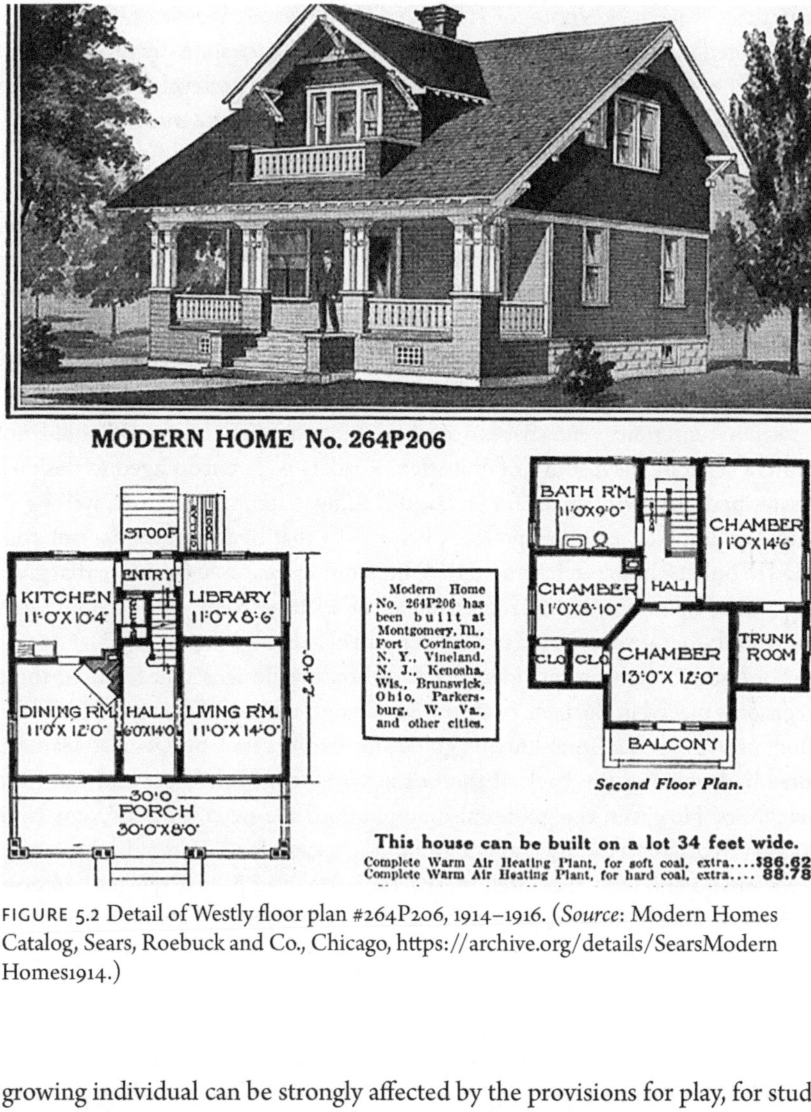

FIGURE 5.2 Detail of Westly floor plan #264P206, 1914–1916. (*Source*: Modern Homes Catalog, Sears, Roebuck and Co., Chicago, https://archive.org/details/SearsModernHomes1914.)

growing individual can be strongly affected by the provisions for play, for study, for sleep, by the opportunities for quiet, isolated activity when that is needed."[29] One ideal home featured in the guide had a separate children's wing, "almost a complete residence in itself."[30] Ford and Creighton acknowledged that many of their featured homes were aspirational and outside of the reach of many middle-class families, but still endorsed the overall principle of obtaining maximum privacy whatever the budget.[31]

For the housing industry, the prevailing discourse of "togetherness" was not as good for business as "apartness."[32] By the late 1950s, builders and architects started to promote housing designs that featured adaptable rooms for individual family members to pursue leisure and work activities on their own. In fact, "apartness" was the keynote for *House and Garden*'s 1962 House of Ideas, which was erected in Franklin Hills, New Jersey.[33] Therefore, despite the promotion of togetherness by social critics, homebuilders and real estate developers promoted larger suburban houses as a way for upwardly mobile, white middle-class families to gain extra space and privacy in the form of separate bedrooms for children, master bedrooms for parents, and the addition of multipurpose rooms. The promotion of apartness is rooted in class (as evidenced by the spatial layout of larger suburban homes that adopted the features of upper-middle-class houses in established suburban neighborhoods), as well as in public health discourse about the negative effects of overcrowding in multi-unit housing, especially for children.[34] Furthermore, housing guides emphasized the need for bedrooms that were large enough to double as a study to allow the father to work at home, as well as entertainment spaces for children, assuming the family could not afford a separate playroom or family den. Readers were encouraged to design a master bedroom with space for "relaxed reading, listening to music, writing or studying, hobbies, or other private pursuits" so that bedroom use is "not confined to only eight or ten hours a day."[35] Illustrations featured furniture that gives the master bedroom the overall character of a sitting room or bedroom / personal study, because it should be "given more of a 'living' character."[36]

Ford and Creighton included practical housing designs that featured three bedrooms placed in the back of the house facing a fenced-off backyard for maximum privacy. Other home-buying guides for families on a budget also featured three bedrooms in the back of the house, away from the street and from the neighbors. However, the guides also emphasized the need for bedrooms large enough to double as study and entertainment spaces for children. In the case of the husband and wife, this often meant a spacious and private master bedroom with an en suite bathroom, as parents needed a retreat from too much "togetherness."[37] Many articles in major and local newspapers featured parent retreats or "dens" to escape the loud music and gangs of teenagers that seemed to take over suburban homes.

The *Saturday Evening Post* in 1959 asked readers, "Are you outgrowing your house?"[38] Newspapers and magazines like *Popular Mechanics* published articles advising homeowners how to finish an attic or add bedrooms for growing families, master bedroom suites for couples, social spaces for the household such as a family or "rec" room, and an office under the stairs to allow the father to work at home.[39] In reminding Americans of their need for a little "aloneness" and for efficiency and harmony within the home, domestic consumerism in the form of housing design and consumption became acceptable and desirable. The housing industry identified new markets in home renovation in the promotion of upper-middle-class apartness and started to market remodeling of standard Levittown-style starter homes that represented "togetherness" to resemble the traditional suburban homes of the upper middle class.[40]

Homebuilders and interior designers reported that their research revealed that couples desired extra rooms to prepare for the possibility of additional children but also wanted multipurpose rooms to use as an office, sewing room, music/entertainment center, or library.[41] Of note is that most of the rooms in that list blur the boundary between work and leisure. Too much togetherness meant smaller homes, less furniture, one television, and a single phone. Newspapers published articles that appealed to the need for domestic efficiency. As the *Atlanta Daily World* argued, "Bringing the family closer together is all very well, but let's not forget that family 'apartness' can be a good thing at times, too."[42] By the mid-1960s, togetherness was out of fashion.[43] Despite the cultural norm of togetherness and prioritizing home over work, the competing ideologies of family life, privacy, and work remained. These conflicting ideologies are apparent in the marketing of office technologies and furniture to middle-class homemakers, which is discussed in the next chapter.

6 • THE BIG BUSINESS OF HOMEMAKING

During the postwar period, married middle-class American women, acting as homemakers, were expected to manage the household. The furniture industry caught on, recognizing the need for workspace for the homemaker to make calls, pay bills, file records, and conduct other household duties, as evidenced by the marketing of home office furniture in newspapers and workspaces displayed in model bedrooms at home design expos.[1] Dedicated workspaces were proposed as solutions to meet the demands of modern living. Even though female consumers were assumed to be married and therefore not part of the workforce, the housing industry recognized that there was work involved in managing a household beyond cooking and cleaning. The home office was touted as a means to save money and time, a necessity for the efficient homemaker to run her "own little household business center" and avoid embarrassment when her husband asks where she has placed important receipts, family records, and bills.[2] Managing a home was compared to running a business and the home office to a space where family transactions took place. Movies, television, and advertising bolstered this belief.

FICTIONAL HOME MANAGERS

Although many women did work during the postwar period, middle-class white mothers were typically represented as home managers in postwar popular culture. Most popular shows and films in the 1950s and early 1960s implied that in upper-middle-class households, domestic workers handled heavy labor—in the form of substantial cleaning (and sometimes cooking)—and that the homemaker managed the household, more like a supervisor. Upper-middle-class television mothers are depicted cleaning up after dinner, often with the help of the father, and preparing meals while avoiding the grunt work because most had some form of household help. Some shows revolved around a domestic worker's relationship to a middle-class family. One of the earliest representations was *The Beulah*

Show (1950–1952), which followed the antics of a black housekeeper named Beulah Brown "as the queen of the kitchen" as she rescued her white employers from many of their domestic failures. The show ran on ABC and was the first sitcom to star an African American woman—first Ethel Waters, then Hattie McDaniel, and finally Louise Beavers. Another significant show was NBC's *Hazel* (1961–1966). The sitcom featured a witty and resourceful live-in maid, Hazel Burke (Shirley Booth), who takes care of the upper-middle-class Baxters in a New York suburb.

By the mid-1960s, popular culture started to slowly reflect feminist ideas in the United States that emerged from second-wave feminism. The women's movement sought equal rights and opportunities for women in the areas of sexuality, family, and work. The growth of feminism was influenced by events such as the Food and Drug Administration's approval of the first oral contraceptive ("the Pill") in 1960, the Equal Pay Act of 1963, the publication of *The Feminine Mystique* by Betty Friedan in 1963, and the passage of the Civil Rights Act of 1964, which included the Title VII prohibition of discrimination based on sex by employers. Arguably, early representations of this emerging shift are evident in films such as *Please Don't Eat the Daisies* (1960), which was discussed in relation to suburban home design in chapter 5. To recap, Kate Mackay (Doris Day), the mother of four boys, is a homemaker married to Lawrence (David Niven), a professor who has left his job to become a drama critic for a major New York paper. Kate does not fit into her husband's new cosmopolitan lifestyle. Other women in Lawrence's professional circle dismiss her because she is perceived as having too many kids and no life outside of her family. Kate tells her husband that "interesting people don't want to meet housewives."

What does it mean that her role as housewife is undervalued in the city? Postwar popular discourse situated married women's role in the private sphere, but, more specifically during this period, their place was in the suburbs. The film reflects this belief, as Kate insists that the family move out of their apartment in the city. Although the family ends up in the country, Kate embraces similar rhetoric about the benefits of the suburbs to justify the move to the country. She argues that the country would be good for the family, especially the children. The country, like the suburbs, represents a space of privacy and leisure, divorced from the perceived ills of the city. It also represents a space where Kate can fully fulfill her role as a home manager, extending her identity as just a wife and mother. For Kate, moving out of the city to a larger house with outdoor space could provide more opportunities to fill time during the day, such as cleaning a larger house, gardening, shopping, and chauffeuring the children to school. Lawrence, on the other hand, wants to stay in the city and continue to socialize with important people in the theater industry. He wants to be successful, a prominent critic, and Kate's desire to focus on the family is holding him back.

While a minor theme in the narrative, Kate's proclamation that being a housewife is not exciting foreshadows Friedan's argument in *The Feminine Mystique* about the "problem that has no name." Friedan describes what drove the collective disillusionment for white, suburban, middle-class women: "It was a strange stirring, a sense of dissatisfaction, a yearning that women suffered in the middle of the twentieth century in the United States. Each suburban wife struggled with it alone. As she made the beds, shopped for groceries, matched slipcover material, ate peanut butter sandwiches with her children, chauffeured Cub Scouts and Brownies, lay beside her husband at night—she was afraid to ask even of herself the silent question—'Is this all?'"[3] Kate wants to embrace her role as homemaker even though she acknowledges it is not considered as glamorous or even meaningful compared to the professional roles of actors, critics, and writers that the men and women hold in Lawrence's professional circle. She welcomes the chance to oversee the renovation of their dilapidated house in the country as she sets out, with the help of her housekeeper, to make a home for her family. Kate enthusiastically helps the local drama club find a play and accepts a role in the production. Her children's school in the country wants the parents to participate in after-school activities. Lawrence refuses and tells the principal that elementary school is for kids, not parents, and this is their chance for a break from their kids. In contrast, Kate volunteers to run an after-school activity one day a week even though she has other obligations. These scenes most likely resonated with suburban middle-class mothers, as they depict the obsession with volunteer work that was common in the suburbs during the postwar period.

Television shows such as *Bewitched* (1964–1972) and *The Brady Bunch* (1969–1974) can be seen as examining the shifting role and conflicting ideological representations of women in households prior to and during the height of second-wave feminism. As discussed earlier, upper-middle-class families often hired a housekeeper to take on the tasks of cleaning the house and cooking meals, allowing the housewife to act as a home manager. This practice helped homemakers married to professionals pursue volunteer work in the community (e.g., for parent-teacher associations), manage their children's extracurricular and school activities, and attend events that furthered their husband's career. Throughout *The Brady Bunch* and in the last two seasons of *Bewitched*, this practice was represented, as both mothers had full-time, live-in housekeepers. *Bewitched* directly addressed the role of housekeepers when Samantha Stephens's (Elizabeth Montgomery) mother-in-law suggests that she hire a live-in maid to make herself more available to help her husband Darrin (Dick York, later Dick Sargent) move up in his career as an advertising executive. By "more available" she means spending more time volunteering on high-visibility organizations in the community and hosting and attending professional dinners and other events with her husband.

Nonetheless, Samantha actively fights the need for a housekeeper for the first six seasons of *Bewitched*. This was a departure from earlier fictional upper-middle-class television homemakers who either embraced their housekeepers or seemed to accept their presence as a given. *Bewitched* underscores this point by featuring three episodes in which Samantha actively rejects hiring or keeping a maid despite the objections of her husband and mother.[4] In "Maid to Order" (S2:E17) Darrin does not want Samantha to do heavy housework while she is pregnant. He suggests that, like their neighbors, they hire a maid. Samantha rejects Darrin's proposal because she does not want a stranger overseeing the management of her house. To convince Samantha, Darrin tells her that she would be in charge: "She won't run it honey, she will just help you run it!" The comparison of housework to management practices assured middle-class women who had left a career to get married that they could also experience the power of managing employees, as their husbands did in the public sphere.

As a witch, Samantha has the ability to magically clean the house but chooses to physically labor to share the experience of most working-class and middle-class women of the period. In the beginning of the first season, Samantha enthusiastically embraces her gendered role in the private sphere, choosing to abandon her life as a witch when she marries Darrin. The act of abandoning magic to support her husband at home mirrored the societal expectation that women stop working after getting married in the 1960s. As the series progresses, however, Samantha increasingly cannot resist the urge to use her magic to solve household problems and help her husband pursue his career. As Lynn Spigel argues, *Bewitched* "seemed to celebrate the sexism of the suburbs" but also "presented viewers with the possibility of thinking about the social constraints of suburban life."[5] By the mid-1960s, feminist ideas started to influence popular discourse on gender roles in the private and public spheres, which included the narrative on *Bewitched*. An early episode, "Help, Help, Don't Save Me" (S1:E5), reveals the internal conflict Samantha experiences in suppressing her magical powers to embrace housewifery. Despite several all-night stints in his study, Darrin is unable to create a successful advertising campaign. She decides to help him by rewriting his slogans and improving on his ideas. They start to argue because Darrin believes she used magic instead of her own inspiration to come up with slogans she believes will impress his boss. Samantha tells her mother, Endora (Agnes Moorehead), that she will finish cleaning the house and cook dinner without magic before putting on the sexiest dress she owns and having a drink with Darrin to convince him that she was wrong and will mind her own business. While Samantha is cleaning, her mother magically places a horse harness around her daughter's neck, joking that she is "working like a horse." Endora's act makes Samantha's embrace of patriarchal privilege apparent to the viewer. Darrin gives up and uses Samantha's ideas after pressure from his boss, but the client does not like the new campaign. This allows Darrin to believe that it could not be Samantha's magic that prompted her ability to create interesting slogans; to his relief, she is just like any other housewife. He states, "You inspire me, and I came up with the idea and that is the way it ought to be!" He dismisses Samantha's intellectual contribution and claims that her love and support inspired him to come up with a new and viable advertising slogan. Samantha fulfills one of the primary duties of her job as homemaker to a professional husband—to support his career advancement at the expense of her own desires and needs.

Although *The Brady Bunch* premiered in September 1969 and relates to seventies culture, the show also evokes earlier family sitcoms from the late 1950s and 1960s through its "wholesome character."[6] Identifying with public discourse on divorce and the rise of blended families, the show tells the story of Mike (Robert Reed), a widower, who marries Carol (Florence Henderson), a divorcee. Mike has three boys from his previous marriage, and Carol three girls from hers. Mike is a successful architect and is able to support his new wife, the six children, and a full-time live-in housekeeper, Alice Nelson (Ann B. Davis), in a well-appointed modern house. Like most fictional television mothers prior to the 1970s, Carol is a housewife and consequently does not "venture into the masculine world of work outside the home."[7] However, in the home, she does adopt the role of home manager thanks to Alice's role as maid to the household. Alice shifts from surrogate mother in her previous working relationship with the boys to employee after Mike marries Carol.

Consequently, Carol is able to take on her new job as home manager, similar to the system of management in the business world, even though dialogue on the show reminds viewers that she is capable of taking care of the house on her own. In the beginning of season one Alice believes that Carol feels uncomfortable, as Mike and the boys automatically look to Alice to resolve their domestic problems. In "Alice Doesn't Live Here Anymore" (S1:E4) Alice tells Mike to ask Carol to mend his shirt. Mike agrees, stating that Carol "surely can sew a button." However, as Mike and the children start to ask Carol instead of Alice for help with skinned knees, homework, and acting as den mother for their scout projects, Alice starts to question the need for her to remain in the household. Alice decides to quit her job and lies to Carol and Mike about a sick aunt in Seattle who needs her help full time; however, Mike thinks that Alice wants more money because her workload has doubled.

The children then overhear Alice talking to a friend about her diminished role in the home. Collectively, the family comes up with a plan to show Alice that they cannot survive without her because Carol and Mike are too busy with their personal lives and raising the children. For example, Carol cannot manage the children's social activities and also cook dinner for eight people. The show equates Carol's job as home manager with caring or emotional labor. She oversees Alice's day-to-day duties, such as cleaning the house, doing laundry, and preparing meals for the family. This allows Carol to fulfill her duties as wife and mother. Although significantly more women were participating in the workforce by the 1970s, *The Brady Bunch* imagines another role for women that does not trespass into the public sphere while also not involving the drudgery of household labor.[8] The job of housewife is imagined as a home manager who, like her husband at work, gets to delegate tasks to subordinates, but who is also able to express love for her family by helping with tasks associated with emotional labor, such as helping with homework and taking children to doctor's appointments.

DEDICATED WORKSPACES AND OFFICE TECHNOLOGY

Although the relationship between homemaker and domestic employee was very evident on postwar television, women did not have a dedicated workspace within the home to manage the household, unlike men, with their study or den. Television sitcoms removed the stigma of domestic labor (associated with the working class) from the middle-class suburban home by disassociating grunt work (labor) from the image of the homemaker. This made the kitchen, historically a workspace, into a hybrid public-private space, subsequently incorporating the public sphere of work into the home. Consequently, women were spatially associated with the home, and specifically with the primary work zone of the house, the kitchen. Although the kitchen had always functioned as a workspace within the house, historically it was treated as a private space, and because it was a space of work and often occupied by servants, the kitchen was considered inferior in respect to other spaces of the home.[9] Examining postwar floor plans for the middle class, we can see that house layouts shifted to reflect the changing relationship of the kitchen vis-à-vis the rest of the house. Instead of occupying the rearmost space of the house or sometimes the basement floor of large Victorian era homes, the kitchen moved next to the living room and became part of the public zone of the home (see figure 5.1). As Barbara Kelly claims, this transformation "paralleled the transition of housework from backstairs to public space, and the concomitant acknowledgement of the housewife as an important actor in America's new commercial villages."[10]

Sitcoms and family dramas depicted the mothers' workspace in the kitchen, but in the selling of new homes or furniture and interior design, homemakers were encouraged to carve out workspace within the home in addition to the kitchen, often in the master bedroom, but also in the study or den, as a shared space for husband and wife. For example, in a 1959 *Chicago Daily Tribune* article, efficient housewives were instructed to have a "properly outfitted office space right in the home," a place where all the transactions of the "big business of homemaking" can happen "with the least amount of confusion."[11] The author claims that having an office space makes recordkeeping "fun." Conflating work and leisure in the middle-class house, the home office purports to provide the homemaker with the same opportunity for fulfilling work that her husband has in his office in the public sphere. Another editorial equated the trend of housewives reserving a working corner in their bedroom to women's experience as secretaries before marriage.[12] Therefore, white middle-class housewives were encouraged to think of themselves as homemakers and to manage their home on a "businesslike" basis. Home economics advocates equated good household management with efficiency, convenience, and good consumer practices.[13] This equates mothering and domesticity with the work in the public sphere. As Spigel argues, "The case of the housewife presents an even more pronounced example of the integration of work and leisure in everyday life."[14] In spatial terms, this translated to allotting an area of the house for office space.

A good home office space necessitated a decent-sized desk, chairs, cabinets or filing drawers, and bookshelves.[15] Advice columns made a point of including a typewriter and telephone to facilitate discussions with insurance brokers, lawyers, and schools.[16] Therefore, adding communication technology such as a telephone extension, a typewriter, and a desk in the bedroom could be seen as a natural way to incorporate prior work experience and skills into home management. Columnists framed these suggestions as common sense because of the already gendered relationship between the typewriter and office work in the public sphere, and consequently further undermined the public-private dichotomy by constructing the home as a public space.[17]

Similar to today's anxiety about the breakdown of work-life balance, privacy and family life due to smartphones and social media, postwar social commentators also questioned the role of communication technology in the breakdown of family life. For *Life* magazine writers, the telephone was a means to illustrate the nature of the atomistic family.[18] The telephone separated the family, distracting the children from playing with each other. It created opportunities for the boss to summon the father to attend a late-night business meeting and for the mother to request outside services to manage needs that were previously handled within the home. A pictorial essay in *Life* magazine compares the modern Parker family to the idealized close-knit and self-sufficient farming family of the past, and laments the dissolution of the "old family functions of home manufacture."[19] This nostalgia for the family economy of the farm or other forms of preindustrial home-based labor, coupled with the contemporary belief that the telephone is disruptive because of its ability to inject the public sphere of the market (production and consumption) into the home, reveals contradictions in the postwar conception of the private-public dichotomy. Within the system of capitalism, spaces of production cannot be separated from spaces of reproduction because they are mutually dependent on each other. Consequently, *Life*'s featured parents, Mr. and Mrs. Parker, "only have one major function left: that of giving their children the affection and care they need until they leave home for college or a job that may be at the other end of the country."[20]

The Southwestern Telephone Company placed advertisements in regional newspapers and magazines during the early 1950s to convince housewives that having a telephone did not threaten the family and that it was in fact necessary to successfully manage the household. The additional cost was worth it because of the "work it does."[21] Many of the advertisements marketed the telephone to "homemakers" for better home management. In one advertisement, titled "How to Save Yourself 76 miles of Walking Each Year," the Bell Telephone Company lists ways that the housewife could be more efficient (e.g., dinner prepared faster, paying bills more efficiently) around the house by installing multiple phone extensions in the home to save time and effort.[22] Although the market for first lines was not saturated, Bell Telephone (now AT&T) believed that marketing second lines would be profitable in certain urban markets. For example, in 1954, Bell's New York branch launched a marketing campaign to promote sales of additional lines in bedrooms, kitchens, and dens (see figure 6.1).[23] By 1960, two-thirds of American households had at least one telephone in the home.[24]

Bell Telephone encouraged its sales force to persuade subscribers to think about their telephone use across the entire home. Salesmen were to appeal to individual family members and depict the home as a space of activity beyond the living room.[25] Bell framed its residential advertising around security, privacy, convenience, and work, recognizing that the home was a space of both labor and leisure. To promote the sale of extensions phones, Bell created illustrations and accompanying text that inadvertently acknowledged the incorporation of work within the home. Bell commissioned advertising effectiveness studies beginning in 1948 through the Pennsylvania Bell System to determine the costs and benefits of various copy and layout treatments. Through the 1950s, Bell found that photographic illustrations that portrayed telephone use in ways that consumers considered realistic within the home were more effective in terms of value and cost when marketing additional phone extensions.[26]

In one effective advertisement that ran in major women's magazines, Bell asks consumers to consider the areas of the home that serve different functions, such as the spaces "where people work—kitchen or den or basement workshop."[27] Specifically, Bell suggested that women imagine trading jobs with their husbands by thinking of the kitchen, "where you do so much of your work," as their "office" at home (see figure 6.2). By the early 1960s, Bell began to heavily market the Princess phone, which it launched in 1959. The Princess was originally marketed to female consumers as a stylish, compact, and convenient phone to be used primarily in the bedroom. In most advertisements, the phone is depicted by the bedside or on a desk or dressing table to promote convenience or safety for women. Nevertheless, by placing the Princess phone on a desk in the bedroom, Bell tacitly acknowledged that bedrooms could serve as home offices for women by suggesting that adding a bedroom extension could "aid in running the home"

FIGURE 6.1 "Home-wide telephone convenience." Bell Telephone advertisement, c. 1950s. (*Source*: Courtesy of AT&T Archives and History Center.)

FIGURE 6.2 "Madam! Suppose you traded jobs with your husband?" Bell Telephone advertisement, 1956. (*Source*: Courtesy of AT&T Archives and History Center.)

FIGURE 6.3 "Where will you put your bedroom phone?" Bell Telephone advertisement, 1963. (*Source*: Courtesy of AT&T Archives and History Center.)

(see figure 6.3). In 1962, Bell started promoting workspaces in the home as other possible locations for a Princess phone (see figure 6.4). Collectively, Bell used advertisements to construct the home as a space for work as well as leisure.

In an internal publication for employees from 1954, the telephone extension is promoted as a means to reduce the amount of work for the homemaker and

FIGURE 6.4 "Any room is *the* room for your Princess phone." Bell Telephone advertisement, 1962. (*Source*: Courtesy of Courtesy of AT&T Archives and History Center.)

make talking on the phone more private and convenient for the entire family, especially for fathers conducting business at home and teenagers keeping in touch with their friends.[28] The "well-telephoned home" was a necessity to meet the needs of modern living. Telephone companies noted that home design in the 1950s emphasized openness, function, and flexibility compared to the defined floor plans of traditional housing originating in Europe. The telecommunications company emphasized that family life had become more informal and incorporated greater amounts of leisure time and work within the home. The model homes emphasized cutting-edge planning in home design by hiding telephone wiring in the walls and preinstalling telephone extensions in the work areas of the house in addition to the bedrooms. Finishing a work assignment, ordering groceries, and making a date could all be done within the convenience of the home. Consequently, communication technology allowed activities typically performed in the public sphere to be done within the private space of the home.

As noted in chapter 4, American typewriter companies such as Remington Rand started to manufacture portable machines for home use in the 1920s. One of the early models was the Remington Portable, which the company marketed to businessmen, school-age children, and "the woman in her home."[29] By the early 1950s, Remington continued to market new portable models to families to use within the home; however, the company's primary focus was on professional fathers who worked at home or needed to take work home and on children and teenagers through its Education Division.[30] On the rare occasions that a portable typewriter was marketed directly to women for home use, Remington Rand described the target consumers as mothers who actively volunteered outside the home.[31] Smith-Corona, the other primary U.S. competitor in the portable typewriter market for home use, also marketed its home office machines for use by students and men in the home during the postwar period. Smith-Corona advertised the Figurematic—an electric adding machine—in *Life* magazine to help housewives manage household finances such as the costs of groceries.[32] Overall, during the postwar period, typewriter manufacturers did not promote their already gendered machines within the public sphere as a way for homemakers to earn money, only as a means to manage the household, and therefore upheld the private/public dichotomy for women within the home.

In contrast, newspapers, popular magazines, and guidebooks encouraged middle-class housewives to participate in paid work within the home using typewriters, telephones, and other office machines to supplement the family income.[33] For example, Isabel Stevens Webster, author of *How to Make Money at Home* and coauthor of *Start Your Own Business on Less Than $1000*, suggested purchasing a "good, legal size mimeograph machine and a good typewriter" to start a small duplicating and mailing house at home.[34] She informed readers that a new mimeograph machine would cost approximately $30 but was worth it, providing an easy way for women who already possessed office skills to make money. In her words, the "minister has sermons to be typed; restaurants have menus changed daily; movie houses send out programs; many clubs want announcements mimeographed; and churches often use mimeographed Sunday morning bulletins."[35]

Scanning the help wanted sections of various papers across the nation reveals a postwar market for homemakers equipped with a typewriter and a telephone to earn money as freelance typists and secretaries.[36] Several articles featured mothers with "old office skills" brushing up on their typing and clerical skills to subsidize their spouses' salaries.[37] These articles mention the homemakers' previous office experience or that job applicants are tested and given the opportunity to take a short course to brush up on their office skills after staying home for several years. In 1954, *Kiplinger's Personal Finance* ran an article titled "Ladies! Earn Cash by Typing at Home."[38] It stressed the need for housewives to take the work seriously and the importance of professionalism. Warning housewives of the many "work at home" frauds advertised in newspapers, the article listed all the equipment needed to work at home, how to determine pay rates, and how to network and find business opportunities in one's hometown. A good typewriter, a duplicating machine, a desk, a comfortable chair, and a telephone extension were considered necessary for a fully functional home business. The magazine also suggested converting a study or extra bedroom as a dedicated space for a home office. In addition to typing correspondence, homemakers were advised to advertise dictating services for professionals over the telephone.

For postwar middle-class homemakers, columnists constructed working at home as both a sacrifice and a necessity. Homemakers worked at home to help pay medical expenses or send a child to college, not out of boredom or to purchase items for themselves. In fact, according to historian Eileen Boris, like their turn-of-the-century counterparts, typists who worked at home did so "because they needed the money."[39] The difference between homeworkers in the postwar period and those in the late nineteenth and early twentieth centuries was that "the universe of women needing to work had expanded to include 'the middle class' and not merely the beleaguered mothers of urban immigrant districts."[40] For example, as described in a 1954 *Chicago Daily Tribune* article titled "Mothers Pay Bills with Old Office Skills," Mrs. Rita Oster started a business in her home office (extra bedroom) hiring housewives to type letters, make appointments, and transcribe recordings at home for local businesses. Defending her decision to hire mothers, Mrs. Oster made the point that if you want to work for her, "you must have a better reason than money."[41] Her employees worked for certain goals, such as "new furniture, down payments on a home . . . and to pay medical bills."[42] Oster's defense of employing housewives reflected postwar public political discourse on the subject of women's place in the home. The article has photographs of Oster sitting at a typewriter in her home office, as well as others showing her employees interacting with their children at home and taking care of household tasks, implying that working at home is something they do in their spare time without neglecting their duties as mothers. Another article argues that working at home is beneficial to housewives as "Her working hours and conditions are pleasant. Her time is her own to plan."[43] Working at home fitted into the life pattern of white middle-class women who had worked in an office before marriage and left the labor force after having children.[44] Homework allowed these women to restart their careers from home. However, newspaper and national magazine articles praising the benefits of working at home often ignored the difficulties involved with simultaneously caring for young children and how men felt about their wives working to supplement the family income. In fact, Boris notes that working at home was not easy for mothers, and many male trade unionists at the time argued that home typists took jobs away from men who needed them as a primary source of income to support their families.[45]

Women's workspaces at home were treated as paradoxical: the middle-class housewife who worked at home was depicted as someone who needed an office with a desk, a typewriter, and a telephone extension and who simultaneously devalued her family and personal work as just "play," conflating her home office with leisure or noncompensated work. The homemaker plays at working, unlike her husband, who has a "real" office in the public sphere. The work of home management—in other words, noncompensated housework—is constructed as a leisure activity that also conceptually slides into compensated work. Even paid work, for the homemaker, is paradoxically made less visible through its association with women's leisure activities within the home, such as chatting on the telephone or using the typewriter to correspond with friends or for other hobbies. Participation in paid labor at home is clearly not dependent on technology alone, but the introduction of machines usually associated with the public sphere also contributed to the growing acceptance of work and leisure as interchangeable forms of consumption within the home, further fusing the leisure/work binary.

7 • JUNIOR-SIZED OFFICES

Modern beliefs about the nature of self were influenced by changes in how Western societies understood childhood.[1] By the end of the nineteenth century, labor laws to protect children were established and policies were adopted to support public schools, kindergartens, and playgrounds. Consequently, spaces of childhood began to emerge as adults increasingly managed children's free time and space.[2] By the mid-twentieth century, clear distinctions between adults' and children's spaces were established. As Sonia Livingstone notes, by the 1950s one of the primary spaces of childhood centered on the home, as fears for children's safety brought about a further retreat from public spaces and the childrearing experts emphasized the necessity for children to have their own space for proper social development.

In 1959, Leonard W. Besinger Jr., son of the founder of the National Association of Home Builders, published an editorial in the *Chicago Tribune* encouraging families to move out of the city into his family's new suburban housing development.[3] To sell houses, Besinger utilized prevailing discourse on the home and the family. Part of his argument emphasized the need for children to "have room to play and grow in safety . . . in an environment conducive to their sound development of mind and body."[4] In addition to yard space and local playgrounds, he contended, children needed their own private space within the home, which was not possible for the average-size family in a crowded two-bedroom apartment.

PRIVATE SPACES FOR CHILDREN

Child development experts wrote editorials and scholarly articles arguing that children needed privacy and a sense of possession.[5] Ideal middle-class children's bedrooms combined spaces for playing, studying, and sleeping (see figure 7.1). This required children's bedrooms to be rather large and furnished beyond the standard bed and dresser, and to have enough room for toys. In a 1955 showcase home in Holmby Hills, California, the children's room includes a large desk area and shelving area.[6] The space is equally divided among work, play, and sleep areas, suggesting that work is of equal importance. In fact, in one photograph a

FIGURE 7.1 Children's bedroom. Showcase home in Holmby Hills, California. (*Source*: Julius Shulman photography archive, 1936–1997, Series IV, job numbers, 1934–2009. © J. Paul Getty Trust. Getty Research Institute, Los Angeles [2004.R.10].)

child is depicted playing while another appears to be writing a letter or doing homework. Therefore, in addition to the private cul-de-sacs of the suburbs, bedrooms took on a particular significance in defining the spaces of childhood. For children, the home was a site of play *and* work. Public discourse on children having their own room and a space to work was framed as necessary for developing a sense of responsibility, security, and "pride of ownership."[7]

Judging from newspapers, home-buying guides, and national periodicals, the general consensus at the time was that teenagers preferred bedrooms that resembled a study.[8] For teenagers, this meant the addition of a "rec" room or a bedroom remodeled as a studio apartment where they could entertain friends, listen to music, watch television, and study. Articles often featured well-designed bedrooms that emphasized music or other aspects of popular culture that would be attractive to postwar teenagers. The bedroom shown in figure 7.2 has the feel of an apartment, as it is furnished with a daybed, suggesting a space for activity, not sleeping. The caption for the featured bedroom also notes that a television or movie projector can be added. The housing and furnishing industries advised families to create spaces for teenagers that addressed their new needs and matur-

FIGURE 7.2 "Teen-age Territory." Accompanying photograph for newspaper article as an example of a teen studio apartment. The text notes that a television or movie projector can also be added. (*Source*: *Christian Science Monitor*, © September 8, 1950, Christian Science Monitor. All rights reserved. Used under license.)

ing interests. Using the gendered language of the era, one adviser writes, "It is ideal if he can have a retreat of his own, a place to concentrate on his studies and hobbies, and where friends of his own age group may visit."[9] Families were advised that a combination bedroom and living room–study, "a separate suite of his own," was the best solution.[10]

During the postwar period, *Seventeen* magazine regularly featured articles on home decorating, primarily on the bedroom. Recognizing that many readers did not have large bedrooms, the magazine ran articles like "Small Rooms and How They Grow"; published in March 1950, it advised teenagers how to organize a small bedroom to create different areas for sleeping, studying, and entertaining friends.[11] Furniture companies such as Ethan Allen ran advertisements that accompanied editorials for the "Living Bedroom"—an all-day space for "teen needs"—featuring a desk area, shelving for books, and furniture to accommodate a television and phone.[12] Creating a "teen apartment" was considered a win-win for parents and teenagers, as both would gain privacy and a place to entertain friends without taking over other public spaces in the home.

Social commentators promoted the addition of televisions, music centers, and telephones to create a space that would be attractive to the average teenager.[13] In addition to telephones and record players in teenagers' bedrooms, a desk and a typewriter often complemented the private space of the studio-like bedroom in advertisements and editorials.[14] Even homebuilders began to integrate technology by adding phone outlets in bedrooms, and phone companies encouraged families to modernize their existing wiring in anticipation of the teenage years, when their children would supposedly spend hours on the phone.[15] As discussed in chapter 6, the telephone industry monetized the desire for privacy by promoting additional extensions as a necessity for a home with adolescents. Family advisers also supported increased autonomy and privacy for children as they grew older and in some cases advocated telephone extensions in the child's room so long as the telephone did not interfere with dinner and other joint family activities. *Newsday*'s advice columnist, Frances Story, advised parents to allow teenagers to have their own private line, as "the universal use of a telephone is both a luxury and a modern convenience—indeed in most cases a necessity."[16] In her response to a concerned parent, Story equates a two-telephone home to the national ideal of a two-car household. She acknowledges that some families cannot afford two lines, but for most middle-class families and teenagers who have summer jobs, having a telephone would mean more privacy, which is important to developing young adults. To support her advice, Story referenced data from a telephone company that two-telephone households were on the rise.

However, on television in the 1960s, telephones were depicted as potential interruptions to family togetherness, drawing members out of the home. On programs such as *Leave It to Beaver* (1957–1963), *Father Knows Best* (1954–1960), and *My Three Sons* (1960–1972), the children do not have an extension in their room and have to use the main phone in the living room.[17] On *Father Knows Best*, middle son Bud (Billy Gray)'s bedroom is outfitted in typical teenage decor: posters, a record player, and a workspace in the form of a desk and chair. However, Bud is forced to talk on the phone in a closet for privacy because the only telephone he has access to is located in the living room. Only teenagers who live in households where their parents ignore them or who have social problems have telephones in their rooms, at least according to *My Three Sons*. In the early episode "Other People's Houses" (S1:E20) middle son Robbie (Don Grady) visits his friend's apartment in the city and is amazed at the size of Hank's bedroom. Robbie is jealous because Hank has privacy, his own phone extension, and a sitting area, which makes the bedroom resemble a studio apartment. Unlike the housing and telephone industries' promotion of privacy for teenagers at home, in this show having an apartment-like bedroom with your own telephone is indicative of family problems. Because Hank lives in the city, it is also implied that he does not have access to neighborhood school friends like Robbie. Being an only child is also cast in a negative light. Having privacy as a teenager and a sophisticated city apartment are not as important as living a carefree life in the suburbs with siblings and a father who spends time with his children.

By the 1970s, *The Brady Bunch*, which was discussed in relation to the role of women in households in chapter 6, was featuring story lines with teenagers desiring a private, apartment-like bedroom with a telephone and a stereo. The show engaged with public discourse that had emerged in the 1950s about the developmental importance of the teenage years and how youth culture was influenced by consumerism. In "To Move or Not to Move" (S1:E23) the writers addressed the question that many viewers were already asking: Why doesn't Mike, an architect, design a bigger house for the extended family? In the episode, Mike notes that he and Carol cannot agree on a house they both like and find a bigger house that they can afford. They need at least one more bathroom and additional bedrooms to accommodate three boys and three girls. Initially, the children are very excited about the possibility of moving. The Bradys put their house up for sale and look at a larger house that would better fit their needs. However, moving would require the children to attend a new school. Furthermore, the children realize that they would miss their current home and the closeness they experience as siblings living at close quarters. The children decide to collectively sabotage the move by first convincing Alice and Carol that the house is haunted and later scaring off a prospective buyer.

By season two, the living arrangement no longer works for Greg, the oldest son. In "Our Son, the Man" (S2:E18), he is upset about the lack of privacy in the family's three-bedroom home. Greg has to share a bedroom with his two brothers and is unable to talk to a friend on the phone in the family room without his siblings interrupting his conversation. Greg asks for his own room, arguing with his stepmother that he is no longer a boy; he is a "man" in high school who needs privacy. Mike reluctantly gives Greg his office space in the den. The space becomes a teenager's dream, complete with seventies hippie decor, a stereo system, and a telephone extension—just as in the interior decorating guides and magazines marketed to the youth of the day. But, as discussed earlier, the show adopts a postwar view of ideal family life and therefore never fully embraces the social and cultural practices of the seventies. Consequently, Greg ends up moving back into the bedroom with his siblings, agreeing with his parents that he is growing up too fast.

The need for privacy cannot be ignored during Greg's junior year in high school, however. Unable to find any private spaces in the house to hang out with friends, Greg asks his father if he can move into an apartment with a friend. Mike thinks that Greg is too young to move out of the home but accepts his proposal to move into the attic. Meanwhile, Marcia, who is a freshman in high school, also wants privacy from her sisters and asks Carol if she can stay in the attic. Unaware that their parents did not discuss their decision prior to giving each of the children permission, both of them start moving their things into the attic. Greg and Marcia refuse to give up the attic space as their new bedroom, prompting their parents to agree that because Greg is the oldest he should get the room first; Marcia can move in after Greg leaves for college in two years. Marcia is very upset about the loss of personal space, which prompts Greg to offer Marcia the room. The two younger boys want Greg to move out, and use phone pranks to convince Marcia that living in the attic would make it difficult to talk with her friends over the telephone because the attic does not have an extension. In the end, Marcia tells her stepbrothers that her desire to move to the attic room was selfish and that their parents were correct in offering it to Greg. During the last season of the show, Greg occupies the attic space with the assumption that Marcia will move in after he leaves for college.

WORKSPACES FOR CHILDREN

Although on-screen children often completed their homework in the family room or kitchen to drive and shape the narrative, parents in the late 1950s and 1960s were encouraged by designers and child experts to create a private space for their elementary-aged children to encourage good study habits.[18] Most of the time, this seems to involve a space in the child's bedroom for a desk and a chair, not a separate study room.[19] Overall, this was a middle-class privilege, as working-class families living in smaller houses or apartments did not have the space. The film *A Raisin in the Sun* (1961), based on writer Lorraine Hansberry's Broadway play by the same name, illustrates this point. The Youngers and their extended family live in a crowded Chicago Southside tenement building. The plot centers on the tension between Walter Younger (Sidney Poitier), who desires to start his own business using a $10,000 life insurance check from the death of his father, and his mother (Claudia McNeil), who wants to use the money to buy a single-family home in a white neighborhood. The Younger's son, Travis (Stephen Perry), sleeps in the living room and studies in his parents' bedroom during the day and on the weekends. One of the primary arguments by the grandmother and Travis's mother (Ruby Dee) in support of moving to a house in a white neighborhood is to provide Travis with his own private space and better educational opportunities.

In the period before World War II, some education professionals advocated abolishing homework.[20] However, during the postwar period, the progressive education movement came under attack for being insufficiently rigorous. By the late 1950s, due to the launch of Sputnik by the Russians, Americans were worried that their position as the most advanced nation in the world was threatened. Education advocates argued that American students were behind their Russian counterparts in math and science.[21] This led to a boost for the pro-homework movement. In the 1930s, Remington Rand's Education Division had begun promoting typewriter rentals directly to high school students, claiming that they would earn better grades and gain more free time, and marketing typewriters as a great Christmas or graduation present from parents.[22] Nonetheless, the majority of the Education Division's marketing efforts prior to World War II were targeted at schools or teachers.[23] By the 1950s, capitalizing on the pro-homework movement, typewriter manufacturers found several ways to promote direct sales of portable typewriters to middle-class families with children. Remington Rand offered weekly and monthly payment plans of $1 per week through authorized dealers aimed at parents of students in order to make their product more affordable.[24]

Television shows began to feature typewriters in children's bedrooms around the same time. For example, on *Leave It to Beaver*, Wally (Tony Dow), the teenage son, is shown studying at his desk, which features a typewriter. Remington ran an accompanying commercial, "Leave It to Remington," featuring two teenage girls talking on the phone about using the Quiet-riter to create an award-winning play aimed at convincing students (and their parents) of the importance of owning a typewriter to do well in high school.[25] Advertisements informed parents that students who type get "38% better grades!"[26] Typewriters were depicted as being just as desirable to children as a brand new toy. In an advertisement for Smith-Corona typewriters that ran during the postwar period, a school-age boy is shown pressed up against a store window looking at several colorful typewriters on display (see figure 7.3). The Royal Typewriter Company went so far as to manufacture a typewriter intended just for children. The Mercury, manufactured by Silver-Seiko for Litton Industries, featured a standard keyboard with a compact design to fit a child's hands. It was relatively lightweight—ten pounds—and retailed for $49.95, half the price of their standard-size portable.[27] Finally, Remington's Education Division created a $35,000 scholarship sweepstakes to promote sales of the lower-cost ($90) Monarch portable typewriter to potential college students.[28] Consumers were persuaded that having a personal typewriter in the home improved grades and increased the chance of getting into and being successful in college. Interestingly, this is the same argument used to sell personal computers during the 1980s, which I discuss further in chapter 12.

Ad copy for Smith-Corona typewriters, unsurprisingly, was often gendered. Portable typewriters were marketed to young women as handsome, easy to use, and practical because, as one advertisement stated, "almost any firm can use a smart young steno."[29] For adolescent girls, having a typewriter in their bedroom not only helped with homework but also provided an opportunity for them to become accomplished typists in preparation for entering the workforce before getting married.[30] Smith-Corona portables used regulation keyboards to ensure that their student customers could transition to standard-sized typewriters used in business offices. In 1957, Smith-Corona introduced the first portable electric typewriter, which was aggressively aimed at two untapped markets: small businessmen and women who worked as secretaries and used electric typewriters at work but disliked switching to manual portables at home. Company executives believed that more women entering the workforce and the "trend toward more

FIGURE 7.3 A Smith-Corona typewriter advertisement from the 1950s that ran in popular U.S. magazines. (*Source*: Image courtesy of Smith Corona Corporation.)

businesslike home management" would translate to growth in sales of electric portables.[31] For young women, the typewriter represented the bridge between nonpaid work within the private sphere, in the form of homework, and future gendered work within the public sphere. Regardless of gender, the postwar home represented a space where children could develop a middle-class work ethic by playing at work, further undermining the public/private dichotomy.

Toy and furniture companies went so far as to create "junior-sized" executive and secretary desks for children to work on hobbies and homework, as well as office-based toys to emulate their parents during the postwar period.[32] The play office set replicated sexist gender norms of the period. According to one product description: "The 'Junior Executive,' #5585, gives Junior [a] replica of everything on Dad's desk, for his pre-executive training. There are the plastic name-plate, lettering for it, a desk blotter, pencils, ball pens, pen-holder, perpetual calendar . . . and—of course—the indispensable credit card. The 'Junior Secretary,' #5586, has most of these items, plus steno book, hairbrush, cosmetics, perfume and cologne."[33] Incorporating office furniture, toys that replicate gender dynamics in the public sphere, and technology associated with the world of business—in this case the typewriter in children's bedrooms—advanced the dismantling of the public/private dichotomy. The office toys merged work and play, introducing middle-class baby boomers to future working practices that would typify the postindustrial economy. The postwar suburban home was also a space where children could develop a middle-class work ethic by receiving an allowance for household chores. Historically, as outlined in chapter 1, children participated in the household economy as a means of "earning their keep." Like their parents, children worked to help ensure that their family had a place to sleep and food to eat, and to generally help the household. Children's chores were historically related to farm duties or home-based industry. By the early twentieth century, chores involved household tasks, and the rationale for why children should receive allowances was introduced: it was supposed to create responsible consumers.[34]

However, it was not until the 1950s that paid allowances for chores became popular, and this coincided with the rise in teenage culture and consumption.[35] Popular postwar sitcoms often dramatized the themes of ethics, consumerism, and work by featuring story lines with children and teenagers working within the household. Grace Palladino explains that during the postwar period the emergence of a distinct teenage social life drove the new teenage market for consumer products and entertainment.[36] By 1965, the teenage market in the United States had reached $11 billion annually and influenced $30 billion of family spending.[37] Most depictions of children earning money on television took the form of chores and negotiating an allowance, but in some cases children were depicted as entrepreneurs. In the early *Father Knows Best* episode "Live My Own Life" (S1:E5), Bud is tired of his family controlling his life and of his lack of privacy and decides that he wants to move out and rent a room over a store for $5 a month in exchange for cleaning the store. In order to lure Bud back home, his parents ask him to fix his sister's radio and help out around the house, giving him things to do to feel like a "man"—in other words, to make him feel he is needed and has a valuable position in the household.

Leave It to Beaver depicted the childhood exploits of Theodore "Beaver" Cleaver (Jerry Mathers), the younger of two sons, who occasionally desires to earn money by creating a home-based business, such as selling water to people in the neighborhood after the utility company shuts off the water. In "Water, Anyone" (S1:E7), older brother Wally needs $3.98 to pay for a baseball uniform. His father, Ward (Hugh Beaumont), does not believe that he "should just hand over $3.98." However, Beaver asks, "Where else can you get money if you don't get it from your father?" The ensuing dialogue provides an opportunity to promote and convey middle-class work ethics. Ward suggests that his sons work to earn the money, and the children appear shocked by the suggestion. By the 1940s, most middle-class children were no longer expected to work to help support the family unit.[38] Between the 1870s and 1930s, because of the passage of child labor and compulsory education laws, urban middle-class children became "economically 'worthless' but emotionally 'priceless.'"[39] There was no expectation that children like Beaver had to work in the public sphere to help support the household. Instead, it was understood that any form of work children performed in the private sphere (e.g., doing chores, delivering papers, mowing the law) was an educational opportunity that "would benefit primarily the child."[40] Ward offers Wally twenty-five cents an hour to clean the house to earn the money for his uniform. Wally does more damage than good, however, making a complete mess of the kitchen in his attempt to clean the fridge, creating more work for his mother. June (Barbara Billingsley) explains to a friend that it really would be easier to give the money to Wally, but working three or four Saturdays to earn it "builds character."

In the same episode, Beaver realizes that he can exploit the need for water because of the hot weather and learns that the water company plans to shut off the water to locate a leak. Like an entrepreneur, he decides to sell water for five cents to people in the neighborhood. His friend objects because he does not think he should have to pay for water, and then Beaver raises the price to six cents after his friend realizes that the water has been shut off. Ward complains to June that Beaver is exploiting people by selling water and running a monopoly, but notes that he gave Beaver the idea by lecturing him about "big business, corporate endeavors, and showing initiative." The dialogue uses corporate language that would be familiar to viewers in the era of "the company man." A neighbor complains to Ward that Beaver's behavior is problematic and could lead to juvenile delinquency or even communism. The show picks up on postwar social conditions and public discourse regarding youth culture to uphold the image of middle-class respectability. According to Beaver's father, this means developing good behavior such as sharing with friends when one has something that others lack.

Beaver recognizes the moral contradiction in pursuing profit at the expense of his friends and neighbors, but proclaims that Ward's friend, the neighborhood grocer, does not give food away to their family or the neighborhood. Defensively, Ward retorts that the grocer is a businessman, and Beaver replies, "So am I."

Children at the time were told to share, be team players, and work collaboratively. Yet, under capitalism, children also had to learn how to compete as individuals to achieve the American Dream. Robert Wuthrow's argument that middle-class socioeconomic success is founded on the concept of middle-class respectability is beneficial in deconstructing this dialogue.[41] Beaver, as a child, must learn hard work, honesty, and perseverance—qualities associated with respectability since the mid-nineteenth century.[42] Respectability constructs middle-class identity in comparison to various "others"—marginal people—who do not conform to middle-class behaviors that promote economic stability. The others in this case are the greedy businessmen, communists, and juvenile delinquents who do not practice or embrace the qualities that define what it means to be a good worker or a good businessman. Ward cannot find a satisfactory response to convince Beaver that what he is doing is wrong. The televisual text cannot offer a real resolution because of the social contradictions evident in a capitalist society.

Postwar television also reflected the cultural trend of voluntarily participating in household work without financial compensation as a means of developing character. When on-screen children and teenagers receive an allowance, they use it to attend the movies, pay for dates, or participate in a hobby. On *The Donna Reed Show* (1958–1966), the Stone children are encouraged to finish their chores without explicitly receiving money in exchange. In the mismanaged homes of the friends of the Stone children, chores are only completed after the children are yelled at and punished. Donna tells her children that they still need to do their chores even when she is nice, and the children fall in line without conflict. We can only assume that Donna's "innate" parenting skills and cheerful disposition are enough to raise compliant children. The lesson taken away is that ideal middle-class parents raise responsible children with a good work ethic.

When children do receive an allowance, the opportunity to teach proper employer-worker relations emerges. This theme is represented in the *My Three Sons* episode "My Three Strikers" (S1:E12). The boys demand higher allowances to buy the latest product marketed to teenagers and to participate in social events with their school friends. They threaten to strike until their demands are met. Asking his children to "come to the table and negotiate with management," Steve Douglas (Fred MacMurray) uses his business savvy and his ability to be a present father, despite his demanding job, to avoid a strike by taking the time to sit down with his children and broker a deal. In his parenting, Steve uses a business model to explain to the children how management and labor relate and can work together. Therefore, the incorporation of the child's responsibility to do homework and receive payment for doing chores (bourgeois labor) as part of suburban home life takes away the negative associations of nineteenth-century child labor practices. The middle class maintained its ideological hegemony by facilitating the enculturation of the work ethic in its children.

Although television sitcoms did not overtly discuss the problems associated with attaining and maintaining a middle-class standard of living, early 1950s family television shows actively tackled the impact of work on family life and the importance of developing an appropriate middle-class work ethic. Images on television solidified the ideological hegemony of the middle class. Television, and sometimes film, attempted to resolve the tension between the postwar idealism of privatized family life and the necessity of work within a capitalist system by representing a space for children to work within the suburban home. This includes representations of domestic workspaces for fathers, which will be discussed in detail in the next chapter.

8 • AN OFFICE AWAY FROM THE OFFICE

Most public discourse on masculinity in American culture sees it as being in crisis, a state that began in the nineteenth century with industrialization and the changing nature of work (see, e.g., Michael Kimmel's *Manhood in America* [2017], Roger Horrocks's *Masculinity in Crisis* [1994], and Sally Robinson's *Marked Men* [2005]). As John Beynon states, "Crisis is constitutive of masculinity itself," as definitions of what it means to be a man are always changing.[1] One key aspect of this crisis is the work-life dilemma and changing definitions of fatherhood in relation to family and work that began in the postwar period. Many scholars have re-examined the long-held belief in the strict division of men and women into separate spheres that began in the nineteenth century; however, there is limited scholarship examining men's presence and role in the construction of what it means to work in the domestic sphere.

Whereas most middle-class white women's lives were expected to revolve around family and home, men's lives were expected to occupy both work and home. As in the late nineteenth century, men in the postwar period were confronted with contradictions, as they were supposed to provide for their family by participating in work in the public sphere—meaning they were often absent from the home for the majority of the day—and simultaneously establish a palpable presence in the home by providing a masculine role model for children and embracing the 1950s ideology of togetherness. The ideology of togetherness dictated that family work be shared equally among married couples, but this did not happen in reality. Social critics argued that ideal family life was best achieved with the father regarding the home as a place of leisure, not a place of work.[2] As Andrew Gorman-Murray argues, "The private space of the home enabled men to negotiate alternative masculinities, where they could be expressive, emotive and engage in domestic labour and child care."[3] For men in the 1950s, supporting the family was the primary role, and togetherness a leisure-time pursuit. This chapter examines attempts to resolve these contradictions in the promotion of togetherness by looking at how television and film portray men bringing work into the home. I also examine surrounding discourse on shifts in the notion of family life, specifically ideas about fatherhood and work-life balance during the postwar period.

According to Jessica Weiss, the Great Depression was psychologically damaging to American men's sense of manhood and their ability to provide for their families.[4] World War II restored their status as the household's main source of income. However, because so many men were absent from the home during the war, childrearing experts and social critics started to question the consequences for society and the impact on children of growing up without fathers living in the home. At the same time, prominent social critics such as David Riesman expressed anxiety about the role of women in the feminization of men. Historian James Gilbert writes, "By invoking a discourse that had come to identify mass consumer society with women, and by adding his own vivid terminology to explain this phenomenon, Riesman implicitly wrote the history of character as a story of the decline of masculinity."[5] After the prolonged absence of men in many households due to World War II, postwar popular discourse implored men to become involved fathers and take their rightful place as head of the family. Fathers were receiving mixed messages—men were expected to play a vital role in the family and at the same time make a contribution to society and reclaim their manhood in the public sphere. Discourse about what it means to be an involved father echoed earlier rhetoric during the Machine Age in the United States, the period between World War I and World War II. Sociologist Ralph LaRossa shows in his research that contradictory and complex notions of what it means to be a father emerged in the 1920s.[6] Yet, by the 1930s, the definition of an "involved father," which included "economic provider, pal, and male role model all rolled into one," became the institutionalized contemporary stereotype of middle-class fatherhood.[7]

In the postwar period masculinity was primarily defined by employment outside of the home despite the consequences of inadequate interaction with one's family. Parenting experts such as Dr. Benjamin Spock noted that male role models were necessary for children to properly develop and that a male presence at home was important for boys in developing masculinity.[8] Male role models were also understood to be good for American society as a whole. Therefore, men had to take their place in the home. Weiss further explains that experts instructed men through newspaper editorials, popular magazines, and self-help books to spend more time at home participating in parenting, thereby modernizing the concept of fatherhood.[9] Editors of popular magazines and authors who wrote for them urged men and women to view parenting as a shared effort within conventional gender roles. Postwar television reflected this trend in shows such as *Father Knows Best* (see chapter 7), emphasizing the role of men within the family. This did not change the belief that the primary responsibility of mothers was to raise the children and that of fathers was to financially support the family, but men were encouraged to help out around the house and spend time with their children. Fatherhood could be about do-it-yourself household projects, hobbies, friendship, and having fun with one's children without jeopardizing one's position outside the home and one's masculinity. Men's role in the home would counteract the feminization of the home.

For some postwar social critics and psychiatrists, men's presence in the home was necessary but had gone too far; they saw the boundary between mother and father as becoming too blurred. A *Life* editorial quotes psychiatrist Dr. Ralph Greenson on the danger of swapping traditional gender roles in the modern marriage: "The [father] confuses being fair with submitting to [his wife's] aggressiveness. Finally he begins to trade roles and to take on more and more of the maternal role with the children, protecting and nurturing and worrying about them."[10] The problem was not the amount of time men spent in the home but the role they played there, and the possibility that children would lose sight of their father as a breadwinner and the head of the family and perceive him as another mother figure. Fathers would destabilize their masculinity by acquiescing to their wives in the home. In the discourse on fatherhood and the role of men in the home, a subversive thread emerged about the role of the home in the feminization of American men.[11] Toward the end of the 1950s contributors to *Playboy* magazine such as Philip Wylie were railing against what they perceived as the takeover of the American home by women and the consequent domestication of America. Wylie argued that women had removed the spaces of masculinity within the home and that all that remained as the center of the home were the master bedroom (which he implies is the domain of mothers and had lost any sexuality), the kitchen, and the nursery, with no consideration of the desires of men.[12] This was happening despite what he argued was the debt that women owed men for freeing them from traditional domestic labor by inventing modern appliances such as the washing machine. Men needed a space to retreat to where they could avoid the constant barrage of feminine influences within the middle-class suburban home.

Even a cursory look at postwar television and romanticized depictions of life in the 1950s reveals that the suburban home was constructed as a space of feminine domesticity separate from the sphere of work—a space of leisure. The spaces within the home are marked clearly as public (kitchen, living room) or private (bedrooms) compared to the hybridized public-private spaces of today. The postwar suburban home is also depicted as a space of childhood and entertainment, especially the act of watching television. But the spaces within the home were not homogeneous. With the incorporation of communication technology into the home in the form of the telephone and television, middle-class families created multipurpose spaces out of necessity to meet modern lifestyles, and this included mixing the practice of everyday life, work, and leisure in the suburban home. In order for middle-class men to take their place as head of the household, be active fathers, and at the same time have successful careers without spending too much time away from home, a solution needed to be found within the suburban house. Consequently, extra bedrooms acting as multiuse rooms or a study served as hybrid public-private spaces within the home.[13]

Editorials in publications such as *Playboy* describe the suburbs as places of isolation, as men were cut off from the traditional masculine spaces of the city that had no counterpart in the suburbs. The only solution was to reinstate the spaces of masculinity in the home: the den, library, study, or bar. But, as noted in chapter 5, newer middle-class starter homes had eliminated these spaces because of costs and limited space. Only the homes of the upper middle class and homes in established suburban neighborhoods retained the study or den. By 1955, some homebuilders had responded to consumer demand and were offering as standard more affordable midrange three-bedroom homes ($15,000–$19,000) with a den, home office, or extra bedroom/multipurpose room. For example, a 1,270-square-foot floor plan described as the ideal house for "living in the present tense" had three bedrooms (including a large master bedroom with en suite bathroom) and a separate study.[14] The bedrooms are located next to workspaces, as are play spaces. As discussed in chapter 9, this spatial arrangement represents a conflation of work and leisure, exemplified by *Playboy* in the bachelor pad.

Even though the den was reintroduced into the middle-class home, this did not necessarily solve the problem. In popular magazines such as *Kiplinger's Personal Finance* and *Life*, writers argued that builders were still failing to create spaces wholly dedicated to the father in the promotion of multipurpose rooms in the modern house. Instead, men had to share space with the family, as the study often served as a study-family-television room due to the limited space in most middle-class homes. Writers complained that men did not really want togetherness; they wanted aloneness. As one bemoaned, "The beauty of a bona fide den is that a man can interrupt a complicated job of work . . . and come back later expecting to find everything as he left it."[15] The telephone and TV started to migrate to other areas of the house besides the living room, and the need for flexible/multipurpose space in the modern household made a space exclusively for men unattainable for most of the middle class, even though men argued that the den should not be shared as a family room.

For junior executives, corporate careers were demanding, requiring considerable time commitments on top of a long commute between home and the office in the city. William Whyte described this lifestyle and the impact of corporations as mass organizational institutions on society in his sociological report *The Organization Man*.[16] The book was a best seller and analyzed what Whyte found alarming about the postwar relationship between work and everyday life. In the opening of the book, Whyte attempts to define the organization man in a passage that I believe is particularly instructive for understanding the origins of today's professional or "creative" class that comprise the ranks of the upper middle class and its accompanying work practices:

> *They are not the workers, nor are they the white-collar people in the usual, clerk sense of the word.* These people only work for The Organization. . . . *They are of the staff as much as the line, and most are destined to live poised in a middle area that still awaits a satisfactory euphemism. But they are the dominant members of our society nonetheless.* They have not joined together into a recognizable elite—our country does not stand still long enough for that—but *it is from their ranks that are coming most of the first and second echelons of our leadership, and it is their values which will set the American temper.*[17]

Further to my ongoing argument that the home is a space of work, I also examine the values and ideals that reflect the relationship between work and the home and which laid the foundation for the live-work lifestyle dominated by communication technology that many writers, social critics, and other experts argue describes contemporary everyday life. Just like the smartphones and laptops of today, telephones, Dictaphones, and typewriters made working at home possible during the postwar period. Whyte goes on to describe the working experience of executives at various professional levels and the impact that work had on life at home. Men reported working on average fifty to sixty hours per week, with an average day at work of 9.5 hours. In almost all of the companies Whyte surveyed, a five-day workweek did not exist, and most men reported that their employers expected them to work on the weekend and in the evening. Many junior executives had work commitments in the evening outside of the office and, when they did go home, described their den or study as a "branch office." A few men even reported equipping their study or home office with dictating machines and calculators in addition to a telephone and a typewriter. Typewriter companies advertised their products for dads to use at home so that they could avoid working late at the office.[18]

In Whyte's study, most executives reported doing the bulk of their reading for work at home and managing subordinates by telephone in their study. As one executive put it, "I do a lot of spot-checking by phone from home." He goes on to say that he has "more time then, and besides most people have their guard down when you phone them at home."[19] One of the earliest uses of the term "home office" appeared in the *New York Times* for September 25, 1960, in an article informing readers of a successful new business venture by a commercial office designer. The designer noted that "many executives try to make their office a home-away-from-home, [but] there is a need for many to try to make their home an office-away-from-the-office."[20] Men in the Whyte study reported trying to be devoted husbands and involved fathers, and were aware that the practice of togetherness was expected, but in reality work absorbed much of their time even when they were physically present in the home, which produced a lot of guilt.[21] Considering the representations of fatherhood on television, it is easy to understand how men could feel guilty based on the mixed messages they were receiving about their social and familial roles and work-life balance.

MASCULINE DOMESTICITY IN POPULAR CULTURE

Popular television sitcoms made very clear the importance of the father in relation to the family, the significance of fatherhood, and the necessity to obtain work-life balance. Consider the following titles that highlight the cultural importance of fatherhood: *Father Knows Best, My Three Sons, Make Room for Daddy* (1953–1956), and *The Bachelor Father* (1957–1962). One could say that postwar television was obsessed with masculine domesticity and finding a space for men in the suburban middle-class home. Television dads were mostly upper middle class by occupation and the sole provider for their family, which included buying the latest consumer products and paying the mortgage on a large house in an established middle-class neighborhood. Like many of their counterparts in reality, television fathers had a den that served as a study or home office. In some shows the den actually doubles as a TV room, as it does for the Nelsons on *The Adventures of Ozzie and Harriet* (1952–1966), or as a bedroom, as it does for the grandfather on *My Three Sons*. In the case of the Nelsons, Ozzie does not seem to need a den for his exclusive use, as his occupation is never defined, and on *My Three Sons* Steve Douglas uses his bedroom as an office.

However, in other depictions of the study, the room represents a space of masculinity and is exclusively the domain of the father. For example, on *Leave It to Beaver*, Ward's study is equipped with a telephone, bookshelves, and two leather chairs facing the desk. There is wood paneling to code the room as masculine compared to the other rooms in the house. The study is a space where Ward conducts family business and lectures the boys after their misguided adventures. Ward does not work long hours at the office or take long business trips. He is home before dinner to spend time with the family. Although Ward does not actively talk about his job often and does not seem to have any problem balancing work and home life, the study does appear to be a space for him to work at home. He is often depicted working in his study, mostly reading reports on the weekend. In the episode "Beaver's Prize" (S3:E4), Beaver spills ink on his father's papers and gets into serious trouble because Ward has made it very clear that his desk is off limits to the boys. On television the study is designated as the territory of the father and a space to establish and assert masculine authority within the perceived feminine sphere of the suburban home.

Although all of the television fathers are portrayed as professionals (e.g., advertising executive, engineer, lawyer, or doctor), roles that normally would demand long hours at work, their jobs rarely interfere with their ability to be physically present in the home. The details of their occupations are glossed over in most cases, and very few depictions of their workplaces are shown compared to their life at home, emphasizing the point that the happiness and well-being of the middle-class family was dependent on the physical presence of the father. To maximize the presence of the TV father, story lines had to diminish his occupation or incorporate a space for work in the home.

The most obvious examples are Dr. Alex Stone (Carl Betz) on *The Donna Reed Show* and Steve Douglas on *My Three Sons.* Alex works as a pediatrician and has a home-based practice. Because of the nature of the medical profession, Alex can work from home and, with the benefit of the telephone, is accessible to his patients in case of emergencies. Key themes of the show are Alex's struggle to be present despite his medical practice being located in the den, Donna's and the children's tolerance of the many interruptions during dinner when patients telephone for medical advice, and Alex being called away from home on weekends and in the evening. Steve Douglas is an aeronautical engineering consultant. He uses his bedroom, outfitted with a drafting table, to complete projects at home and maximize his ability to be present during the evening and weekends. Although he does occasionally go on long work trips, for the most part his schedule seems to be flexible and not the typical nine-to-five workweek.

In both cases the fathers are characterized as hardworking and busy professionals who, despite the demands of their jobs, are able to be present for their families. They are not condemned for bringing work into the home and are contrasted with the fathers of their children's friends and other men in the neighborhood or from the father's workplace, who are collectively depicted as workaholics. The other fathers are portrayed as failing to balance home and work life by their continued absence from the home or by working additional hours in the evening or on weekends. Failing to be present in the home is a failure of fatherhood. This message is driven home when Ward occasionally has to discipline Beaver's friend Larry (Rusty Stevens), whose mother struggles to raise him well because his father is often out of town on business. Working at home is allowed for noble professions such as medicine, but working many hours at home to get ahead or satisfy a materialistic boss is also represented as a failure of fatherhood. Missing a son's baseball game on a Saturday is portrayed as a serious threat to the father's work-life life balance and ultimately the well-being of the family.

In *Living Room Lectures,* Nina Leibman notes that advertisers and the marketing departments of major networks heavily influenced television narratives during the 1950s.[22] Because many television fathers were employed as managers or executives, advertising and corporate culture in general could not be portrayed as a source of social problems. However, the ideology of family togetherness was central to the middle-class value system at the time. Therefore, the neighborhood fathers on shows such as *Leave It to Beaver* and *The Donna Reed Show* who spend too much time at work are portrayed with contempt. Also, 1950s family sitcoms often featured narratives that portrayed employers and clients negatively. Employers who expected unreasonable workloads and took television fathers away from their homes outside of normal business hours were portrayed as threats to the primacy of the nuclear family and the practice of togetherness.

One subtheme that has emerged from this examination of work in the home is that market-based work is recognized as a necessary and natural aspect of men's role in society. In reflecting the postwar emphasis on togetherness, television fathers maintained a continued presence in the home, effectively domesticating white middle-class men and associating masculinity with what was traditionally characterized as the feminine sphere. However, by incorporating a space for work in the home, the father's status as a knowledge professional—performing one of the celebrated occupations in the public sphere traditionally associated with men—mitigated any threat of the feminization of middle-class white fathers within the suburban home.

The postwar suburbs are understood to be bedroom communities separated from work and the public sphere. Despite the assumed separation of the private and public spheres within the postwar middle-class home, by examining the integration of communication technology within the home, the relationship of gender and space, the enculturation of the work ethic in middle-class children, and representations of work within the home in popular culture, I have shown that spaces of production did transgress the boundaries of the privatized home. White middle-class families were encouraged by companies such as Bell Telephone to create multipurpose spaces out of necessity to meet modern lifestyles, and this included mixing everyday life, work, and leisure in the suburban home. In an attempt to resolve the tension between the postwar idealism of togetherness and the necessity of work within a growing system of consumerism, mass media depicted various hybrid spaces within the home that enabled different kinds of work. At the same time, the proliferation of communication technology within the home complicated the relationship between work/leisure, public/private, and togetherness/apartness within the domestic sphere. Despite the ideological push for togetherness and the promotion of family life over the office, work was always present in the home, facilitated by the growing use of technology within the domestic sphere. Early communication technology in the form of the telephone and the portable typewriter mediated the practices of everyday life in the postwar period. Consequently, this reveals the interdependent relationship between the private and public sphere within late capitalism and the impossibility of maintaining the tenuous dichotomy.

PART 3 THE BIRTH OF THE LIVE-WORK LIFESTYLE

9 • REAL MEN LIVE IN THE CITY

By the early 1960s, representations of masculinity in popular American culture were grounded in the space of the city, and as Elizabeth Fraterrigo argues, *Playboy* magazine served as the guidepost.[1] *Playboy* led, and many imitators in popular culture followed. Alan Baker (Frank Sinatra) in *Come Blow Your Horn* (1963), Matt Helm (Dean Martin) in a series of 1960s spy spoofs, and James Bond (most famously played by Sean Connery) all embodied the characteristics of the playboy bachelor: well-dressed, womanizing, successful professionals living in well-designed modern apartments. Popular films such as *Pillow Talk* (1959), *Boys' Night Out* (1962), *Come Blow Your Horn*, and *Diary of a Bachelor* (1964) depicted unmarried men in bachelor apartments seducing women, drinking, and living the good life while trying to avoid marriage and the perceived feminized world of the suburbs. For example, in its opening scenes *Boys' Night Out* underscores the belief that living in the suburbs is emasculating for men. Three married friends and a divorced man, Fred Williams (James Garner), commute each workday by train from Greenwich, Connecticut, to New York City. To convince the audience that their lives lack something essential to masculinity, we see a glimpse of how each of them lives in the suburbs. George (Tony Randall) and his wife, Marge (Janet Blair), interact in their bedroom as roommates, not lovers. It is implied that George is sexually frustrated because his wife would rather do crossword puzzles in bed than have sex with him. Fred is recently divorced and lacks autonomy and privacy because he lives in the suburbs with his mother. Doug (Howard Duff) wants the satisfaction of completing home repair projects himself, but his wife, Toni (Anne Jeffreys), cares about appearances and would rather hire someone to maintain their home. Finally, Howie (Howard Morris) is unable to enjoy old-fashioned home cooking because his wife, Joanne (Patti Page), is constantly on a diet. The men learn that Fred's boss has rented an apartment in the city to conduct an affair with his mistress. Dissatisfied with their lives, they fantasize about pooling their money to rent their own love nest in the city.

However, because most films of this era featuring bachelors were romantic comedies, the bachelor apartment in the masculine space of the city provides only a temporary reprieve from emasculated life in the suburbs. *Playboy,* by contrast, anchored masculinity in the city and eschewed the idea that the only valid form of masculinity was linked to family and life in the suburbs. At the time, popular writers such as Philip Wylie and Robert Moskin railed at the intrusion and growing dominance of women in the workplace and other spaces in the city traditionally occupied primarily by men. To the proponents of masculinity in crisis, "America's females [had] pushed and heckled their way into every private male domain."[2] This was due to the perceived loss of masculine spaces in the home, shifting gender boundaries, and more women participating in social activities and work in the public sphere that were traditionally closed off to them because of their gender.

In his infamous essay "The Womanization of America" (1958), Wylie outlines the feminization of the public sphere by his definition of "every private male domain": the men's clubs and drinking places.[3] Interestingly, Wylie identifies the commencement of this transformation with industrialization, and argues that it was "completed by feminism." Industrialization brought unnatural social values and restrictive sexuality, which he ascribes to female influence and "Victorian prissiness." Men once had their separate spaces as a haven to escape this oppression associated with industrialization. Now those spaces of escape are gone, and masculinity is in crisis. Moskin also believed that growing sexual freedom for women threatened definitions of masculinity and the dominant social order, arguing that men "will have to invent new meanings and myths for maleness."[4] By placing the bachelor in the city, *Playboy,* in Fraterrigo's words, "addressed both the apparent encroachment of women into the public sphere and the 'feminized' spaces of suburbia."[5]

The glamorization and positive representation of life in the city as a temporary or permanent space of masculinity provided a counternarrative to public anxiety about the threat to American masculinity and the decline of American urban centers.[6] As Fraterrigo claims, "If some presaged an urban wasteland, *Playboy* offered an urban wonderland."[7] *Playboy* constructed the white, successful unmarried man in the city as the savior of American masculinity and as an alternative narrative to life in the suburbs. The *Playboy* penthouse apartment was a key feature in imagining the city. As George Wagner writes, the "penthouse sits above but within the city—in it but not of it—and allows the bachelor a controlling gaze of the urban spectacle."[8] For Wagner, the bachelor never completely integrates *into* the city but takes a position of power *over* the city. This conceptualization of the relationship between the white male and the city ignores the problems associated with the racialized city and the possibility of the reversal of Western decline through white masculine surveillance and control. By the postwar period, American cities were associated with African Americans, crime, and poverty in public discourse because of government policies and historical developments. This included the promotion of the suburbs as the economic and cultural future of the white middle-class family, which resulted in the decentralization of metropolitan areas, and the fact that blacks were discouraged from owning property in the suburbs through racially discriminatory economic and government-supported lending policies. In addition, because of the rise in crime due to the economic decline of urban centers and lack of jobs, crumbling infrastructure, and the threat of nuclear annihilation brought on by the Cold War, cities were depicted as dangerous and declining.

Therefore, contradictory narratives regarding the city emerged at the end of the postwar period: on one hand, the deterioration and predicted decline of urban centers, and on the other hand, the glamorization of the city primarily for young white singles in the pursuit of the good life. Pamela Wojcik notes that in film and television during the postwar period, cities, especially New York City, became a "key symbol of America's prosperity and optimism."[9] Wojcik argues that this was due to the destruction suffered by European cities during World War II and their subsequent decline, with New York City becoming the economic and political capital of the world. Although I do not disagree with this interpretation, I would argue that the relationship between cities and representations of masculinity during the 1960s should be further examined within the context of work, leisure, and the home.

A SPACE TO WORK AND PLAY IN THE CITY

Playboy promoted an image of the city as a place for young, primarily white, single men to experience sexual freedom and career opportunities of urban living. The magazine's influence extended to public discourse in leading newspapers, which during the 1960s and early 1970s also featured articles on urban single men living desirable lives where work and leisure appeared seamless. An interior decorator in Chicago claimed that many young men with high salaries "yearn[ed] for the kind of set-ups they associate with spreads in men's magazines and the movies."[10] These setups featured single men living in well-appointed apartments, experiencing domestic bliss outside of the institution of marriage. The opening line of an article featuring four affluent single men in New York City living the good life echoes the sentiment that a wife was not necessary to establish domesticity in the city: "An interesting city apartment apparently doesn't require a woman's touch."[11] Articles featuring bachelor pads bolstered their association with masculinity by emphasizing the amount of physical labor and ingenuity professional men applied to designing their apartments. For example, John Full, a photographer tired of living with roommates who left to get married and presumably moved to the suburbs, decided to rent his own apartment in the city and remodel it as a bachelor pad. John's apartment is a do-it-yourself project.[12] He built most of the furniture, the stereo cabinet and system, and the bar for entertaining women, such as the stewardesses featured in one of the photographs accompanying the article. The author asks, "But what's it all for? Why go to all the trouble?" He proposes that it would have been easier to adopt a hobby like building model airplanes. John explains that he did it to achieve a lifestyle, a way to entertain and work comfortably in his home, reflecting public discourse on bachelor pads influenced by films and men's magazines.

Playboy's promotion of the bachelor pad and the corresponding lifestyle was very influential judging by the number of television shows and films that featured bachelors living in modern and sophisticated apartments during the 1960s. Television shows such as *Family Affair* (1966–1971) and films such as *Pillow Talk* (1959) and *If a Man Answers* (1962) featured successful bachelors living the good life in New York City apartments. In *If a Man Answers,* Gene Wright (Bobby Darin), a young photographer, lives in an apartment that has been converted into a live-work space to accommodate his studio and darkroom. His apartment and lifestyle are more realistic than many other representations of bachelor life in the city. His apartment is modestly furnished with a daybed and a small table, and has a dirty kitchen. In an argument with his soon-to-be wife, Chantal (Sandra Dee), Gene asserts that having a clean kitchen or a stocked pantry is not necessary because he lives in the city. Gene has access to housekeepers and restaurants to support his lifestyle as a bachelor. Chantal argues that he would be better off married, but he counters that bachelorhood is the natural state for men, especially in an urban setting. The message is clear: marriage is an institution for "unnatural" men and women who live in the suburbs.

Pillow Talk also imagines the city as a space of masculine domesticity but goes further by making the connection for the audience that marriage and life in the suburbs fundamentally change men. Brad (Rock Hudson) is a songwriter who works predominantly from home. He lives in a modern bachelor pad with a second-floor loft bedroom and a well-stocked bar. Modern art and leather-bound books line the wood-paneled walls. Brad fully embraces being single in the city even though his friend Jonathan (Tony Randall) claims that mature men want to be married and have children. For Jonathan, what it means to be an adult is to have a wife, children, and a house. Even though *Playboy* magazine countered the prevailing expectation that men must marry, Hollywood would only push against the dominant ideology to a point. In the end, Brad willingly destroys his masculinity, symbolized by his "pregnancy" announcement, which is misunderstood by a doctor and nurse who think he is a medical first, a pregnant male. The film frames Brad's playboy lifestyle as only temporary. For men, falling in love means acceptance of the inevitable: marriage, children, and life in the suburbs.

In fact, it is in the suburbs where the audience witnesses Brad's failure to seduce Jan (Doris Day), the interior decorator he is pursuing under false pretenses. An early scene with Jan and a wealthy suburban client hints at what forms of domesticity are permitted in the suburbs versus the city. The client naively wants to place an African-inspired sculpture in her remodeled living room. Jan tells her that she does not need a fertility goddess in Scarsdale, a New York City suburb. The narrative operates on the assumption that when people think about the middle-class home, they most likely are thinking about sex within the context of the family because the suburban home is imagined as feminine, the space of reproduction. Historically, fertility goddesses represent sex and procreation, but in the film sex is decoupled from reproduction and becomes a form of leisure. Audience members recognize the connotations associated with the suburbs and the bachelor pad and therefore get the joke: there is no need for a statue to promote fertility in a space already dominated by children. This new historicized notion of sex as leisure, I will examine later in this section, is significant not only in popular culture but in the reconstruction of our notions of the private sphere.

The pilot episode of *Family Affair* establishes Bill (Brian Keith), a civil engineer, as a playboy bachelor type. He lives in a spacious bachelor pad in an upscale New York City neighborhood and employs a valet. His bachelor lifestyle is disrupted, however, when his nephew and two nieces move in after losing their parents in an automobile accident. Despite his change in circumstances, dating and pursuing a career are still possible to Bill as a new parent. The show hints at the concept of work-life balance that would enter public discourse in the late 1980s and 1990s. Bill is able to incorporate the children into his busy lifestyle even though he travels often for work. His day-to-day schedule is flexible, and therefore he is able to reschedule important meetings to attend school functions during the day. Bill also conducts business at home, but has to use a desk in the living room because the den is now a bedroom for one of the children. The household is able to manage without the presence of a woman because Mr. French (Sebastian Cabot), his valet, also acts as a nanny, stepping in when Bill is unable to parent the children.

Like television, *Playboy* for the most part situated masculine consumerism for single men in the domestic realm of the city. *Playboy* promoted the "Playboy Penthouse" and bachelor pads as the center of operations for the bachelor. As the magazine's editors saw it, for bachelors, living in a penthouse or an apartment in the city was the "pinnacle of urban living."[13] The inaugural December 1953 issue firmly placed the magazine's readership in the domestic sphere by declaring, "We like our apartment," and publishing editorials on the problem with houses in the suburbs. From the mid-1950s through the early 1970s, *Playboy* featured a series of sophisticated modern bachelor pads (actual homes and architectural renderings) in the city. For example, a series of articles titled "Playboy on the Town," which featured photo editorials of major cities, made life in the city seem exciting and glamorous compared to popular representations of life in the suburbs.[14] The luxurious interiors and the emphasis on "opulent leisure distinguished them as idealized habitats for a new breed of male consumer."[15] These bachelor apartments in *Playboy* served as a setting for a lifestyle that combined work and leisure and provided easy access to everything the city had to offer.[16]

In September 1956, *Playboy* featured the architectural plans for the quintessential bachelor pad, the "Playboy Penthouse Apartment." Although the magazine promoted the image of the bachelor playboy as the man about town, through its editorials, features, and pictorials *Playboy* presented the bachelor pad as the key setting for the playboy lifestyle of professional work, entertainment, and consumerism. The apartment was conceptualized as "a man's world that fits your moods and desires, which is a tasteful, gracious setting for an urbane personality."[17] By situating the bachelor apartment in the city, the bachelor pad and the sophisticated lifestyle that became associated with it became linked to urbanism, unlike the house in the suburbs, which was associated with marriage and family life. In "The Dream House and How to Avoid It," *Playboy* writer Shepherd Mead tells readers that the suburban single-family house is emasculating: "It takes a heap of living to make an apartment a home, but it takes a heap less than if you are driven into a freestanding house. . . . You will discover, however, that every woman wants a house of her own. From the very moment you move into your apartment she will make it clear that she thinks of it only as a temporary expedient."[18]

As mentioned in chapter 8, Philip Wylie, another prominent contributor to *Playboy*, goes further, explaining that the problem was not only the loss of the public spaces in the city and the feminization of the suburbs but also the emasculation of the physical space of the home. "Where once man had had a den, maybe a library, a cellar poolroom, his own dressing room . . . to protect his privacy he now found himself in a split level pastel creation with rooms often created by screens his wife moved about as often as she changed her flower arrangements."[19] Wylie mourned the loss of the traditional compartmentalized Victorian layout when cohabiting but favored the open layout for men-only spaces. For Wylie, the loss of masculine spaces within the home was associated with the takeover of domestic design by women and gay decorators he described as "males in form only—males emotionally so identified with the opposite sex they could rout reluctant husbands because their very travesty made men uncomfortable."[20] *Playboy* set out to rectify this situation by declaring, "A man's home is not only his castle, it is or should be, the outward reflection of his inner self," and by creating a magazine "for the edification and entertainment of urban men."[21] Consequently, *Playboy* promoted an urban form of masculine consumerism within the walls of the bachelor pad.

By publishing editorials and articles on home design, technology, and the latest gadgets, and filling its advertising pages with furniture, entertainment equipment, and home accessories, *Playboy* attempted to educate its readers on new forms of masculinity and recapture the space of the home from what it believed was the feminization of the domestic sphere. In addition to advertisements and columns on domestic gadgets, clothing, entertainment devices, and furniture, *Playboy* featured semiregular pictorials on architecture and interior design.

These features were very popular, as evidenced by circulation numbers and letters to the editor. In promoting interest in fashion, furniture, and home decor as masculine, *Playboy* blurred the line between what constitutes the feminine and masculine domains.

Playboy was not limited to the "entertainment of urban men" but set out to teach men that they could live meaningful lives outside of marriage in the suburbs.[22] Hugh Hefner, as creator and editor, differentiated *Playboy* from typical magazines for men that promoted traditional images of manhood "thrashing through thorny thickets or splashing about in fast flowing streams."[23] Instead, *Playboy* unapologetically promoted conspicuous consumption in the domestic realm: "We don't mind telling you in advance—we plan on spending most of our time inside."[24] Surveying the pages of *Playboy*, it is evident that this meant that men needed to learn how to entertain, cook, and shop, as well as decorate their homes in the city. As Elizabeth Fraterrigo notes, men in the 1950s were given the opportunity to embrace domesticity in the suburbs primarily through hobbies and do-it-yourself projects as a means of home improvement. This form of suburban domesticity was unacceptable to *Playboy*, as this type of activity served the family, not the individual.[25] Furthermore, these activities were spatially limited to the garage or basement within a suburban single-family home.

The bachelor pad was culturally significant, as it represented the model of "forward-looking and 'liberated' masculine consumerism."[26] The rise of a consumer-based economy that promoted leisure, conspicuous consumption, and immediate gratification did not support old norms of masculinity that promoted moderation and frugality. For Bill Osgerby, the bachelor pad was the spatial embodiment of a "consuming masculine subject" that emerged during the explosion of American consumerism in the 1950s and 1960s.[27] Nevertheless, this relationship between the bachelor and the domestic sphere was problematic for men trying to maintain their public characterization of heterosexuality, as gay men (and women) were traditionally associated with fashion, furniture, design, and other forms of consumption and lifestyles within the domestic sphere. Osgerby notes that to maintain its heterosexual credentials, *Playboy* used nude pictures and constant references to sex to mark the magazine as masculine and heterosexual. This allowed readers to feel secure in their heterosexual identities while participating in domestic consumption.[28]

In popular culture, the bachelor pad is represented as the public expression of the bachelor's personality and the embodiment of his lifestyle.[29] The concept of the bachelor pad represented in the pages of *Playboy*, in films, and on television during the 1950 and 1960s was largely a "mythological construct," as in reality only economically elite men were able to afford such luxurious and technologically advanced apartments.[30] However, as Osgerby claims, the bachelor pad is still important in understanding the far-reaching "imagined identity" of the playboy bachelor in the city. *Playboy* and family sitcoms during the 1960s reconstructed the notion of masculine domesticity. The men they portrayed were mostly upper middle class by occupation. Sitcoms featuring single men represented the new professional middle class and the privileges that went with it because of capitalism's ideology of upward mobility and a shifting economy based on the valuation of knowledge. Transitions between work and home life appeared seamless in popular representations, as work could be conducted in the home (often in a converted bedroom or den). Therefore, popular culture stressed the value of merging work and leisure in the city and depicted professional lifestyles as flexible, rewarding, and desirable.

10 • PSEUDO-BOHEMIAN BACHELORETTES

Domestic urbanism in the form of the bachelor pad and the apartment of the single career woman connected work and leisure (sex and consumption) through the inclusion of the telephone and entertainment technology, blurring the boundary between public and private spaces within the home. In order to understand this transformation, it is necessary to recognize the significant social changes beginning in the late 1950s and early 1960s and their relationship to the space of the bedroom and home office. A critical social change was the separation of the act of sex from its reproductive function into a form of leisure and the subsequent transformation of the private sphere. The control and creation of sexual norms associated with the Victorian era were a means to ensure the health and survival of the bourgeoisie. By the late postwar period, this dominant ideology was being challenged and began to shift. According to Steven Seidman, there is significant historical evidence documenting sexual behavior outside of the institution of marriage in the United States, but it was not until the late postwar period that this behavior gained social legitimacy.[1] For example, as noted in chapter 9, publications such as *Playboy*, launched in 1953, started to challenge the dominant ideology. By the 1960s, scientific discourses and media representations of sexuality emerged that "constructed sex as a domain of pleasure, self-expression and communication."[2] The shift began with the research of Alfred Kinsey in the late 1940s and early 1950s and continued with that of scientists such as William Masters and Virginia Johnson during the 1960s and 1970s and the publishing boom in sex manuals such as *Everything You Always Wanted to Know about Sex (But Were Afraid to Ask)* (1969) and *The Joy of Sex* (1972).

With the benefit of hindsight, scholars, specifically feminist ones, have noted that the "sexual revolution" in America was not as revolutionary as the term implies. However, significant social changes did occur during the 1960s and 1970s. Historian Stephanie Coontz argues that "taken together, the rearrangements in marriage, childrearing, inter-generational relations and responsibilities, sexuality, and reproduction have been tremendous, far-reaching, and unprecedented."[3] One significant social change important to the discussion in this chapter was what Seidman calls the "eroticization of female sexuality," which undermined the double standard for female sexual behavior outside of marriage.[4] Easing the double standard ultimately opened up the possibility of living arrangements outside the norm of the family and more independence for women, and extended the period between leaving the parental home, marriage, and having children as part of the family cycle. Even though the changes were not radical, in that double standards still existed for women, and marriage was still the norm, the social transformations during the 1960s and 1970s may have seemed dramatic and appeared to have such a sweeping impact on society as a whole because of popular culture. The culmination of social movements over the course of the twentieth century and increased representations of single life in the city converged in the 1960s and 1970s and helped to redefine sexual activity as a means of individual satisfaction and made it ripe for consumerism.[5]

SELF-FULFILLMENT AND LIFE IN THE CITY

The popularity of bedroom comedies such as *The Seven Year Itch* (1955), *Pillow Talk* (1959), and *Some Like It Hot* (1959) in the mid-1950s, followed by sex farces such as *If a Man Answers* (1962) and *Sex and the Single Girl* (1964) during the early 1960s reflected changes in social relations as traditional norms about gender, sexuality, and individual identity were being challenged by the sexual revolution and the emergence of second-wave feminism. Unlike television, which still reflected the dominant trends of the 1950s, Hollywood films in the 1960s portrayed the increase in sexual liberalization in American society.[6] In addition to the acceptance of premarital sex among young people and the demand by women to have more economic and sexual freedom, the emergence of a singles culture significantly accelerated sexual liberalization during the 1960s.[7]

Unlike their parents, Americans coming of age in the 1960s were encouraged to focus more on personal self-fulfillment instead of the family. Seidman writes, "Whereas their parents might have pursued [self-fulfillment] through work and homemaking, the younger generation, encouraged by an expanding entertainment and leisure industry, looked more to personal avenues of self-fulfillment."[8] This focus on self-fulfillment was rooted in a longer history: the appearance of what historian T. J. Jackson Lears calls the "therapeutic ethos" in the late nineteenth century that influenced the rise of consumer culture in the United States.[9] The therapeutic ethos legitimized a culture of consumerism and leisure, "imagining that the path to betterment was through the increased acquisition of goods."[10] During the postwar period, the economic boom, encouraged through advertising and pro-consumption discourse, accelerated the growth of the leisure market and a consumerism-based notion of the good life. Therefore, by the 1960s, as the market for big-ticket household items such as refrigerators slowed, advertisers started to focus on the next big growth market, individuals. Thomas Frank drives home the point: "If American capitalism can be said to have spent the 1950s dealing in conformity and consumer fakery, during the decade that followed, it would offer the public authenticity, individuality, difference, and rebellion."[11] Television followed with shows such as *Bachelor Father* (1957), *The Lucy Show* (1962), *That Girl* (1966), *I Dream of Jeannie* (1965–1970), and *Family Affair* (1966–1971) that "partition[ed] the mythical family of the 1950s into as many different varieties and subsets as possible."[12]

The white-collar sector of the economy was taking off, and subsequently, young middle-class whites were encouraged to move to the cities to pursue professional opportunities.[13] American urban centers provided the possibility of social and sexual freedom for young women and career advancement for men. Magazines and news media plugged cities such as New York as the places to participate in the new "singles scene." Newspapers featured articles on bachelorettes, often referred to as "single girls" or "career girls," living in the city on their own, describing their lifestyle and living arrangements and the dating scene.[14] In the urban singles scene, the single girl was imagined as the ideal companion for the playboy bachelor. According to Katherine Lehman, the term "single girl" replaced the unappealing "spinster" to characterize the unmarried woman as "youthful and playful well into her thirties."[15] Characterizing single women as "girls" was a way of redefining the period between school and marriage as one of "extended adolescence" during which more women delayed marriage and childbearing.[16]

By the 1970s, with more American women delaying marriage or divorcing, the percentage of single women in their late twenties and thirties in the workforce increased. This trend was prompted not only by feminist influence in the public sphere but also by the maturation of capitalism in the growth of white-collar jobs, a decrease in blue-collar jobs, and high inflation in the 1970s.[17] Ultimately, these trends placed single women at the center of consumer and economic life.[18] As discussed in chapter 9, many contemporaneous social critics believed that white American males were in crisis during the 1950s because of the turn toward family life in the suburbs and the perceived feminization of the public sphere. The public perception of the decline in masculinity of the American male also served as a proxy for the threat of the reorganization of the established social order. The promotion of singles culture in the city by influential publications such as *Playboy* and *Cosmopolitan* and popular representations of urban bachelors in 1960s film and television seemed to be an attempt to reclaim urbanism, which ultimately meant a resurgence of capitalism, as urbanization is arguably its material manifestation.

In 1962 Helen Gurley Brown published *Sex and the Single Girl*, which quickly became a number-one best seller. The book emphasized the joys of being single and the gratification that a career could provide women. At the time the average white American woman married in her early twenties, forgoing career ambitions even after attending college. Although Brown's book was ultimately about snagging a man (but not necessarily to get married), it also advised young women to pursue a life of sexual freedom, leisure, and work well into their thirties before settling down to get married. Therefore, life as a single working girl was understood not to be a permanent state. Brown's advice was supported by her own life as a successful forty-something advertising executive who married at the age of thirty-seven after pursuing a career in her twenties and thirties.

Brown's message pushed back on the prevailing ideology that educated middle-class women should use their skills and intellect to support their husband and raise a family. During the Great Depression, social scientists, educators, and feminists encouraged white women to attend college, and government officials promoted citizenship and eugenics in the belief that educated women were more likely to vote, volunteer, and produce healthier future generations.[19] African American women were encouraged by the black press to attend college to further the important work of racial uplift. Between 1900 and 1940, annual female college attendance in the United States increased from 85,338 to 600,953.[20] By the postwar period, dissatisfaction with housewifery started to emerge in public discourse as even more women started to attend college. Writer and editor Edith M. Stern addressed this issue in a 1949 essay in *The American Mercury*, a satiric magazine that critiqued American social, political, and economic life:

> When a man marries and has children, it is assumed that he will do the best work along lines in which he has been trained or is at least interested. When a woman marries and has children, it is assumed that she will take to housewifery. But whether she takes to it or not, she does it. Such regimentation, for professional or potentially professional women, is costly both for the individual and society. . . . Perhaps even more deplorable is the loss to society when graduate nurses, trained teachers, lawyers, physicians, artists and other gifted women are unable to utilize their prolonged and expensive educations for the common good. Buried in the homemade cakes the family loves, lost among the stitches of patches, sunk in the suds of the week's wash, are incalculable skilled services.[21]

By equating housewifery to slavery, Stern argued that housewifery was actually forced on women and left them with no opportunities to feel satisfied with their lives, in comparison to their professional husbands.

It is not surprising that in her 1963 book, *The Feminine Mystique*, Betty Friedan claimed that "fulfillment as a woman had only one definition for American women after 1949—the housewife-mother."[22] She contended that women could not be fully satisfied until they were able to pursue careers outside the home. Friedan recognized that being a housewife is not a profession, despite a focus in junior colleges and all-women colleges on education in the 1940s and 1950s on courses on marriage, home economics, and family life, and despite advertisers' efforts to convince housewives to think of themselves as professionals to encourage the sale of new products.[23] Friedan, like Stern, believed that married women could balance work outside of the home and family life. There should be no need to choose one or the other. Unlike Friedan and other feminists at the time, Brown believed that Americans needed to adopt a more open sexual culture to expand women's personal freedom. Sexual freedom and the opportunity to delay marriage gave women opportunities to explore their identities in pursuit of a meaningful career. Brown advanced the single working girl as the new and modern woman transforming prevailing gender stereotypes. Although popular, her book was considered controversial, as Brown promoted sexual freedom along with her message of consumerism and gainful employment for women as a means of self-fulfillment.

According to Lehman, urbanism was central to the single woman narrative in the late 1960s, as the city signified new social and career opportunities as well as sexual liberation.[24] The single girl was a unique character in popular culture, as she was directly linked to the city and actively negotiated the city alone.[25] In *Sex and the Single Girl*, Brown, who lived five minutes from her office, tells her readers to live as close to work as possible. Living close to work allows the single girl to transition quickly between her private life and work. Brown felt that "to be a glamorous, sophisticated woman that exciting things happen to, you need an apartment and you need to live in it alone!"[26] Living alone signaled independence, and for Brown financial independence translated as "sexy" to eligible men.

Brown's book is full of pronouncements on everything from appearance, cooking, and dating to decorating the ideal apartment. In every case, Brown argues that in order for women to live "the good single life" they must be willing to work hard. *Sex and the Single Girl* acted as a guidebook for the emerging single working girl in the city. Unlike the typical married woman, who was financially dependent on her husband, the single girl had to work hard at her job and budget accordingly to pay for her apartment and the trappings necessary to live the good life. A job was necessary, as it gave "a single woman something to be," an identity outside of marriage.[27] For Brown, working single women could forge an identity independent of men; unlike married women, they could be known for what they did rather than for whom they belonged to. Brown articulated a lifestyle for women outside of relationships. Sexual freedom was important to Brown, but in her writings, she also encouraged women to pursue careers—both sex and work were necessary for a fulfilling life. If women worked hard, no matter what level they started at, career advancement, and consequently the "good single life," as Brown phrased it, were possible. The working single girl was an ideal, an "economic dream . . . not a parasite, a dependent, a scrounger, a sponger or a bum. She is a giver, not a taker, a winner, not a loser."[28]

Women's occupational choices were more limited than men's, and often associated with everyday life in the private sphere. Therefore, Brown instructed her readers to develop their minds in addition to their appearance as a means of socioeconomic advancement: the single girl "can read Proust, learn Spanish, [and] study *Time*, *Newsweek* and *The Wall Street Journal*. Most importantly, a single woman, even if she is a file clerk, moves in the world of men. To secure a man she knows their language—the language of retailing, advertising, motion pictures, exporting, shipbuilding."[29] Brown understood that most of her readers were not executives or in well-paid positions like herself and could not afford a glamorous professionally decorated apartment in an ideal location in the city. Therefore, she advised young women to avoid expensive neighborhoods, encouraging them to live in ethnic neighborhoods and places where artists and other creative types sought inexpensive housing. However, she did expect her readers to adopt a creative sensibility in home design and furnishings, advising them to sink money into important items of furniture, such as a good-quality modern sofa, but to avoid high-end accessories and entertainment equipment by shopping strategically in places such as secondhand shops.

In 1965, Brown became the editor of *Cosmopolitan*. She revamped the magazine to appeal to the modern woman, focusing on the single working girl, and it became the counterpart to *Playboy* in the 1960s. I agree with Elizabeth Fraterrigo's argument that *Playboy* characterized men as powerful and deserving of male privilege and that it marked the city as a space of masculinity. However, popular female media figures such as Brown countered this image of the city by promoting a life of fulfilling work and sexual freedom for urban single women. Even *Playboy*, as Fraterrigo noted, had to encourage the presence of single women in the city for the bachelor to take part in *Playboy*'s construction of the good life.

Cosmopolitan focused on women's issues primarily relating to self-improvement, sex, fashion, travel, and careers. Although it did not feature as many articles on home design, cooking, and household maintenance as *Playboy*, the magazine did offer practical advice and inspirational pictorials to provide the single girl with decorating ideas and advice on maintaining an apartment, such as hiring a maid. Brown felt that the new household appliances and products sometimes created more work and needed a person to operate them. To balance a career and social life, she suggested that for the single career woman "hiring a good cleaning lady is a wonderful boon to your life, as unexpendable as" a weekly trip to the hairdresser.[30] Career women were encouraged to treat their maid as an employee, not "the help," as their mothers did in the 1950s.[31] This meant treating her with respect, being thankful, and paying into her Social Security retirement account. Brown did not think that career women should have to do housework and should embrace having help to maintain their apartments in the city; however, she also recognized that housework is labor and that women working as maids deserve respect and adequate compensation.

Many articles framed the single girl's apartment as a creative space. "Two Creative Pads That You Can Copy" featured the apartments of a freelance illustrator and an assistant art director. The accompanying photographs feature rooms with eclectic furniture and accessories. There are antiques, pieces from the family attic and secondhand stores, and "well-shopped investments" such as a $600 "lavishly upholstered corduroy sofa."[32] There is an abundance of textures and fabrics. In the mid-Manhattan efficiency apartment, a handmade room divider separates the living and sleeping areas. The workspace is composed of a desk made from a "hollow-core flush door." Overall, this representation of the single girl's apartment and the choice to feature creative professionals suggested the kind of pseudo-bohemian lifestyle depicted in televisual and cinematic spaces of single working women during the 1960s and 1970s.

THE TELEPHONE, WORK, AND THE SINGLE GIRL

As noted in chapter 9, in *Pillow Talk*, Doris Day stars as Jan Morrow, a single woman in her thirties living alone in an upscale apartment in New York City. The plot revolves around her dispute with Brad Allen (Rock Hudson), a playboy Broadway composer, with whom she unfortunately shares a telephone party line. Jan complains to a telephone company employee that she needs a private line because she often works at home. She has a home office adjacent to her bedroom and uses the phone to work with clients (see figure 10.1). A successful interior decorator, she is often unable to make or receive business calls due to Brad's constant chatting to women on the line. When confronted by Brad over the telephone, Jan argues that she is content with her life, contrary to Brad's claim that she has "bedroom problems." Brad assumes that a professional woman in her thirties who lives alone must be lonely because she is not married and therefore lacks a sex life. Jan's status as a successful businesswoman, content living alone, is potentially transgressive, challenging established social norms about the role of women in society. Brad undermines this possibility, reminding the audience that Jan cannot be single and happy and is in fact jealous of his bachelor lifestyle.

Alma, Jan's maid, after eavesdropping on the phone call, argues that Brad is right; there is nothing worse than a woman who lives alone and says she likes it. Jan asks what she is missing. Alma responds, "When you have to ask, believe me, you're missing it!" Jan argues that of course she likes living alone; she has a good job, a lovely apartment, dates, and access to the theater and restaurants. Jan is not a virgin, and therefore what she is missing must be love, or what all women of the period should want—a husband, children, and a life in the suburbs. Jan's character has many qualities indicative of emerging second-wave feminism, echoing Helen Gurley Brown's belief that living in the city offered single career women the good life. The film potentially undermines patriarchal ideas about the role of women in society, as Jan embodies the contradictory representations of postwar

FIGURE 10.1 Jan Morrow's home office in *Pillow Talk*. (*Source*: *Pillow Talk* [Universal Pictures, 1959].)

women—she is both modern and traditional. Nonetheless, *Pillow Talk* is a text of its time, and like other films of the same genre, ultimately undermines its feminist message by contributing to the collective societal belief that pursuing a career and delaying marriage are unnatural for women. Jan cannot remain in her unmarried state and falls for Brad despite his deceit in pursuing her. The film ends with marriage and pregnancy and, in the minds of viewers, the assumption that Jan will assume her role as housewife in the suburbs.

If a Man Answers features a college-educated half-French, half-American young woman torn between adopting a pseudo-bohemian lifestyle as a model and pursuing the traditional institution of marriage. Chantal is a blend of her parents—her mother was a Parisian dancer, and her father is a conservative businessman. Her father represents postwar tension between emerging second-wave feminism and patriarchal ideology, evident by his disappointment with her serial dating and resistance to getting married. After moving to New York City, Chantal meets her future husband, Gene, while window shopping on Fifth Avenue. Comedy ensues when Gene expresses interest in her appearance and offers Chantal $10 an hour to meet him at his studio apartment. Gene, realizing that Chantal is offended because she misunderstands his intentions, quickly introduces himself as a photographer interested in working with her because he has assumed she is a fashion model. Unable to suppress her desire to marry, Chantal accepts his offer to model and introduces herself as "Chantal Stacy with the Stacy being temporary."

The remainder of the film follows Chantal's failed attempt at modeling and her use of eccentric methods, influenced by her mother, to train Gene to acquiesce to his new role as a married man. Marriage means that Chantal must stop modeling and conform to middle-class norms even though Gene continues to work as a photographer and to live his bohemian lifestyle, using their home to

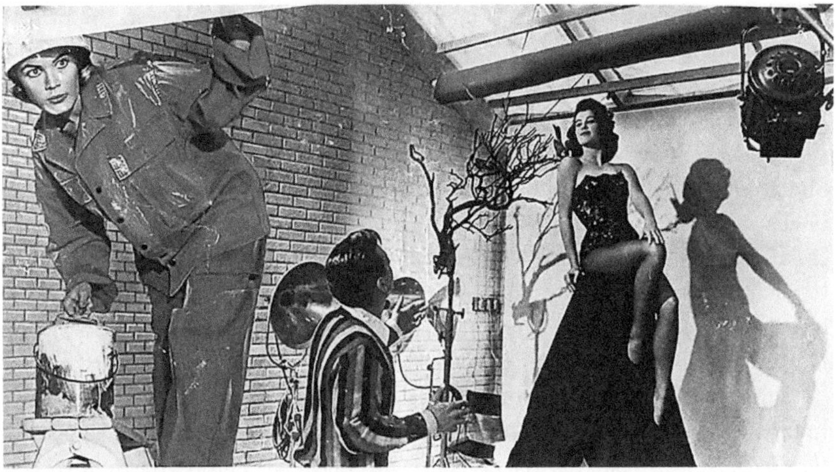

FIGURE 10.2 Chantal and Gene's studio apartment in *If a Man Answers*. (*Source*: *If a Man Answers* [Universal Pictures, 1962].)

work with attractive female models while Chantal cooks and paints the apartment (see figure 10.2). As a wife, she has loss her status as a single career woman in the city. Following the narrative formula of the period, Chantal is pregnant at the close of the film, and the audience can assume that the couple will eventually move to the suburbs.

Television examples of single career women include Marlo Thomas's character as an aspiring actress in *That Girl* (1966–1971) and Mary Tyler Moore's role as an associate producer at a TV station in Minneapolis on *The Mary Tyler Moore Show* (1970–1977). The formula was very successful and socially relevant. Even *The Doris Day Show* (1968–1973) decided to radically change its format by season four by recasting Day's character as a single working woman (minus her two boys) living in an apartment in San Francisco. No longer a secretary, Day is reimagined as a staff writer and later an editor for a fictional magazine. Television shows attempted to address the key goals of second-wave feminism: workplace equality, autonomy, and financial independence for women. Sitcoms created story lines that lightly address women's struggles for equality in the workplace. However, conventional media's dependence on depictions of successful white middle-class single women as representative of the feminist movement "minimized the movement's relevance across lines of class, race, and marital status."[33] As Lehman argues, the popular sitcoms suggested that women had "made it" in an androcentric world.

ABC's *That Girl* was groundbreaking, as it was one of the first shows to focus on the life of a college-educated single working woman. Ann Marie leaves her family in the suburbs to live in New York City to pursue her dream of becoming an actress. The sitcom depicts her struggles as an actress and her relationships with her boyfriend, friends, and family. Many scenes take place in the private realm of her apartment or the local restaurant she frequents with her boyfriend. Ann Marie, referred to as "Miss Independent" by her father, lives alone (unlike earlier female leads who lived with roommates or family members) and must support herself by working a variety of temporary jobs in between acting gigs. She lives in a spacious one-bedroom apartment decorated with an eclectic but unglamorous mix of inexpensive furniture and accessories and the personal and creative touches of a young woman just starting out. This form of gendered urban lifestyle is familiar and natural in present-day depictions of single women living and working in the city, for example, in HBO's *Girls* (2012–2017) and Comedy Central's *Broad City* (2014–2019).

Although Ann Marie has a boyfriend, she lives a chaste, virginal life compared to the lifestyle of sexual liberation proposed by Helen Gurley Brown in *Sex and the Single Girl*. Instead, her relationship with her boyfriend is an extended version of the romantic bachelor comedies that were popular in the 1960s. At the end of the series, Thomas—as star of the show and unofficial executive producer—wanted to leave her female viewers empowered with the message that they can have a successful career in the city that does not have to end in marriage, as it does for the characters in *Pillow Talk* and *If a Man Answers*, for example. Therefore, the last episode, "The Elevated Woman," ended with Ann Marie getting engaged to her long-term boyfriend Donald (Ted Bessell) instead of with a wedding, which the show's sponsor, Clairol, and ABC executives pushed for. In Thomas's words, getting married was "a portrayal to all the young women who have been following this show and finding their own independence. If we get married in the last show, what we're saying is that's the only happy ending there is. That is dangerous."[34] For viewers, Ann Marie's character represented a bridge between tradition, in her focus on familial and romantic relationships, and progress, in her decision to live on her own and pursue a career in the city.

Unlike on *The Mary Tyler Moore Show*, Ann Marie's story line was not depicted in the workplace due to her ongoing struggle to make it as an actress. Her acting gigs seem few and far between, so to maintain her independence she has to work a variety of temporary jobs to pay the rent. She does some of these jobs at home. For example, in one episode she gets a telemarketing job—conducting phone surveys on electric appliances. Ann Marie's short-term jobs represent typical opportunities for women to work in their bedroom or at their kitchen table, such as typing and mail-order services advertised in publications such as *Cosmopolitan* and local newspapers.[35] Thus, as a single woman, Ann Marie is able to earn a living without curtailing her personal life.

The telephone is very prominent in the narrative of many *That Girl* episodes. Anne Marie's status as a single woman living alone provides opportunities for the public realm to enter the privatized space of the apartment. The telephone connects Ann Marie to potential acting jobs and temporary gigs, keeping her in touch with the realm of production even though she is primarily situated within the domestic sphere. Ann Marie also spends a lot of time on the telephone placating her father and connecting with her boyfriend. Even though the telephone, like other forms of technology, is not "consciously encoded with political qualities," it still helps to "reproduce economic priorities or power relations inherent in the social formation."[36] Through communication technology, her apartment becomes a private-public space, merging her familial and romantic relationship and her career ambitions within the space of the home.

Jan Morrow's (*Pillow Talk*) and Ann Marie's chaste lifestyle and relationship to the telephone are strikingly different from those of most cinematic depictions of single women living alone struggling to survive in the city. The relationship between sex, work, and leisure is apparent in the character of the call girl. Although prostitution has existed at least since the beginning of written history, the call girl is a unique figure, as she merges sex (as a leisure commodity) and work (reproductive labor as productive labor) made possible by communication technology. During the 1960s and 1970s, the phenomenon of the call girl is well documented in newspapers and referenced in popular books such as *Sex and the Single Girl*. A call girl is the main character in several popular films of the period, including *BUtterfield 8* (1960), *Breakfast at Tiffany's* (1961), *Boys' Night Out* (1962), and *Klute* (1971). In each case, the character of the call girl is constructed by her domestic space (primarily the bedroom) and her relationship to the telephone. As Pamela Wojcik claims, Audrey Hepburn's character in *Breakfast at Tiffany's*, Holly Golightly, is apparent in relation to her home. Her relationship with her neighbor Paul "exist[s] in and through the space of the apartment."[37] Holly's life is empty, and so is her apartment; in fact, the primary piece of furniture is her bed. Holly claims: "I don't want to own anything until I find a place where me and things go together. I'm not sure where that is but I know what it is like. . . . It's like Tiffany's." What she does own, what is essential to her character, is a bed, a suitcase, and a telephone. (See figure 10.3.) Holly Golightly, the call girl, is reimagined as a party girl and thus represents a life of leisure, a single woman living in the city. She is depicted dodging her "dates" and throwing wild parties in her empty apartment. Sex work is sanitized and celebrated as an exciting source of income for single white women.

Gloria Wandrous, played by Elizabeth Taylor in *BUtterfield 8*, is also imagined as a party girl. In the opening scene, Gloria wakes up in the bedroom of Weston Liggett, a wealthy businessman. Weston has left, presumably for work, leaving Gloria $250 on the nightstand. Insulted, Gloria angrily writes "No Sale" in lipstick on the mirror. Gloria insists that she is not paid for her "dates" and instead is a model. However, with the exception of her mother, no one believes that Gloria is just a model, as she has a reputation for partying with numerous men. Although angry at him, Gloria likes Weston, and in desperation tells her answering service to put him through if he should call. The telephone connects the

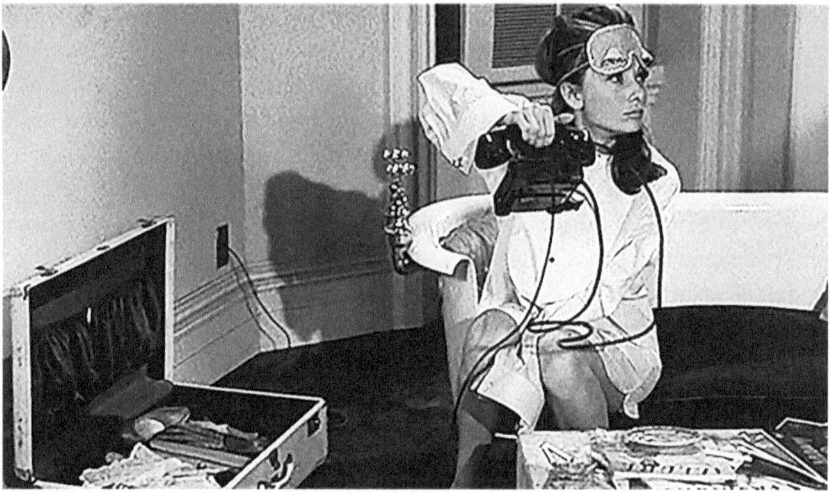

FIGURE 10.3 Holly Golightly's apartment in *Breakfast at Tiffany's*. (*Source: Breakfast at Tiffany's* [Paramount Pictures, 1961].)

possibility of work and the possibility of redemption in the form of heterosexual love. Gloria's business and identity are linked to the telephone. An advertisement for *BUtterfield 8* states, "Some women never give a name—just a phone number." In this case, the call girl is directly associated with work (in the form of sex for money in the bedroom) through the use of technology. If a man wants to make a date, the transaction is initially brokered over the telephone either directly or through an answering service. For the call girl, work is primarily conducted within the private sphere—in a bedroom at home or in a private hotel room.

Like *BUtterfield 8* and *Breakfast at Tiffany's, Bells Are Ringing* (1960) features a story line driven by the use of telephones and the suggestion of prostitution. The film stars Judy Holiday as Ella Peterson, a switchboard operator at Susanswerphone, whom the police mistakenly believe works for an escort service in New York City. Again, women's productive labor is domesticated, transformed into a practice associated with the private sphere. Editorials of the period complained about the growing problem of call girls conducting business in upscale apartment buildings in reaction to citizen campaigns to close city brothels.[38] These acts essentially shifted sex work from the public sphere, where men ventured out to seek sex, to the private sphere, where sex could be arranged discreetly through the telephone. The telephone transformed the space of reproductive labor into a space of productive labor.

In the opening scene of *Bells Are Ringing*, the answering service is associated with professionals and glamorous lifestyles in the city; however, the answering service office is located in the basement of a run-down brownstone house on a block with razed buildings and empty lots. Ella and her female co-workers take calls and messages for residential and business customers in the city, merging the public and private spheres. Ella also merges her work and her personal life, as she is unable to avoid becoming involved in the lives of the answering service customers. For example, she develops a crush on Jeffrey Moss (Dean Martin), a playwright, after interacting with him and taking phone messages. This merging of the public and private spheres extends to Ella's living arrangement—she lives in the building, presumably upstairs in an apartment above the answering service business.

Collectively, *Pillow Talk, If a Man Answers, BUtterfield 8, Breakfast at Tiffany's,* and *Bells Are Ringing* are comments on the increasing role of the telephone in managing work and personal obligations, anticipating contemporary use of the smartphone. The films represent the telephone as a means to extend the self, by creating social connections that maintain personal relationships and provide opportunities to earn a living. In other words, the telephone is framed as a necessity and an instrument that can merge practices usually associated with work or private life.

11 • WORK WHERE YOU LIVE

The apartment in popular culture as a material space blurs the public-private dichotomy. Pamela Wojcik writes that the apartment plot in film "blurs distinctions between public and private, work and home, masculine and feminine, inside and outside."[1] A prime example is the studio apartment, as the entire space functions as a bedroom-study. Representations of domestic spaces are not limited to the apartment plot in film and television. They are also present in depictions of urban lifestyles in newspapers and popular books and magazines from the late 1950s to the early 1970s. These representations of the apartment offered an image of home as transient, visible, and permeable compared to the impenetrable, private, permanent space of the middle-class suburban home, especially when considering private spaces such as the bedroom. In this chapter I look at representations of work and communication technology in apartments in popular culture as a specific form of urban domesticity to examine how media representations of ideal urban domesticity actively incorporated aspects of the public sphere—work life and entertainment.

Hugh Hefner's *Playboy* philosophy represented a backlash to the contemporaneous work culture that valued conformity and turned workers into "organization" or "company" men as described by William Whyte in his 1956 book *The Organization Man.* For junior executives or middle managers trying to climb the corporate ladder, work is described as very demanding, requiring on average 9.5 hours a day. The remainder of their waking hours were spent commuting due to the society norm that promoted life in the suburbs for families over living in the city close to employment. Whyte found this relationship between work and everyday life problematic for most middle-class men. For Whyte, organization men were the "dominant members of society" where future leaders would emerge and "set the American temper," even though he contended that at the time they had not "joined together into a recognizable elite."[2] Hefner was such a worker; he started his own company out of dissatisfaction with postwar work culture and the emphasis on men giving their lives to companies to support their families. In 1953, working from his apartment in Chicago, Hefner founded a small publication, *Playboy.*[3] The magazine was soon a commercial success. By 1959, circulation reached 1 million and surpassed that of its primary competitor, *Esquire* magazine.[4] The *Playboy* brand continued to grow, becoming a huge corporation with sales of close to $200 million annually by the 1970s.[5]

Hefner did not completely reject corporate culture and the importance of capitalism's work ethic in driving American economic success. In fact, he embraced hard work as necessary for individual fulfillment. Elizabeth Fraterrigo's research points out that, unlike members of the Beat Generation, those who followed the *Playboy* philosophy did not reject society or challenge the dominant economic order by dropping out.[6] Through *Playboy*, Hefner promoted the emerging consumer ethic "not by advocating unbridled hedonism, but by articulating the link between work and play, a connection that in effect granted permission for pleasure."[7] However, I would extend her argument and claim that *Playboy*'s construction of the bachelor in relation to his home acted as a guide to understanding the lifestyle and work ethic of the new emerging upper middle class.

Two opposing forces were operating in 1950s and 1960s America: the enduring work ethic, which valued hard work, moderation, and familialism, and the ascendant consumer ethic, which emphasized the attainment of pleasure, self-fulfillment, and individualism. However, as early as 1933, *Esquire* linked the notion of leisure with the possibility of increased consumer spending by commodifying the emergence of male free time due to the Great Depression.[8] Still, leisure or adult play was constructed as a reward for hard work. Work hard first and enjoy the rewards later—this was the natural order, with work and play existing in separate realms. Fraterrigo noted that one aspect of *Playboy*'s lasting influence was to contribute to the blurring of the spheres of work and leisure by creating a middle ground between an enduring cultural work ethic that valued moderation, self-restraint, and hard work and the growing consumerism of postwar America.[9] Transforming play into work and work into play provides justification for consumerism, imbuing a lifestyle that places consumption and the good life at the forefront with the virtues and ideals usually associated with work.

In economic and sociological literature, the new middle class that adopted the artistic work ethos is often referred to as the knowledge class, intellectual workers, cultural and social professionals, or the creative class.[10] Income levels in relation to the lower and upper classes have traditionally defined the middle class. However, as Richard Florida argues, the conditions of the new economy also create the necessity to define class by economic function and common interests. Knowledge workers do not control any significant means of production or property. They generally do not produce tangible products, and their means of production and property are "thinking" and the creation of ideas. Knowledge workers are paid to think for a living, as opposed to the members of the working class, who are paid primarily to produce material goods and to carry out their job according to well-defined plans.[11] Knowledge workers include, but are not limited to, writers, musicians, designers, engineers, lawyers, bankers, teachers, and entertainers. This group has played a substantial role in postindustrial patterns of consumption, acting as a force behind economic growth, and consequently has become a leading influential class in U.S. society.[12]

The postindustrial economy—now commonly referred to as the information or knowledge economy—brought about socioeconomic reorganization. The postindustrial economy is marked by a shift in producing goods to delivering services during the 1970s.[13] These services are increasingly driven by knowledge and ideas. Economists define the knowledge economy by the increasing interdependence of a two-tier system (the service class and the new middle class), the growing service class, and the subsequent decline of the working class.[14] What is of importance to my argument is that the new middle class, sometimes referred to as the knowledge class, emerged concurrently with the postindustrial break in the late 1960s and early 1970s and the beginning of gentrification (renewed interest in urbanism) in former industrial cities.[15] As I discuss in later chapters, this group shifted public discourse about the role of work in domestic space, the role of communication technology within the home, and the idea of domestic urbanism. The pages of *Playboy*, beginning in the 1950s, represented the emergence of the knowledge-cultural professional and elements of this transformation to the new economy.

Fraterrigo's emphasis on the role of play and consumerism in the making of the good life provides the foundation for my arguments about the role of work within the domestic sphere in constructing the good life and the wide-ranging cultural and social implications, primarily the emergence of the knowledge-cultural professional and renewed interest in the city. I propose that in addition to promoting consumption as a lifestyle, *Playboy* magazine also constructed the knowledge-cultural professional and reconstituted home in the form of the bachelor pad as a public/private space of work through communication technology—what is now understood as a major aspect of the live-work lifestyle. Specifically, Hefner portrayed the live-work lifestyle as the good life practiced by the new middle class who enjoyed the arts and culture, had access to the latest communication and media technology, and joined play (leisure) and work within urban domesticity. Hefner himself compared *Playboy* to early Sears, Roebuck catalogues that offered Americans a seemingly endless variety of consumer items. In his words: "Playboy has always been a wish book, or a dream book. A book of aspiration and fantasy."[16] Hefner believed that American men deserved to live the good life displayed in the pages of *Playboy*. Yet, the *Playboy* lifestyle was first and foremost aspirational. It resonated with many Americans due to increased prosperity in the widening of the middle class, the growing influence of consumerism, and the emerging importance of ideals of what constitute taste and status in framing hierarchies within social classes and importantly, I would add, the construction of the new middle class.[17]

Although the *Playboy* philosophy was that everyone should have access to the good life by participating in consumerism, Hefner believed that the lifestyle represented in the pages of his magazine was a reward for hard work. In his words, "*Playboy* was not planned as a publication for the idle rich, so much as in recognition that with the prosperity of post-war America, almost everyone could have a piece of what we described as the playboy life—if he were willing to expend the necessary effort."[18] *Playboy* promoted individual initiative. Its editorial content did not emphasize ways that men could earn money (although Hefner showcased what I would argue are ideal professions for the emerging knowledge economy—editors, architects, lawyers, professors, etc.); rather, the magazine focused on entertainment, leisure activities, and the bachelor's domestic environment. However, as editor, Hefner claimed, *Playboy*'s articles "on the creature comforts and the infinite variety of man's more elegant, leisure-time possessions, clearly stress that these are the prizes available in our society in return for honest endeavor and hard work."[19]

An examination of *Playboy* reveals that for postwar men the good life was associated with living in a well-designed apartment in the city, owning expensive clothes and the latest home and entertainment technology, good food, travel, and access to beautiful women. Hefner believed that the aspirational lifestyle portrayed in the pages of *Playboy* provided motivation for men to pursue economic success through work and ultimately advance American capitalism. But more importantly, *Playboy*'s philosophy regarding the role of work was culturally significant, and its influence is still meaningful today. Hefner, through the pages of *Playboy*, espoused a new work ideal. Work was no longer just a means by which to earn money to purchase necessary goods and a place to live, and to support a family. More specifically, *Playboy* introduced an urban-centered domesticity as ideal for aspiring knowledge-cultural professionals and an idealized live-work lifestyle within the home, which I contend is part of our contemporary understanding of what constitutes working life for upper-middle-class professionals.

Playboy depicted the playboy as a young, educated professional, often employed in creative and cultural fields, living the good life. Perhaps this was intentional on Hefner's part, as he depicted himself, the editor of a successful magazine (or as Pierre Bourdieu would classify him, a "cultural intermediary"),[20] as the playboy archetype in magazine editorials and related publicity. *Playboy* ran pictorials during the 1960s featuring the bachelor pads of single successful men. Besides being white, young, and male, the men also shared similar professions. Although the typical "company man" and men in working-class occupations also read *Playboy*, their lifestyles were not represented in the magazine. Instead, *Playboy* featured photo essays of, for example, architects' homes in Malibu and Connecticut, a freelance photographer's apartment in New York City, and a lawyer's home in Palm Springs, California.[21] In the pages of *Playboy,* it is evident that Hefner constructed the audience of his magazine as urban and sophisticated. *Playboy* targeted professional, college-educated men from the very beginning.[22] It conducted reader surveys for marketing purposes and to determine its base readership. Carrie Pitzulo's research reveals that during the 1950s and 1960s, the average reader was twenty-nine years old. Nearly 75 percent of readers were college-educated or employed in professional fields.[23] On average during the postwar period, 52 percent of reader households surveyed had annual incomes over $10,000.[24] The median income for American families in the mid-1960s was $6,900.[25]

In a 1958 *Playboy* essay, Philip Wylie lamented that in the pursuit of money to purchase all the luxuries demanded of families, "America's leading men, more than males elsewhere, abandoned the arts, sciences and so on—for business enterprise."[26] The magazine promoted hard work and professional success, but favored careers that incorporated creativity and higher education, as the *Playboy* lifestyle was ultimately about the merging of work, play, and pleasure. In *Playboy*'s own words, the ideal reader was "a sharp-minded young business executive, a worker in the arts, a university professor, an architect or engineer. . . . [H]e must take joy in his work, without regarding it as the end of all living . . . a man who—without acquiring the stigma of voluptuary or dilettante—can live life to the hilt."[27] Hefner's vision incorporated leisure and creativity into work for men. His vision was perceptive considering that business experts in the early 1960s started to be concerned about the lack of creativity in the workforce.[28] In fact, Thomas Frank found that some large corporations during the immediate postwar period were actively taking measures to remove creative individuals from white-collar professions.[29] According to *Playboy,* the noble pursuits of men of the past—the arts, music, literature, and philosophy—were no longer held in public esteem. In the past, "education was esteemed above riches," and "merchants usually fell far below in the classic list of public esteem."[30] Wylie argued that men were thus being emasculated because these domains were being ridiculed and feminized. America was anti-intellectual and antisexuality and undermined male authority—men did not read and take part in the arts anymore.

The *Playboy* lifestyle embodied old ideals regarding work and financial success but embraced new ideals about play and leisure. Household and personal commodities and leisure activities promoted in the magazine became symbolic codes that defined the *Playboy* lifestyle. In his 1984 book *Distinction,* Bourdieu notes this shift in his discussion of the new petit bourgeoisie in Europe. The old petit bourgeoisie followed a "morality of duty" and practiced restraint in fear of pleasure relating to the body.[31] The new cultural intermediaries—represented in this case by *Playboy*—urge "a morality of pleasure as a duty."[32] *Playboy*'s representation of the good life bridged the gap between the American tradition of hard work and the ascendant consumer ethic. Bourdieu's claim that the most likely way to enter the dominant class from a lower social position is through the liberal professions, as they tend to transmit both economic and cultural capital,[33] is enlightening considering the average *Playboy* audience and the bachelors depicted in the magazine's editorials. *Playboy* embraced the liberal professions (for example, attorneys and architects) because of their attainment through higher education, but also depicted playboy bachelors as cultural producers (musicians, writers) and cultural intermediaries (critics, editors). Therefore, the ideal playboy bachelor embodied the old bourgeoisie represented by the liberal professions and their corresponding work ethic and tastes in art and leisure, and embraced the new middle class, as conceptualized by Bourdieu,[34] adopting pleasure and the new consumer ethic.

Therefore, one key aspect of the imagery of the bachelor is his socioeconomic position as a knowledge/creative professional, often working at home, situated in the city and living the good life. In bedroom comedies such as *Pillow Talk* (1959), *If a Man Answers* (1962), and *Under the Yum Yum Tree* (1963), the bachelor works for a living at home. In *Pillow Talk*, Brad, a Broadway composer and a confirmed bachelor playboy, works at home. Even though he has a separate bedroom, his work and seduction occur in the main room, a hybrid work/live studio furnished with a desk, a piano, and an automatic sofa bed. Brad uses the telephone and his push-button automated apartment primarily for leisure pursuits. His life at home is sexualized, mixing work and leisure, as he is depicted playing ballads for numerous women as a form of seduction. His work and private life are seamless; in fact, it is hard to tell when he is composing a song for income or to seduce one of his many paramours.

WORK AND LEISURE ZONES

For scholars such as Steven Cohan, the bachelor pad in films like *Pillow Talk* is a space for the playboy to perform heterosexual masculinity. This performance was necessary because of postwar anxiety about the stability of American masculinity, "underscoring the homophobia that structured the cultural meaning of masculinity as the opposite of femininity."[35] However, I propose that the 1960s bachelor and his domestic space can also be read as an indicator of the emerging dominant social order and socioeconomic relationships: in this case, the interplay between work and leisure in the home, the role of communication technology and home entertainment in the evolution of vernacular space, and the emergence of the knowledge-based economy. Applying Wojcik's notion of domestic urbanism, the bachelor pad "occupies an indeterminate space, which is neither fully public nor fully private,"[36] for two primary reasons. First, representations of the bachelor pad act as public-private spaces because of the incorporation of work and technology into the private realm—the customary site of leisure and reproduction. Second, as Fraterrigo contends, the bachelor pad helped undermine the urban-suburban dichotomy by masculinizing the domestic realm within the city.[37]

Playboy featured a modern townhouse in the May 1962 issue that is emblematic of the weakening of the public-private dichotomy. The modern townhouse is depicted between two grand nineteenth-century brownstones. The front of the townhouse has floor-to-ceiling windows, giving it a sense of openness and continuity between the private space of the home and the public space of the city, compared to the closed feeling evoked by the stone walls of the brownstones. This continuity is notable considering the competing myth of the home as a space of privacy and the contemporaneous transformation of the home into a recognized space of work. The interior of the bachelor pad represented a destabilization of the public-private dichotomy, or, as I described earlier, our former understanding of the relationship between leisure and work.

A 1964 *Playboy* feature on an architect and his bachelor pad illustrates this point. Fred Lyman, the architect, is depicted working (and painting a portrait) in his bedroom-study.[38] According to the article, Lyman "wanted to design a home in which it would be enjoyable to work as well as play."[39] This is evident in the accompanying photo essay, which depicts different areas of the house that serve as work and leisure spaces. For example, the open-concept kitchen and dining areas, described as spaces for entertainment, include an area that acts as a compact office in addition to the other work/leisure space in the home—the bedroom-study. Lyman states that his home was "designed so that every aspect of life within it could be experienced joyously. Where every social and solitary activity—dining, relaxing, sleeping, working, and even bathing—could be celebrated and savored."[40]

Playboy's open-concept design is a rejection of the conventional suburban floor plan of "separated rooms for various purposes." There are no "cell-like rooms"; instead, the floor plan of the bachelor pad is divided into "function areas" (active and quiet zones) that interact as a whole and invite "individual as well as simultaneous use."[41] Cohan claims that the division of the apartment into active and quiet zones "accommodates a divided masculinity."[42] This, he claims, further "interiorizes" the gendered division between the private and public realms.[43] Yet, the incorporation of work within the home, technology, and the conflation of active and quiet zones within the bachelor pad make the notion of the public-private dichotomy problematic. *Playboy* collapses the three traditional zones—social (living room, dining room), work (kitchen, study), and private (bedroom/bathroom)—into two zones. In the bachelor pad, the active zone includes the open areas of the house: the living room, kitchen, and dining room. The quiet zone includes the bathroom, the bedroom, and, most importantly, the study, categorized by the lack of permanent walls between the study and the bedroom.

The first significant breakdown of conventional boundaries is the incorporation of the kitchen in the active zone, which implies the social and public space of the home. As discussed in part 1, historically, a clear demarcation of the kitchen and laundry room from the living or family room compartmentalized household labor. Unpaid household labor, traditionally not considered productive (unlike paid labor traditionally performed by men, and situated in the public sphere since industrialization), was associated with the private sphere and therefore with women. Consequently, the kitchen was designated as the domain of women. In the bachelor pad, the kitchen becomes a part of the social space—a space for entertaining guests.

Playboy's attempt to create a space for heterosexual masculine domesticity necessitated the erasure of nonproductive household labor to eliminate the possibility of queer interpretations of the bachelor living alone. In the words of *Playboy*, "This is a bachelor kitchen, remember, and *unless you're a very odd-ball bachelor* indeed, you like to cook and whomp up short-order specialties to exactly the same degree that you actively dislike dishwashing, marketing and tidying up."[44] The magazine simultaneously established the playboy bachelor as heterosexual, masculine, and, by extension, someone who naturally dislikes housework. Because of modern technology such as the "ultrasonic dishwasher" that uses "inaudible hi-fi sound," there is no need to manually clean dishes: "no soap, detergent or hot water required in the three-minute washing and drying cycle."[45] By eliminating the need for soap or detergent, *Playboy* further distances the image of the bachelor from the representations of the housewife and the proliferation of associations to household products in postwar advertising.

The second significant breakdown is the inclusion of the study in the quiet zone (the private space of the home) and the lack of walls between the study and the bedroom (see figure 11.1). The bedroom and study are separated by an accordion door, but designed to merge as a continuous large room because of the wall-to-wall carpeting and matched draperies "tying it all together."[46] The study is described as a "sanctum sanctorum" where the bachelor can work or "just sit and think." *Playboy* describes the study as a private space in which to work with business guests undisturbed. In the bachelor study there is "ample storage for typewriter, Dictaphone, stationery, [and] office supplies."[47] Therefore, the bachelor can type correspondence and dictate instructions for his secretary from home. Because the study is an extension of the bedroom, the bedroom-study acts as a space of work and leisure. The study has a built-in bar and a small refrigerator to "have a romantic nightcap with a chosen guest."[48] Again, work and pleasure coincide. Working from home is a pleasurable experience ameliorating the drudgery and monotony associated with work. The bedroom-study acts as a space that allows the bachelor to participate in leisure, work, and consumer activities on his own time. This is evidenced by (1) the presence of the desk, typewriter, space for files, and a telephone extension for work; (2) the built-in

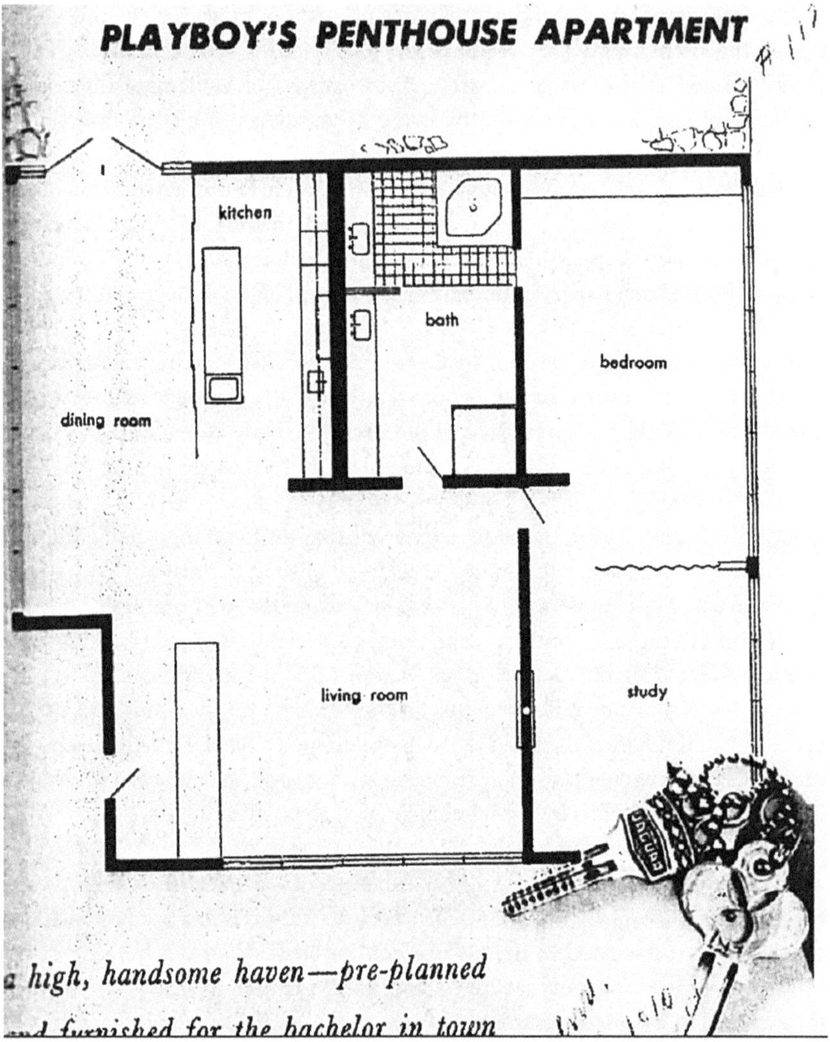

FIGURE 11.1 Partial image of floor plan of *Playboy*'s Penthouse Apartment. (*Source*: "Playboy's Penthouse Apartment [Part I]," *Playboy*, September 1956, 53–60. Library of Congress Rare Books and Manuscripts Collection.)

storage space to accommodate the bachelor's hobbies and collections, such as "record albums, stamp albums," and "picture books"; and (3) the act of including a study within an already masculine space—the bachelor pad in its totality.[49] The bachelor pad represents the quintessential idealized modern space: increased privatization and spatial mobility through the convenience of having communication technology within the home.[50] Advances in communication technology promise portability and greater flexibility in integrating work and leisure, blurring the boundary between work and play in new ways.

Playboy continued to publish variations of the bachelor pad throughout the 1960s and 1970s. However, the Playboy Mansion in Chicago represented the ultimate bachelor pad. Hefner featured his home throughout the 1960s to illustrate the good life. For Hefner, this meant the ability to combine work, leisure, and self-fulfillment within the private sphere. The mansion represented a very public "private" space—a space where Hefner could illustrate and perform the good life. Lifestyle articles featuring the Playboy Mansion attempted to position Hefner as a professional and emphasized his work ethic in reaction to the public criticism of his sybaritic lifestyle. In January 1966, *Playboy* published an article titled "The Playboy Mansion," describing where Hefner "resides and presides over every phase of his *Playboy* operation" or empire.[51] Portraying him as "never tiring of his work," the article points out that Hefner went from a weekly wage of $50 to $12 million per year in nine years through creativity and initiative.[52] The opulent mansion is dubbed the "grand manor" and the aspiration of teenage boys. Thus, the mansion represents hard work and a nod to the past, the gentleman's country home, a space of leisure and a material testament to economic success.

In keeping with the *Playboy* lifestyle, the article features celebrities and bunnies attending decadent parties, as well as the entertainment spaces of the mansion, such as the home movie theater. However, the majority of the article focuses on Hefner working within the mansion in the dedicated and hybrid spaces with technologies that facilitate this lifestyle. Hefner surrounds himself with executive-style telephones, electric typewriters, a built-in office screen and projector, and audio and video (TV and recording) connecting his master quarters and executive offices. He appears to seamlessly integrate work and leisure within the mansion. Even while attending an editorial meeting in the conference room, he combines work with everyday activities such as getting a haircut and manicure from an assistant.

Even though the mansion has dedicated workspaces such as conference rooms and executive suites, work extends into its private spaces: the master's quarters, which consist of a study, bedroom, bath, and sitting room. In one article and image Hefner is depicted in his master bedroom on a circular rotating bed talking on the telephone and editing transparencies for an upcoming issue while a black domestic employee serves him in the background (see figure 11.2). *Playboy* illustrates the depth of Hefner's work ethic and the seamlessness of his work and private life. He works in his pajamas, surrounded by numerous objects of his work life. The circular bed is symbolically significant, as it has no beginning or end—for Hefner work and private life are continuous. All things being equal, Hefner works on his bed, sleeps on his bed, and has sex on his bed. Work-life balance is not the objective; in fact, work is integrated into all aspects of life. Moreover, even the specialized bed is not enough, as Hefner "never tires of his work . . . put[ting] a desk in his bedroom, on which he can work with the drawing

FIGURE 11.2 Hugh Hefner working in bed. (*Source*: "Playboy Mansion," *Playboy*, January 1966. Library of Congress Rare Books and Manuscripts Collection. © Burt Glinn/Magnum Photos.)

board, slide viewer, crayons or electric typewriter."[53] Work is consuming, but that is okay because work equals pleasure in the *Playboy* ethos.

The headboard and its many iterations featured speakers for the hi-fi system located in the living room, as well as a radio, shelving for books, a telephone, and hinged doors that folded down to create working space. The bachelor could control his apartment from the bed using remote controls and push-button technology. This hands-off approach to technology allowed the bachelor to act on his domestic environment and accomplish everyday tasks and activities without the need for proximity and physical exertion that characterized previous social constructions of masculinity, labor, and technology. The use of domestic technologies in the home produced additional figurations of masculinity besides the image of masculine exertion in the form of productive labor in interaction with technologies of labor outside of the home. Also, I argue that because of the gendered nature of domestic labor, masculine use of domestic technologies needed to be constructed as hands-off and exercising control without proximity and exertion to uphold existing gendered hierarchies within the domestic sphere.

By the 1960s, illustrations of the bed evolved into the iconic circular "Playboy Bed" that originally appeared in the November 1959 issue and made its real-life appearance in the Playboy Mansion in 1965. Now, in addition to a telephone and radio, the circular party bed included a television, filing cabinets, a minibar, and a refrigerator. In Hefner's version, the bed could fit twelve people, rotated 360 degrees, and featured an intercom-phone system with a telephone programmed to call two hundred numbers. The bed rotates to face north, south, east, and west and effectively creates four rooms: east creates the entertainment space facing the built-in television/entertainment wall; north creates a sitting room; west creates an office/dining room with a stationary headboard expanse that can be a desk or a table; and south creates the conventional bedroom facing the fireplace (romance/sex implied).

The bachelor could sleep, entertain guests, or watch television, all from the comfort of his bed. He could "take his ease . . . yet not be completely cut off from the niceties and conveniences of apartment living."[54] The telephone and table space allowed the bachelor to conduct business from the bedroom. The Playboy Bed embodied the *Playboy* philosophy of the good life. The bed combined leisure in the possibility of sex, play as a form of masculine consumerism, and work in eliminating the necessity to commute to the office. Essentially, Hefner is a public figure who never goes out. *Playboy*'s representations of his lifestyle and the mediated mansion embody the conditions of modernity—what Raymond Williams describes as an "at-once mobile and home-centred way of living: a form of mobile privatization."[55] This is the paradox of modernity: increased privatization exemplified by the domestic sphere and spatial mobility as a result of technologies of transportation and communication. As discussed in part 1, this paradox is a result of the social and economic forces of industrialization. The home was no longer the productive space of the family economy, and because of the reorganization of labor practices during the Industrial Revolution, the economic preservation of the family shifted primarily to the public sphere.

DOMESTIC TECHNOLOGIES

According to cultural studies scholar Raymond Williams, television offered a resolution to this modern paradox by bringing the public sphere into the private sphere.[56] However, in the case of the mediated spaces of the Playboy Mansion, the presence of communication technologies such as multiline telephones, audiovisual recording and monitoring equipment, electric typewriters, and ubiquitous screens is more complicated than television's ability to bring information and images of the public sphere into the home. The cross-fertilization of technology—communication networks within the home and connections to the outside world—as well as merging productive and reproductive spaces such as the bedroom, executive office, private study, and screening room, creates the conditions for a trans-spatial public-private mobility that allows for simultaneity of experience. Hefner's mediated environment allows for a lifestyle that is simultaneously public and private, combining uninterrupted opportunities to merge work and leisure—the conditions of work for many professionals in the knowledge economy.

The Playboy Mansion contains multiple spaces of work, and Hefner seems to inhabit all of them. In addition to working in his bedroom-office, he is depicted in his study with a typewriter working on an installment of the editorial column "The Playboy Philosophy," which was published in twenty-five installments from 1962 through 1966.[57] Through the "philosophy" and the content of the magazine, Hefner's publication focused on the advancement of the individual through careerism, sexuality, and consumerism. In Hefner's words: "*Playboy* exists, in part, as a motivation for men to expend greater effort in their work, developing their capabilities further and climbing higher on the ladder of success. This is obviously desirable in our competitive, free enterprise system, for only by each individual striving to do his best does the country itself progress and prosper."[58] In the February 1963 installment, Hefner ties individual work ethic, careerism, and consumerism to the success of American capitalism and frames this as embodying the American Dream. Affluence is achieved through work, and careerism becomes the catalyst for men to raise their social status. Hefner defends materialism, arguing that there is no ethical conflict between "the pleasure a modern American finds in material things and his struggle to discover a *new scientific truth, or evolve a new philosophy, or create a work of art . . . as the good life*, the full life, encompasses all of these."[59]

As in the previous statement, references to the humanities and sciences are found throughout the magazine, side by side with references to materialism and sex. Hefner wants to be portrayed as a hard worker, but also wants readers to see him as more than a bachelor obsessed with women and sex. In managing his image, Hefner is portrayed in his study, filled with "reference books on psychology, sociology, comparative theology, political science and law for use in writing 'The Playboy Philosophy.'"[60] Therefore, Hefner equated his work as a cultural intermediary to the liberal or knowledge professions. *Playboy* promulgated an idealized form of careerism that incorporated the arts and valued knowledge, dismissing a career in sales or generic "business" as unfulfilling and demeaning to masculine identity.[61] The magazine reflected a belief in a growing threat to white middle-class men because the historical domains of masculine work, the liberal professions, and creative endeavors were including more women in their ranks. Ultimately, women were not displaced from these professions; however, the rhetoric of *Playboy* was telling in that it represented a space where the working-class male was no longer the symbol of masculinity and no longer represented the backbone of the economy. The magazine's pages reflected the emergence of the knowledge-cultural professional through its promotion of consumerism and the rise of the service class.

The Playboy Mansion was designed to seamlessly integrate work and leisure and to convey to readers the depth of Hefner's commitment to living the good life and finding self-fulfillment through work and leisure within the private sphere. This is demonstrated by Hefner's decision to design his home with his automated bedroom connected by a door to the "Electronic Entertainment Room." An article describes the room as the mansion's "nerve center," which arguably could be considered a basic early model of today's home automation devices, such as Amazon Echo.[62] The room featured the latest audio and video technology, such as multiple color televisions and recording equipment to monitor and record activities in the home and on the air. The nerve center also linked the master quarters with the executive offices. Essentially, the nerve center was a networked space of technology that allowed Hefner to communicate, monitor, and regulate his self-contained environment, a space where he could exert power and control over his empire. Hefner created a self-contained live-work space that afforded him the ability to work from home, interact with his employees, and connect to the outside world, essentially incorporating the public sphere of production into the private sphere.

The bachelor pad was laden with the latest consumer gadgets and push-button technology that reflected the 1960s love of high tech. Illustrations of typical suburban homes at the time featured one or two telephones, a television in the living room, and a radio or record player, in contrast to the bachelor pad, with its multiple executive-style telephones and electric typewriters, televisions in the living room and bedroom, and every room wired for hi-fi. As Bill Osgerby notes, the obsession with technology in the bachelor apartment corresponded to changing perceptions of technology: "Breaking with traditional notions of machinery as bulky and cumbersome, the 1960s concept of the 'gadget' conceived technology as a convenient consumer product—precise, functional and emblematic of stylish cool."[63] Yet the bachelor pad not only designated technology as convenient and cool; it placed technology at the center of living—an essential element of contemporary life—and undermined old representations of technology that were associated with the labor conditions of the working class.

After visiting the Playboy Mansion in 1965, journalist Tom Wolfe claimed that Hefner was setting a new trend, replacing the "old approach to status with a new way that America's new Haves can pick up on."[64] Wolfe claimed that Hefner's amazing success was not simply equated to sex, as many of critics of Hefner—and by extension of *Playboy*—claimed. Hefner offered more than sex: "a fantasy of a potentate's control of the environment—all of a sudden made plausible by the new style of life."[65] Using "money and technology to convert his habitat into a stage . . . [t]hrough the more and more sophisticated use of machines," Hefner and, to a smaller degree, the middle class turned their homes, the private sphere, into "almost complete status spheres all their own."[66] The implications for the new middle class are the ability to access novel forms of technology because of rising financial means, creating the possibility to incorporate aspects of the public sphere, work, and leisure into the private sphere, and a growing sense of control of their socioeconomic status.

Representations of urban living in *Playboy* featured the apartment, specifically the bachelor's home, during the 1960s and early 1970s, recognizing that the domestic sphere operates as a space of work. The urban apartment also became an important site in the imaginary of consumerism and the good life, a key site in the negotiation of masculinity, feminism, representations of race and class in relation to technology, and the shifting boundary between work and leisure. Therefore, an important argument in this chapter is that these representations of urban domesticity and the influx of communication technologies into the home were indicative of broad social changes in the arrangement of market-based work in relation to the domestic sphere. From this premise, work, education, and leisure are increasingly organized around access and representations of the central role of technology within the domestic sphere. From this organization emerged the knowledge-cultural professional and the live-work lifestyle as the embodiment of new definitions of the good life.

Playboy's construction of urban domesticity for men undermined the urban-suburban dichotomy and subsequently created new models of urban domesticity for upper-middle-class whites, both women and men. By the early 1980s, the young upwardly mobile urban professional (yuppie) lifestyle was associated with urbanism in the form of gentrification and conspicuous consumption.[67] Neil Smith defines gentrification as the process by which inner-city lower-class neighborhoods that had previously experienced a middle-class exodus are reclaimed and subsequently refurbished by the private capital of the new middle class.[68] David Ley identifies this group as the "cultural new class," which overlaps with definitions of the knowledge-cultural professional.[69] Some theorists looking for explanations see a correlation between the development of the new middle class and gentrification and understand the phenomenon to be the result of postindustrial social restructuring.[70] Therefore, by the 1980s gentrification became an essential part of urban economic restructuring. This was necessary, as many urban economies in advanced capitalist countries experienced a substantial decrease in the manufacturing labor market and a corresponding increase in the professional and service markets, the latter represented in its early stages in the pages of *Playboy*.

Playboy's target readership, *Sex and the Single Girl*'s audience, and corresponding characterizations in film and television represented what Mike Featherstone calls a "stylization-of-life form of lifestyle" built on practices of consumption and symbolic codes.[71] The playboy bachelor archetype is an early representation of a lifestyle that utilizes the acquisition of consumer goods as "cultural signs" that Featherstone argues are associated with postmodern consumer culture. Instead of adopting a lifestyle based on habit or one's socioeconomic membership, Featherstone contends that "the new heroes of consumer culture make lifestyle a life project and display their individuality and sense of style in the particularity of the assemblage of goods, clothes, practices, experiences, appearance and bodily dispositions they design together into a lifestyle."[72]

In conclusion, representations of urban domesticity imagined a space for a seamless relationship between work and leisure in the home. Advances in communication and entertainment technologies and the rise in consumer culture contributed to the emergence of the knowledge-cultural professional and the subsequent emergence of the knowledge economy in the 1970s. Furthermore, postwar celebration of urban domesticity and the live-work lifestyle in popular culture contributed to current definitions of the idealized good life—that of the successful upper-middle-class knowledge-cultural professional who is able to achieve work-life balance by combining work and leisure through consumer practices and technology within the home.

PART 4 NEOLIBERAL DOMESTIC WORKSPACES

12 • THE ELECTRONIC COTTAGE

Apple Computer Inc. started the personal computer revolution with the introduction of the Apple II in 1977.[1] IBM followed with its first personal computer (PC) for use in the home, office, and schools in 1981.[2] In the beginning, home computers were associated with hobbyists. As the market increased, home use expanded beyond tinkering with the machine to playing video games and word processing. Marketing of the personal computer adopted ideas similar to the television about its role and function in the gendered domestic sphere.[3] In the private sphere, early personal computers were used for entertainment. For example, *Antic*, a publication for Atari home computers, described the PC as a machine on which to play sports, fantasy, and competitive games, to do programming, and as a piece of equipment for hobbyists. Computers also carried with them the cultural and social associations of masculinity and technology. William Dutton, Everett Rogers, and Suk-Ho Jun, who researched the impact of personal computers in the home during the 1980s, found that males were more likely to purchase and use home computers.[4] The personal computer was initially associated with typically masculine activities such as video games but also with work and education. Social science researchers studied the impact of video game use in the home. Families reported that fathers usually encouraged the purchase of video games for children. However, many mothers reported that "men wanted to play the games themselves, as well as have them available for the family."[5] Some researchers observed that home computer use started to replace traditional forms of leisure activity such as watching television, listening to the radio, reading books, and participating in outdoor sports and recreation.[6] Considered as a whole, this constitutes early evidence of computer usage as a form of leisure activity.

By 1980, Apple Computer started to realize its goal of making personal computers a household item for ordinary people, expanding the market beyond leisure and scientific applications.[7] Peter Schuyten wrote in the *New York Times* that the Apple III was "hardly a machine aimed at the hobbyist."[8] It was priced at $4,300 to $7,800, a huge increase from the Apple II, which cost $2,200.[9] Schuyten went on to say that "the new computers, like the Apple II, complete the upward migration of the home or personal computer from a creature of the hobbyist to a small business machine."[10] Apple executives believed that the world was changing from "an economy based on the foundations of the petrochemical industrial revolution to a new economy where information services and information products [will] become the building blocks that shape a very different world."[11] Therefore, Apple wanted to legitimize the idea of the personal computer, shifting consumer understanding of the computer from a machine for scientists or hobbyists who were mostly male to "a productivity tool" that "should be accessible to everyone, even children."[12]

Computer companies were aware of their consumer base. For example, in the early 1980s Apple Computer determined that its target audience was predominantly male college graduates, twenty-five to forty-nine years old, earning at least $25,000 per year.[13] The company asked retailers to advertise specifically to professionals, including doctors, lawyers, stockbrokers, real estate agents, middle managers, teachers, professors, engineers, and small-business owners.[14] Apple noted that early computer adoption correlated with education and professional status. This trend continued into the late 1990s, when 88 percent of households with incomes over $75,000 had at least one computer.[15]

Although the rate of personal computer adoption in the 1980s did not equal the rapid adoption of television in the postwar period, the federal government did recognize the social and economic significance of home computing.[16] In October 1984, the government added a series of questions to the Current Population Survey to gauge the level of ownership and use of home computers.[17] In 1989, approximately 15 percent of all U.S. households reported owning a computer, double the proportion in 1984. Similar to market research reports by computer companies, U.S. government researchers found that computer ownership was highly correlated with class and educational attainment. In addition to telecommuting, ownership of a home computer was linked to occupational status. In the 1980s, people who held professional or managerial positions were the most likely to own and use a computer at home.[18] In the late 1980s persons with at least a bachelor's degree (17.7 percent) and with professional jobs (18.2 percent) reported relatively high levels of computer use in the home for work. The most significant finding was the high rate of use among persons with four or more years of college or those who held a professional or managerial position, 71.2 percent and 71.3 percent, respectively. By the late 1990s, the most highly educated persons were still the most likely to own and use a computer at home. Seventy-eight percent of people with at least a bachelor's degree had access to at least one computer at home compared to 46 percent of people holding only a high school diploma.[19]

Early computer usage by the family was associated with education and upward mobility through work. Apple Computer and its competitors jumped on the educational market. This is not surprising considering the increasing convergence of computing, work, and education in the economy. Market researchers advised computer companies to "keep in mind that early adopters tend to be highly educated, and that this would be a desirable attribute to pass along to the children in the household," and that "positioning the product in an educational context would be effective."[20] Consider the evolution of the magazine *Family Computing*, launched in 1983 by Scholastic, an educational publisher. Scholastic repositioned the magazine as *Family and Home Office Computing* before changing the title to *Home Office Computing* in 1989.[21]

Because of capitalism's ideology of upward mobility and a shifting economy based on the valuation of knowledge, successful parenting naturally focused on educational opportunities for the upwardly mobile middle class. This point was constantly addressed on the popular 1980s sitcom *The Cosby Show* (1984–1992). The show heavily emphasized the importance of a college education, highlighting schools such as New York University, Princeton University, and Temple University. The emphasis on historic black colleges was also significant as a means to establish the Huxtables' legacy as an educated black family. In addition to the educational possibilities of television, Bill Cosby promoted the potential of home computers even though it may have been hard for many Americans to afford one at the time. In 1983 he appeared as a spokesperson on television and in print ads for Texas Instruments Home Computers and the company's software library. The advertising campaign's target audience seemed to be the educated professional middle class.

Early Apple Computer advertisements targeted the same audience by associating the personal computer with the American Dream through the acquisition of knowledge. For example, Apple marketed the Apple IIe as "the most powerful mind-expanding tool since the book" to "take your family further."[22] Apple told middle-class families why every child should have an Apple computer to use after school. Coleco's marketing strategy for the ADAM family computer system promised to prepare kids for college and help pay for it by providing $500 scholarships. (See figure 12.1.) Parents who purchased personal computers reported that their children spent more time studying and demonstrated an increased interest in schoolwork. Dutton, Rogers, and Jun concluded that "since adopters are more highly educated than nonadopters, computing reinforces a family's orientation toward both children's and continuing education, thus perhaps displacing other educational activities."[23] The advertising messages were effective. In 1989, 48.6 percent of children with a college-educated parent or parents had a computer at home compared to 30.4 percent in 1984.[24] By the late 1990s, access to a computer at home for children of parents with four or more years of college increased to 75.7 percent.[25]

To legitimize the necessity of buying personal computers for home use, Apple, along with other computer companies such as IBM and Commodore, employed marketing methods similar to those that launched the telephone and

FIGURE 12.1 Coleco computer advertisement, 1984. (*Source*: http://www.vintageads browser.com.)

television in the first half of the twentieth century. For example, a 1912 advertisement for the Telephone Herald Company showed a family using the telephone to access entertainment and educational programs. (See figure 12.2.) Similarly, early advertisements for televisions depicted families gathering around the set, promising to bring the excitement of drama, sports, music, and educational pro-

FIGURE 12.2 "Telephone Herald." (*Source*: *Morning Oregonian*, July 7, 1912.)

gramming into the living room. By the 1980s this narrative seemed familiar, as new forms of domestic communication technology were marketed as entertaining and educational, but most importantly, practical and necessary. Thus, ads for the personal computer were also linked to the image of the family. This association made the computer a familiar aspect of everyday life.

Advertisements typically featured family members working individually on the computer or parents and children using it together. (See figure 12.3.) However, *Family Computing* (which served as a how-to guide to help families incorporate the computer into the domestic sphere) embodied the changing relationship of communication technology in the home. The cover of the premier issue (September 1983) portrayed a family embracing their computer as if it were a child. The computer became a member of the family. Technology not only acts as a gateway, bringing the public sphere into the home, but also realizes its place as part of the family unit. A comparison of typical advertisements that feature individual family members using a computer with the cover of *Family Computing* reveals the contradiction in how we view technology: it both unites and divides us. Composite images of family members working independently seem to portend our current problematic relationship with technology—the prevalence of individualized relationships with communication technology. The *Family Computing* cover seems idealized and representative, as the computer keeps the family together and becomes an integral part of everyday life.

Advertisements for personal computer use in the home directly conflated work and leisure for professional consumers. In a marketing brochure, Apple instructed potential customers to "take [the computer] by the handle. Carry it into your study (or into any other room of your house). The same Apple IIc that teaches and entertains your children can help you write letters and maintain personal records. You can even sneak in a little work on the side."[26] To appeal to educated professional middle-class families, Texas Instruments promoted its computer as "a tutor, an accountant, a librarian, a file clerk and pro football team in your home."[27] Another salient example is a 1985 advertising booklet for the Apple IIe.[28] To make the point that the Apple IIe could "handle the business of running a home" and "become a home for running your business," Apple used a picture of a house constructed with filing cabinets. Each drawer was labeled with a common household category (for example, utilities, taxes, bills, home repair, vacation) or with a category related to a job or running a small business. The accompanying copy listed Apple software programs to plan your next vacation, "take the drudgery out of paying bills," and play various games for family entertainment, as well as a "powerful telecommunications package" to manage a business from home. Other notable examples include an Apple computer advertisement that stated, "It's a home computer, a business computer, a classroom computer, your computer."[29] IBM told consumers, "With IBM PC at the office and PCjr at your house, you can take work home on your little finger."[30]

As more households purchased a personal computer, the need to find a space for this new work-life machine became problematic. The computer, like the

FIGURE 12.3 IBM Personal Computer advertisement, c. 1985. (*Source*: Reprinted courtesy of International Business Machines Corporation, © International Business Machines Corporation.)

communication technologies before it, needed to "negotiate a preexisting set of gendered power relations already expressed in the home's geography and daily routines."[31] Early advertisements and articles in computing magazines situated the machine in ambiguous settings,[32] suggesting locations that were problematic because of existing social and gendered practices, or recommending the construction of new spaces dedicated exclusively to the computer.[33] Placing the personal computer in the living room meant that it competed with the television, and placing it in a child's bedroom limited the parents' ability to work from home. Placing the computer in the kitchen meant sacrificing privacy for a mother working at home. Placing it in the bedroom of a heterosexual married couple signified "bringing business into the bedroom," threatening the room's traditional use as a space for intimacy and relaxation.[34] The marketing solutions illustrated spatial instabilities in the home, "obfuscat[ing] the quandaries these insertions provoked in zones that were claimed by others or already delineated as shared space."[35] Although Marsha Cassidy argues that the material placement of the computer revealed the difficulty of surmounting the gendered spatial divisions of the home, this quandary could be mitigated by placing the personal computer in an extra bedroom or a study.

The housing industry seized on the opportunity to accommodate personal computers in the home. Builders started constructing model homes equipped with computer rooms or home offices. The tenth annual Home Restoration and Remodeling Show, held in 1986, featured firsthand demonstrations on how turn an extra bedroom into a computer room.[36] Homebuilders surveyed professional women, asking them what they desired in home design. What would the home look like? In addition to the master suite with walk-in closets, two bedrooms, and open floor plans for the common space, a home office was a must-have in the ideal home. To emphasize the point, one working mother was quoted as saying, "We all end up doing some work at home, and you need a separate place to do it."[37] Real estate developers reported that the number of people purchasing homes with more bedrooms than needed increased. More couples with no children or with small families requested homes with three or four bedrooms, planning to use the extra space for in-home offices or media rooms. Notably, during the 1980s the primary market for larger homes was dual-career couples and the self-employed.[38] In fact, data from the U.S. Census Bureau's American Housing Survey shows that in homes of those in the middle- and upper-middle income brackets, the average number of bedrooms increased from two to three and from three to four, respectively, between 1973 and the 1990s. During that same period, the number of household members declined, and the number of single and child-free households increased.[39] The number of home offices increased significantly, and by 1995 the U.S. Census started reporting the number of rooms used part-time or exclusively for business in single-family houses.

LIFE AND LABOR FLEXIBILITY

In *Elsewhere, U.S.A.*, sociologist Dalton Conley defines the personal computer as the device that "came along to change the possibilities of home work."[40] I agree. However, as I have claimed in previous chapters, it is important to acknowledge that the groundwork was laid with the introduction of the telephone and office equipment such as typewriters, and with the incorporation into the home of leisure activities previously associated with the public sphere. As Lana Rakow argues, "Technologies, themselves an effect of a particular social order, are not autonomous, self-developing phenomena. They are used for various purposes by social actors with differing constraints and opportunities."[41] Increased participation in paid labor at home is not dependent on technology alone. It is also dependent on growing acceptance of leisure pursuits as a form of consumption since the postwar period and a blurring of the boundaries between public and private life. By 1973, as Lizabeth Cohen argues in *A Consumers' Republic*, Americans were spending more time in "the new public place of the shopping center," where "consuming and leisure were becoming inseparably intertwined."[42] Instead of being a privilege for the wealthy, leisure had become more accessible to an increasing number of Americans since the postwar period. Leisure practices expanded beyond time off from work to relax or go on vacation, and now included buying and using commodities such as personal computers.

The emergence of the electronic cottage is surprising because theories on the development of industrial capitalism understood the appearance of the private sphere as a result of the rise of the modern market. The separation of business and leisure was necessary to create a market for consumption and to monitor the means of production to maximize capital. The household has always been a part of what Roger Silverstone, Eric Hirsch, and David Morley refer to as the "moral economy," where households act as economic units that take part in the transactional and social systems of the public sphere or the public economy.[43] However, the perceived clear boundaries between the private and public spheres have eroded because the private sphere itself has become commoditized, part of the expanding reach of the capitalist market.[44] This is evident in a 1995 America Online (AOL) commercial that featured a father in his home office extolling the benefits of home Internet service to a friend before catching a sports game.[45] The voice-over told consumers that home Internet meant "instant access to the world of sports, finance, and entertainment." The father told his friend that he could finish work assignments, help his children with their homework, find sporting buddies in the chat room, and look up the latest stock quotes, demonstrating AOL's slogan, "Making it easier for people to live, work, and play."

The "process of neoliberalization" that emerged after the economic crises of the 1970s brought about an increasingly postindustrial and service-oriented economy.[46] In *A Brief History of Neoliberalism*, David Harvey defines neoliberalism as "a theory of political economic practices that proposes that human well-being can best be advanced by liberating individual entrepreneurial freedoms and skills within an institutional framework characterized by strong private property rights, free markets, and free trade."[47] Changes in the economy, among them the growth of technology and the entertainment industry, the changing nature of labor markets, increased social polarization and privatization, more flexible labor market laws, and the globalization of culture, have had far-reaching consequences.[48] This late stage of capitalism is mainly characterized by a high degree of mobility of labor and capital, and what Harvey calls "time and space compression," where advances in technology have significantly reduced the time needed to travel across great distances, communication happens almost instantaneously, and disparate parts of the world are being absorbed into an increasingly homogenized global village.[49]

The changing labor market is represented by the emergence of the knowledge-cultural professional, a class of workers Richard Florida describes as the appropriation of formerly excluded groups such as artists and nonconformists and their work ethic into the very center of the labor market.[50] In economic and sociological literature, members of the new middle class who have adopted the "no-collar" artistic work ethos are often referred to as the knowledge class, the creative class, intellectual workers, or cultural professionals.[51] Increased privatization and flexibility in the labor market produced the "no-collar workplace"—with its form of "soft control"—for many of the new middle class.[52] As Mark Andrejevic describes, in the traditional industrial workplace, employees were compensated by wages according to the rate of production, and monitoring became necessary.[53] Home and work space needed to be separated for laborers to be satisfactorily disciplined and for labor power to be more efficient. The separation of business and leisure was necessary to create a market for consumption and to monitor the means of production to maximize capital. In contrast, members of the knowledge class generally do not produce tangible products; their means of production and property are "thinking" or the creation of ideas, as opposed to the working and service classes, whose members are paid primarily to carry out their jobs according to well-defined plans. This new middle class includes but is not limited to writers, designers, computer programmers, engineers, lawyers, bankers, scientists, academics, and entertainers. This group has played a substantial role in postindustrial patterns of consumption, an increasing force behind economic growth, and arguably has become the most influential socioeconomic class in the erosion of the public-private dichotomy.

As Donna Haraway argues, this expansion of the marketplace and the restructuring of labor patterns are indications that "factory, home, and market are integrated on a new scale."[54] Computer companies contributed to the reshaping of the market by convincing their customers, both individual consumers and commercial clients, that with the right equipment they could "work at home with the same efficiency they achieve at central office complexes."[55] As early as 1984, Apple Computer used the slogan "It goes with you. It grows for you" to market the mobility of the Apple IIc.[56] By using an Apple modem along with their personal computer, potential customers were told, they could communicate with computers at their company office from the comfort of their home, quickly get whatever information they needed ("whenever and wherever"), and send the results back to their main office.[57] By the 1990s, Apple fully embraced neoliberal ideology about the changing nature of work. In a presentation to commercial clients, Apple sought to persuade business customers to adopt mobile computing for their employees to help them "improve productivity on a personal and professional level" and to recognize employees' desire for work-life balance by increasing flexibility and reducing stress.[58] To sell computers, Apple sales representatives argued that mobility had "become an essential dynamic of work and life" because "professionally and personally, it feels like we're all having to get more done in less time." Apple argued that "a major shift is occurring in the way work is performed." The concept of work had transformed because the traditional workday had become obsolete, the traditional workplace was changing, and the traditional worker was being redefined.[59] Apple used economic and labor statistics to support its argument that businesses risked going under if they ignored these global trends in the economy. The company recognized that perceived clear boundaries between the private and public spheres had eroded because, in Harvey's words, "neoliberalization has meant, in short, the financialization of everything."[60]

Unlike the introduction of the telephone into the home, which acted as a channel for communication to the outside world, or of the television, which transmitted the public sphere into the home, the personal computer facilitated a two-way relationship between the public and private spheres. Unlike television viewers passively watching the screen in the living room or bedroom, computer users could take advantage of expanded work opportunities in addition to leisure. The use of computers in the home further transformed work practices in the domestic sphere that had emerged during the postwar period. Personal computers in the 1980s offered a substitute for watching television, replaced the typewriter, and ultimately linked the telephone to personal computing. The personal computer represented the amalgamation of work and leisure and contributed a new dimension to public discourse on work-life balance.

13 • ADAPTABLE PARENTS, FLEXIBLE JOBS, AND ADAPTIVE HOMES

Why the media fascination with the "electronic cottage" and the abundance of television shows, news, and magazines articles about the work-at-home professional in the 1980s? How can we understand the explosion of home offices in the residences of professionals during this period? Futurist Alvin Toffler predicted the decentralization of the workplace due to technological advances in communication and coined the term "electronic cottage,"[1] which was widely used in mass media to describe the work-at-home phenomenon as more members of the middle class started to work from home part-time or full-time. First, it is worth noting that the parents featured in these articles were often creative or knowledge professionals. Second, the families described were often upper middle class. The *Chicago Tribune* argued that the phenomenon of the electronic cottage was "propelled by a growing concern among Americans about family responsibilities and the quality of life."[2] Ideology about family and work-life balance, the changing workforce, and economic and political conditions were factors in the increase in Americans working from home. However, the relationships between gender and class, technology, and domesticity were also significant.

In his best seller *The Third Wave*, Toffler predicted "a return to cottage industry on a new, higher, electronic basis, and with it a new emphasis on the home as the center of society."[3] Toffler proposed that the electronic cottage was the solution for the modern family. Responding to social critics at the 1979 National Assembly on the Future of the Family regarding the demise of the nuclear family, Toffler and feminist Betty Friedan argued that the structure of the family was evolving in response to technological, economic, and social transformations. The nuclear family "perfectly fitted the needs of a mass-production society with widely shared values and lifestyles, hierarchical, bureaucratic power, and clear separation of home life from work life in the marketplace."[4] The families of the future would take on multiple forms that would better fit the needs of a postindustrial society characterized by decentralized markets, increased specialization, advanced technology, the decline of the factory, and the subsequent increase in the valuation of knowledge and skills. Toffler further argued that in order to restore the nuclear family, society needed to forego technological advancement, subsidize manufacturing, and reverse the rise of the service sector.[5]

Despite the emergence of the electronic cottage in the 1980s, the majority of Americans did not work at home. However, a noteworthy group of Americans increasingly did more work at home, whether through formal arrangements or as extensions of their workday, and were often represented in popular culture. An examination of the growth of home workers reveals disparities in the relationship and access to technology and the meaning of work within the home because of unequal opportunities due to class, race, and gender. In 1985 the U.S. Bureau of Labor Statistics conducted a one-time survey and found that 17.3 million of the nation's 97.7 million nonfarm workers worked some hours at home.[6] By 1988 that number increased to 24.9 million people working at home at least part time.[7] In 1985 only 7 percent of those who worked at home were employed full time. By 1988 that had increased to 24 percent. The data from 1985 also revealed that 54 percent of those who reported telecommuting were in the professional fields, while 28 percent were employed in sales or clerical positions.[8] In 1995, the U.S. Department of Transportation started to collect data on telecommuters through the National Household Travel Survey in response to the growing trend. Home-based workers were most likely to be white, males, persons in high-income households, and/or suburbanites. By 2001, close to 70 percent of telecommuters who reported working some time at home were in technical or professional fields of employment.[9]

Although the data reveals that some of Toffler's predictions were remarkably prescient, his arguments reflected a strong belief in technological determinism. Technological advances in communication technology did not radically decentralize the economy. As media scholar Mark Andrejevic claims, "The advent of digital interactivity does not challenge the social relations associated with capitalist rationalization, it reinforces them and expands the scale on which they operate."[10] Yet, Toffler's ideas were very popular and influential in economic and policy circles. For example, in 1994, then Speaker of the U.S. House of Representatives Newt Gingrich recommended *The Third Wave* as required reading for Congress.[11] Conservatives such as Gingrich embraced Toffler's ideas regarding home-based work and computer technology in promotion of decentralized capitalism even though Toffler's ideas promoted new forms of family structure that most conservatives rejected. Instead of destroying the family, as detractors of the telephone and television had predicted in the 1950s, technology could save the family. The digital revolution, in Andrejevic's words, "contributes to the fantasy of friction-free capitalism by offering to make labor markets fluid and flexible" in allowing "for the increased economic productivity of spaces of leisure and domesticity."[12] As a political project, the location of market work within the home aligned with the principles of neoliberalism—decentralization, social freedom, the free-market economy, and the family.

BEST OF BOTH WORLDS

As early as the 1960s computers were predicted to be useful tools to help homemakers run more efficient households. Women would use them to "prepare dietetically balanced menus, check prices for a particular item at all stores . . . place orders, [and] do their banking," as well as for diversion or to "attain an advanced degree at a university, all via a computer and without leaving the home."[13] In other words, in the pre-existent gendered space of the home, the computer was originally imagined as helping to streamline "women's work" in the reproductive sphere, not as a machine to be used for wage-based work. However, second-wave feminism demanded changes in women's relationship to the domestic sphere. As the number of working mothers climbed steadily during the 1970s, the discourse on motherhood shifted. The picture of ideal womanhood—a middle-class mother focused on the home—was threatened by the image of the "vanishing mommy," the working woman who has "gone out to work," supposedly "neglecting the children she used to mother."[14] Social critics referred to the research of child development experts such as René Spitz and John Bowlby to support growing concern that by working outside of the home, mothers were harming their children. In their view, maternal deprivation, or the absence of the mother, especially during the early childhood years, was the root of all future problems. Women's vocation was the home.[15] In 1976, historian Christopher Lasch summed up the overall fear expressed in dialogue on the working mother thus: "If she leaves, there is nobody home."[16]

By the 1980s, neoliberal postfeminist arguments about the role of women in society began to take root in response to the dilemma of the working mother. Judging by the abundance of articles on the subject in the popular press during the 1980s, the solution to the working mother's work-life dilemma was the rediscovery of home-based work through the revival of the cottage industry. News articles depicted working mothers smiling, surrounded by young children, while on the telephone or typing on their desktop computers in makeshift offices in their bedrooms or living rooms.[17] As one working mother stated, "It's the best of both worlds for a husband . . . your wife's at home, and she's not a vegetable."[18] Politics followed, as the ban on six types of industrial homework was lifted in the 1980s under the Reagan administration.[19] The professional or clerical mother seated comfortably at a computer in her home office replaced the image of the immigrant woman toiling at a sewing machine in a dark bedroom in a tenement building. The personal computer was supposed to free women, allowing them to be good mothers and earn income within the home. This was never realized because, as Marsha Cassidy claims, the personal computer was initially "incompatible with the gendered interiors of domestic space."[20]

The introduction of the computer in the home revealed contradictions in the conceptualization of the home as a gendered space. The home has historically been imagined as feminine, the space of reproduction. Nevertheless, women do not have spaces of their own, as the home is composed of shared spaces (living room, kitchen, and master bedroom), masculine spaces (den, study, and garage), and childhood spaces (bedrooms, playrooms). Television representations of working mothers during the 1980s and early 1990s validated this perception of the home. Even *Family Ties* (1982–1989), which depicted Elyse Keaton (played by Meredith Ann Baxter), a professional mother working primarily from home, did not show her having a space dedicated to work, unlike Cliff Huxtable on *The Cosby Show* (1984–1992) or Jason Seaver (Alan Thicke) on *Growing Pains* (1985–1992). Elyse, a freelance architect, worked primarily at a desk or table in the kitchen even though the fictional Keaton home had an extra bedroom / guest room that could have been set up as a home office. Unlike in the homes on *The Cosby Show* and *Growing Pains,* which have a study for the father, as their counterparts did in 1950s television (e.g., Ward Cleaver in *Leave It to Beaver*), Elyse's workspace is in the kitchen, as advised by various experts in the popular press during the 1950s. She did not have the privilege of owning a personal computer and having a dedicated space in which to work.

I would argue that in addition to the gendered nature of the home, women's relationship to leisure and technology also shaped the meaning of home-based work. As I argued in chapter 11, historically, work and leisure for men within the home merged through communication technology. For women, the home is a space of "unproductive" labor, not a space of leisure. Lynn Spigel makes this argument using television advertisements—for example, the image of the housewife washing the dishes while watching TV as opposed to her husband in his easy chair waiting to be served.[21] This depiction of married women continued on sitcoms during the 1980s even for those who had jobs outside of the home. For example, in the family sitcom *Growing Pains,* Jason Seaver works at home to allow his wife, Maggie, to return to work. Despite working full-time outside of the home, Maggie is depicted doing the laundry and straightening up the house while Jason and the children watch television in the evening.

Technological advances such as fax machines, data lines, and personal computers were touted as the answer to the working mother's dilemma—making it possible for her to earn a living and pursue a career without abandoning the family. Digital technology was unique in that it expanded the possibilities of home-based work beyond clerical work supported by the telephone and typewriter. The personal computer made it possible for more women to work at home to pursue a career and manage the family. As Cassidy argues, "The home

PC was also advanced as indispensable to successful parenting, a pledge mollifying postfeminism's suspicion that women's liberation threatened effective childrearing."[22] In reality, gender and class shaped the meaning of home-based work. For professionals, who were predominantly men, home-based labor meant individual freedom and work-life balance without sacrificing income potential. However, for most women in the 1980s, home-based work was clerical in nature or an extension of their normal workday. Consequently, working at home meant lower wages. In historian Eileen Boris's words, the "image of the telecommuter was more fantasy than reality."[23] Despite the predictions, working at home did not become a godsend to most mothers. Feminists noted in the popular press that working at home would not solve childcare problems facing working mothers.[24] Without childcare, the "workday" extends into the night. The widely circulated images of the smiling mother working productively at her computer with children underfoot were often a myth.

THE NEW FATHER

One influential social change that helped reconstruct the home as an acceptable space of production for professional families was the emergence of the men's movement in the early 1970s and 1980s and the ideology of the "New Man" (sometimes referred to as the "New Father") in the 1990s. According to Jessica Weiss, one of the central themes of the men's movement was the proximity of the father to the family.[25] Scholars such as Andrew Singleton and JaneMaree Maher argue that the emergence of the "New Father" was in response to late-1960s second-wave feminist critiques of the role of gender within the institution of the family.[26] During the late 1970s and the 1980s, newspapers featured national men's groups such as Free Men and best-selling author and psychologist Herb Goldberg, who published *The Hazards of Being Male* in 1976. Authors like Dr. Goldberg and others in the emerging men's movement criticized the feminist movement for stopping too soon and not doing anything to help men dismantle masculine stereotypes.

As early as 1972, newspapers published reports about fathers opting to work from home, declaring these "husband-at-home families" a "return to old-fashioned family life."[27] The fathers were often writers, illustrators, doctors, and dentists who lived in the suburbs and wanted to spend more time with their families by working at home and eliminating grueling commutes to the city. These men possessed extra space to set up an office or studio in a bedroom or basement and could afford office equipment and a dedicated phone line. They were applauded for their decision to support their families both financially and emotionally. In April 1982, *New York* magazine's cover story "Home Is Where the Office Is" featured an investment banker and two young children in his home office. Kirkpatrick MacDonald appears happy and productive, surrounded by stacks of paper, binders, two telephones, and his personal computer.[28] He has the best of both worlds: professional success and time with his family. The article featured MacDonald and other professionals who chose to work at home setting up offices in spare bedrooms, living rooms, and dens. Telecommuters were touted as part of a new and growing development—the revival of the cottage industry. The article promoted telecommuting as the solution for fathers who wanted to spend more time with their families and to avoid traffic jams and grueling commutes from the suburbs. The arrangement was often romanticized. For example, a wife is quoted saying, "I can't understand the sympathy I get from other women . . . I think I'm the luckiest women in the world to have him home."[29] However, there were issues of family privacy. Client phone calls interrupted dinner and family time. There were also problems establishing boundaries between work and leisure. One father summed up the problem succinctly: "I soon discovered that the problem for me was to get myself to stop working."[30] Home-based work was championed by the mass media as an excellent option for fathers to spend more time with their families; however, many editorials mentioned the disadvantages of working from home—primarily the psychological difficulty of separating private and professional life.[31]

The feminist critique, women's increased labor force participation, and the changing role of fathers within the domestic sphere are evident in depictions of fatherhood in popular culture, beginning with Dustin Hoffman's portrayal of a single father in *Kramer vs. Kramer* (1979) and Michael Keaton's role as a stay-at-home dad after losing his job in *Mr. Mom* (1983). By the late 1980s, the fictional fathers (and father figures) in *Blossom* (1990–1995), *My Two Dads* (1987–1990), and *Full House* (1987–1995) have flexible schedules and the ability to stay home during the day because of their careers as knowledge-cultural professionals.[32] Blossom's father in the pilot episode was an accountant before the show took a different direction and recast him as a musician. Between gigs, Nick Russo (Ted Wass) composes music at home in his living room, which is equipped with a piano and sound and recording equipment. Michael Taylor (Paul Reiser) and Joey Harris (Greg Evigan) of *My Two Dads* manage to raise the teenage daughter of an ex-girlfriend because of their financial means and flexible work life. Michael is a financial adviser, and Joey is an artist. In *Full House,* Danny Tanner (Bob Saget) works as a morning sportscaster. Because he works outside the home, his brother-in-law and a friend take care of the children during the day. Jesse (John Stamos) is a struggling musician who does freelance work in advertising and sometimes gives music lessons in his bedroom. Joey (Dave Coulier) is a stand-up comedian who works primarily at night. When he needs to work on his comedy material he retreats to his bedroom-studio space in the converted garage.

During the 1990s, Mary Douglas Vavrus reviewed hundreds of television news treatments that featured "Mr. Moms" and noted that not one featured a nonprofessional family.[33] Without a doubt there were many working-class families that had a father at home because of necessity, but media representations at the time featured families that were purported to have chosen this "new" middle-class family arrangement. Vavrus mentions the influential role of *Mr. Mom* in her research but primarily situates the emergence of the "Mr. Mom identity" as a reaction to "significant societal shifts vis-à-vis gender and domesticity occurring during the 1990s."[34] I argue that those societal shifts and the possibility of Mr. Mom as a masculine identity are rooted in the postwar period, with the emphasis on involved and present fathers in mass media such as newspapers, periodicals, and television as argued in chapter 8. Mr. Mom was permitted to stay at home and participate in the domestic sphere without contributing income only after representations of the work-at-home father materialized in popular culture. Therefore, emergent social changes were shaped by ideological messages of fictionalized representations of the work-at-home father as well as news accounts in mass media.

Since the 1960s, the United States has experienced significant social changes, such as rising divorce rates, the legalization of abortion, increased use of birth control and a subsequent decline in birth rates, a rise in the number of unmarried mothers, greater participation of women in the workforce, more single-parent families, and increased visibility of same-sex relationships. Many scholars describe the political climate of the 1980s as a culture war between differing conservative and progressive visions of the future of America. As Stephanie Coontz argues, there was a national "call to revive commitment and responsibility through a 'rediscovery' of family values."[35] For example, sociologist James Davison Hunter claims that the Reagan administration legitimated the "conservative cultural revolution."[36] Under President Reagan politics and public policy moved to the right, but American culture moved to a more secular and pluralistic order. One of the central values of the conservative movement was the preservation of the heterosexual nuclear family.

Growing Pains and *The Cosby Show* are particularly significant in examining the reinsertion of the father as the central role in family sitcoms during the 1980s and early 1990s through their depiction of the home office and work-at-home fathers. *Growing Pains,* a family sitcom broadcast on ABC, featured the typical upper-middle-class suburban family with a twist that reflected the social changes of the period. After staying home for fifteen years, Maggie Seaver (Joanna Kerns) decides to return to work as a reporter. Her husband Jason (Alan Thicke), a psychiatrist, supports her decision by working at home to take care of their three children.[37] The show featured story lines that addressed the parents' difficulty in achieving work-life balance. The fictional family experiences "growing pains," but, more significantly, the show reflects the perceived growing pains of society at large. *Growing Pains* legitimates the mother's decision to work outside the home by allowing the father to both support the family financially and adopt a central role in the domestic sphere, preserving the nuclear heterosexual middle-class family.

The fictional fathers on popular shows such as *Growing Pains, The Cosby Show, Family Ties, Blossom,* and *Full House* represented the domesticated New Man. The ideal partner for the New Working Woman, the New Man participates in domestic activities by doing his fair share of housework and parenting. For example, in *Growing Pains,* Dr. Jason Seaver is portrayed as a well-meaning father who has to prove that he can see patients and take care of the kids and the home without Maggie's help during the day. As Andrew Gorman-Murray claims, "The New Man is, thus, a new model of hetero-masculinity moulded through perceived greater participation in domestic activities and labour. As a result of his domestic masculinity, the home is also expected to be de-feminised, and housework de-gendered."[38] Therefore, many story lines featured Jason trying to establish the boundary between being a cool father and a disciplinarian and learning to cook and do laundry while struggling with his wife's new role as busy professional.

Jason argues that he can take care of the kids both emotionally and physically—he *is* a psychiatrist. The show establishes Jason's identity as a professional and an expert and reminds the audience of his masculinity even though he works at home. To emphasize Jason's status as a doctor and to establish his masculinity, he is shown conducting his psychiatric practice from a study at the front of the house. It is decorated in dark masculine colors. There is an abundance of wood shelving for his books, and a telephone and a globe are prominently displayed on his large desk, echoing earlier postwar images of television fathers' domestic space. Within his study, Jason uses his professional knowledge to counsel his children (just like Ward Cleaver) and discuss important topics with his wife. Jason's professional experience extends to his management of the domestic sphere—a refashioned image of the postwar father. Although experts at work, television husbands often left home management to their wives, as revealed in close readings of postwar family sitcoms. Jason represents the new model of fatherhood, fully capable and competent in both domains because of his professional status.

In addition to addressing new forms of masculinity, sitcoms that foreground the father's role in the family also ignore the role of socioeconomic status in providing opportunities for work-life balance. *The Cosby Show* debuted September 20, 1984, on NBC and aired for eight seasons. It had the highest average Nielsen ratings of any 1980s sitcom during its five consecutive seasons from 1985–86 through 1989–90. The sitcom featured an affluent black two-income couple and their five children living in Brooklyn. Bill Cosby played Dr. Heathcliff "Cliff" Huxtable, married to a lawyer, Clair Huxtable (Phylicia Rashād). Watched by 30 million households during its peak, *The Cosby Show* was a mass media success that crossed demographic markets such as race, age and class.[39]

Despite *The Cosby Show*'s commercial success, it was criticized by media commentators as a "sanitized '50s-style white show in blackface."[40] Cosby widely admitted that the show deliberately avoided overtly talking about issues of race and the problems associated with being a black family in America. According to Cosby, his "first defense is that the show is about Americans . . . I won't deal with the foolishness of racial overtones on the show. I base an awful lot of what I've done simply on what people will enjoy. I want to show a family that has a good life, not people to be jealous of."[41] This unwillingness to overtly engage in race and class seemed to drive the popularity of the show across racial and socioeconomic demographics. As media scholar Bambi Haggins argues, "*The Cosby Show* reconfigured race and, in so doing, threw the issue of racial representations in the faces of the audience, televisual consumer and critic alike."[42] Cosby defended his decision to feature an affluent black family as a more difficult marketing choice than depicting typical representations of a black family as a working-class maternal household. For Cosby, family, not race, was the primary focus of the show. In many ways, the show reflected his life. Cosby, although not a medical doctor in real life, did earn a doctorate in education from the University of Massachusetts at Amherst in 1976, arguing that television has the ability to educate people.[43] His wife, Dr. Camille Olivia Cosby, is also a professional like his fictional wife, Clair.

The Huxtable family's affluent lifestyle on *The Cosby Show* was not typical of the average African American family or in fact of most American families, as they are clearly depicted as upper middle class. The merits of hard work and education were a consistent theme on *The Cosby Show*. The children were depicted doing chores to learn lessons about responsibility. These televisual representations emphasizing the importance of education and hard work are important in understanding the social construction of the knowledge-cultural professional in the postindustrial economy in relation to the home as a site of work. There are signs of the importance of work and education throughout the house. Cliff runs his medical practice from the English basement of their brownstone. The children's bedrooms are furnished with bookshelves and desks for studying. The master bedroom has a small writing desk as well as an office-size desk with an electric typewriter and a telephone. The living room also has a desk. Finally, Cliff is always on call for work, as he carries a pager on his person and is available to his patients through the many telephones located throughout the house.

Now, in popular culture, success is found in knowledge-based professions and the live-work lifestyle in affluent neighborhoods in the city or inner/close-in suburbs. This point is further underscored by Cliff and Clair's disappointment with the decision by their oldest daughter, Sandra, and her husband to disregard their educational training in law and medicine, respectively, to run a camping equipment store. For Cosby, being a professional is tantamount to the good life. His decision to make Cliff's character an obstetrician whose practice is located in the home allows him to portray Cliff as integrating his professional and private life in an ideal representation of work-life balance. Cliff Huxtable could not be a present father, actively involved in parenting and filling in the maternal space vacated by Clair's status as a working mother, without his ability to be at home for most of the day.

Growing Pains and *The Cosby Show* make visible the possibility of paid work within the home for upper-middle-class men. In examining the home as a space of work in popular culture, it is apparent that during the late 1980s and early 1990s knowledge-cultural professionals (especially creative and cultural workers) started to replace representations of the "Company Man" of the previous era. Unlike their predecessors, these new television fathers were able to actively parent their children without sacrificing their careers, avoiding the "deadbeat dad" moniker. In contrast to the Mr. Moms who are embedded entirely in the domestic sphere, these television fathers did not have to give up work, as the idea of "stay-at-home parenting is simply not 'natural' for men."[44] The story lines of the new generation of family sitcoms were also less child-centered and consequently dedicated more time depicting the fathers' working and personal lives. Representations of the new father showed them achieving work-life balance by keeping one foot in the public sphere and maintaining their stake in the market while simultaneously reestablishing the patriarchal hierarchy of the domestic sphere. Consequently, these shows normalized greater participation by males in managing the household and further erased the boundaries between work and leisure, public and private life.

14 • URBAN PROFESSIONAL LIFESTYLES

On December 31, 1984, *Newsweek* dedicated its year-end issue to "The Year of the Yuppie," that is, the young, upwardly mobile urban professional. The yuppie lifestyle was associated with gentrification and conspicuous consumption. The new middle class, which included yuppies, emerged concurrently with the shift to the postindustrial economy in the late 1960s and early 1970s, and the beginning of gentrification in former industrial cities.[1] In 1971, before the term "gentrification" caught on, the *New York Times* used "Brownstoneurbia" to describe the restoration of the city's brownstones by young professionals.[2] The neighborhoods were attractive to young professionals for obvious economic reasons, but also for their distinctive architectural features and their proximity to Manhattan. In the early 1980s, the popular press started reporting that suburban sprawl was reversing in some metropolitan areas. As the journalist Wolf von Eckhardt argued, "For all the acres of free parking space, for all their unending commercial strips and Muzak-drenched shopping centers, the suburbs have not replaced the variety and the refinements that an affluent people expect."[3] Young professionals were renovating old houses in cities from Boston to San Francisco. Editorials declared that gentrification was not "a passing fad."

Ruth Glass is widely credited with coining the term "gentrification" in her 1964 book *London: Aspects of Change*.[4] She noted that many working-class neighborhoods in London had been taken over by the middle and upper middle classes. Geographer Neil Smith defined gentrification as the process by which inner-city lower-class neighborhoods that had previously experienced a middle-class exodus are reclaimed and subsequently refurbished by the private capital of the new middle class.[5] Many urban theorists see a correlation between the emergence of the knowledge class and gentrification and understand the phenomenon to be the result of postindustrial social restructuring.[6]

Futurist Alvin Toffler, conservative critics, and policymakers had written off cities during the 1980s. Toffler argued that cities would become economically irrelevant as computers and developing communication technologies made it possible for a growing number of people to telecommute. The rise of the Internet in the first half of the 1990s added credibility to the theory of urban decline led by advances in communication technology. But across the country, experts on technology and urbanism have noted an increase in Internet connections in urban centers populated by well-educated, affluent people, reinforcing the intellectual and economic leadership of a handful of urban centers such as New York, the Boston-Cambridge area, the Washington, D.C., metro area, San Francisco, Dallas, and Seattle.[7]

Many urban theorists questioned why the new middle class was attracted to inner-city bohemian neighborhoods. David Ley argued that the reclamation of the central city by the new middle class was a "statement of social identity and cultural politics"—the spatial expression of the rejection of suburban everyday life by the 1960s student movement in favor of culturally authentic city neighborhoods.[8] He identifies this group as the "cultural new class," which overlaps with Richard Florida's definition of creative professionals.[9] Ley includes professionals in the fine and applied arts, teaching, the media, and other social services sectors that share a calling to improve quality of life. It is their "imagineering of an alternative urbanism to suburbanization" as both producers and consumers that has helped to develop new inner-city communities.[10]

Neil Smith observed in *The New Urban Frontier* that the process of gentrification was a surprising reversal of most twentieth-century urban theorists' predictions of the fate of the city. As a result, gentrification was widely debated in magazines, newspapers, and scholarly journals. Gentrification became so controversial in New York City during the 1980s that the Real Estate Board of New York placed a large advertisement, "Is Gentrification a Dirty Word?," in the *New York Times* justifying gentrification to the public. The copy explained that underpopulated, shabby, and/or dangerous neighborhoods were not good for the future of the city, and stated, "We also believe that New York's best hope lies with families, businesses and lending institutions willing to commit themselves for the long haul to neighborhoods that need them. That's gentrification."[11] The Real Estate Board allied gentrification to private capital and middle-class families.

The possibility of white middle-class families returning to the city was a boon to urban planners and government officials. Promoting a conventional notion of family as the image of the revitalized city countered the prevailing narratives of violent black men and "welfare queens" that captured the attention of the New Right during the 1980s. Popular culture also reified these narratives during the 1970s and early 1980s with sitcoms about black families that were situated in the city—*Good Times* (1974–1979), *What's Happening!!* (1976–1979), and *Sanford and Son* (1972–1977), to name a few. Poor and working-class African Americans were visually associated with urban decay, representing all that was wrong with the city: high unemployment, poverty, crime, and broken families. These representations reflected conservative rhetoric. In the words of President

George H. W. Bush, "The major cause of the problems of the cities is the dissolution of the family."[12] Revitalizing the city meant restoring the middle-class nuclear family.

By the 1980s, gentrification became an essential part of urban economic restructuring. This was necessary, as many urban economies in advanced capitalist countries experienced a substantial decrease in the manufacturing labor market and a corresponding increase in the professional and service markets. Gentrification was an integral part of larger global processes. As Saskia Sassen notes, gentrification became the essential characteristic of the new global city.[13] Therefore, by the 1990s, artists' communities in places such as New York City served as the "beachhead of choice for residential gentrification."[14] Knowledge-cultural professionals who could afford to live in the suburbs instead fully embraced urban neighborhoods that their parents most likely would have abandoned.

Consequently, two contradictory narratives about cities existed during the 1990s. First, cities were racialized—places of crime, poverty, and dysfunctional families. Second, urban centers represented the possibility of renewal, culture, and authenticity and the space of the new middle class, the young, educated professional. In the late 1980s, popular culture adopted new narratives that reflected public discourse on the second form of urbanism. Television and film presented the city as a space of possibility for the middle-class family, although in new forms. The film *Three Men and a Baby* (1987) and the television shows *Full House* (1987–1995), *My Two Dads* (1987–1990), and *Blossom* (1991–1995) were commercial successes about unconventional middle-class families consisting of heterosexual white men (sans mothers) and children living in the city. Popular culture rediscovered fatherhood. Although these popular texts are a nod to 1950s sitcom fathers, the absence of mothers and the relationship between work and leisure make these representations of the private sphere noteworthy. Instead of locating the fictional homes in the suburbs, *Full House, My Two Dads,* and *Blossom,* as well as the most popular show of the 1980s, *The Cosby Show* (1984–1992), were all located in the city. As I noted in chapter 9, cities are symbols of economic prosperity for the nation. These sitcoms became the face of the "revitalized" city. Urban centers could not be abandoned to black men, gay men, and unwed black mothers. The resurgence of fatherhood in gentrified urban centers constructed a new imagery—the city home as a natural space for young urban professional men to raise a family, at least for the early years.

LOFT LIVING

By the late 1980s, lofts appear as a legitimate space for families in television sitcoms. Therefore, the media also participated in the spread of aspirational representations of loft living by depicting urban professionals living in hip bohemian spaces that characterized upper-middle-class postindustrial lifestyles. For example, in *My Two Dads*, Michael Taylor (Paul Reiser) and Joey Harris (Greg Evigan) collectively decide to raise their daughter, Nicole (Staci Keanan), in Joey's SoHo loft.[15] Michael works in finance, is portrayed as traditional, wears a suit, and is focused on money. He lives uptown. Joey is an artist, carefree and fun-loving, and wears jeans all the time. As an artist, he seems to practice a form of seamless and unalienated labor. Joey and Michael represent the merging of the managerial professional and the artisan/cultural worker. One episode clearly illustrates this point. Michael and Joey attempt to bring their divergent social worlds together by hosting a poker game for their friends. One of Michael's yuppie friends defends his lifestyle to an artist: "We are regular guys just like you except we are running the country." The yuppie realizes the cultural value of the artistic lifestyle and declares, "We should be treating each other as equals" after discovering that one of Joey's artist friends was the subject of an article published by his college newspaper.

Three Men and a Baby, a box office hit, also represented upper-middle-class professional lifestyles. Architect Peter Mitchell (Tom Selleck), actor Jack Holden (Ted Danson), and cartoonist Michael Kellam (Steve Guttenberg) are roommates living in a hybrid penthouse/loft apartment in New York City. They all have creative jobs and are not tied to an office and the nine-to-five lifestyle. Their bedrooms have computer desks and are set up to enable the men to work at home. Michael's bedroom is decorated to reflect his job (cartoonist), hobbies, and interests. Peter's room has a drafting table for work and also functions as a media room with three TVs and a huge collection of videotapes. They have a pool table, a jukebox, workout equipment, and other masculine toys in their home. (See figure 14.1.) The bachelor apartment serves as a space of work and leisure. Their lifestyle adopts the goals of work-life balance: the ability to be flexible, to work nontraditional hours, to integrate work and home, and to maintain social relationships. This representation made working at home seem normal and desirable to optimize family life, even in nontraditional family units.

To understand the emergence of this formerly unconventional space's transformation into a space of televisual domesticity, it is necessary to examine its genealogy. In the last half of the 1980s, the terms "live-work" and "live-work situation" began to appear in real estate advertisements in New York City. In 1986, in its Working at Home series, the *New York Times* featured a 7,000-square-foot loft occupied by Richard Wurman, an architect and publisher, Mrs. Wurman, a writer, and their four children. The article featured photographs of their home and floor plans as a "lesson in successful home and office integration."[16] Particular attention is paid to the emphasis on privacy and integration of communication technology, such as the multiple phone extensions and data lines. Twenty years earlier, artists desiring affordable places to live and work began illegally taking

FIGURE 14.1 Peter, Jack, and Michael's leisure space and adjoining kitchen in their New York City apartment in *Three Men and a Baby*. (*Source: Three Men and a Baby* [Buena Vista Pictures, 1987].)

up residence in industrial buildings in the SoHo neighborhood. In 1971, the city amended the zoning regulations to permit visual artists to live and work in their SoHo residences.[17] By 1986, the area became so popular that the city was forced to grandfather legal status to nonartists.[18]

Loft conversions in New York City date back to the postwar period but became popular as a domestic lifestyle in the late 1970s and the 1980s. Since the 1970s, "loft living" has become a familiar term in cities across the United States and in western Europe. The spread of loft living across American cities by national actors, particularly architects, designers, developers, and civic planners, depended on a "symbolic system of imagery in the practice of aesthetics, social locations and lifestyle."[19] As Julie Podmore notes, loft dwellers were generally cultural elites residing in specific urban centers "but more broadly connected to a global habitus of shared dispositions and social practices through the mass media and other communications technologies."[20] The sheer amount of publicity from the mass media influenced the popularity of loft conversions in New York City. Initially most of the articles, as James Hudson claims, "champion[ed] the struggle of artists to secure themselves a place in American society."[21] By the mid-1970s, the media shifted its focus to promote SoHo as a hip downtown destination. In 1974, *New York* magazine published an article declaring SoHo "the most exciting place to live in the city."[22] SoHo became a tourist area complete with maps and guidebooks to rival other tourist traps in the city. Between 1961 and 1983 over 150 articles were published in the *New York Times*, the *Village Voice*, and the *New York Post* on loft conversions in Manhattan. More importantly, the media not only promoted the loft as a domestic space in New York City; it also helped redefine urban industrial buildings as live-work spaces. Therefore, what began as an effort by creative professionals to find affordable space to live and work in the city developed into a lifestyle imitated by countless others in urban centers across the United States and in other Western countries.

According to scholars such as Sharon Zukin and James Hudson, city administrators and developers across the nation recognized that loft conversions could "stem the course of urban decay and deterioration."[23] Loft living started to attract educated and affluent middle-class professionals who desired urban lifestyles associated with the culture industries. Neglected manufacturing neighborhoods could be renewed and transformed by the middle and upper middle class. Early data supports this analysis. In 1978 a survey was conducted of several hundred loft residents in Lower Manhattan. Even before the explosion of nonartist residents in the 1980s, 96 percent of adult loft residents had a college education (compared to 19 percent in New York City as a whole), 33 percent had professional or technical occupations (compared to 14 percent citywide), and their median household income was over $22,000 (the citywide median was $8,400).[24] The revitalization of SoHo and other manufacturing areas in Manhattan made the inner city attractive to knowledge-cultural professionals. Therefore, as Andrew Ross writes, "non-artists could now purchase many of the trappings of a creative, bohemian life without having to work at living it."[25] In response, the real estate industry romanticized the life of the struggling artist and co-opted loft spaces, even though working as an artist is often financially insecure, and converting an industrial space into an inhabitable home is difficult.

The popularity of loft conversions spurred the publication of how-to guidebooks in the 1970s and 1980s. Similar to their postwar counterparts examined in chapter 5, these how-to publications offered floor plans and guidance on finding a space, financing and leasing options, and decorating. However, one major difference from 1950s books on finding the right suburban home was the emphasis on do-it-yourself renovations. Loft how-to books stressed the amount of labor necessary to make industrial space habitable. The other major difference was highlighting the pioneer status of loft converters. Postwar home guides constructed moving to the suburbs as joining an already existing community with desirable amenities and like-minded middle-class neighbors even though many communities were still in the planning stage or in development. In comparison, public discourse on loft living represented middle-class Americans looking for housing in industrial centers as explorers in the urban wilderness. Consider the title of the 1977 guidebook *Pioneering in the Urban Wilderness* by Jim Stratton.[26] The frontispiece features an illustration of Native Americans and presumably Dutch explorers on what is now called Manhattan Island in the sixteenth century. The reverse side of the page features a couple in an unrenovated loft with peeling paint and a rubbish-strewn floor. The point is further made in the first chapter with a quintessential photograph of urban industrial decay: an abandoned warehouse in a section of a city (presumably New York).

Gentrification of old urban residential neighborhoods by middle-class households and subsequent investment of private capital were fueled by neoliberal urban renewal practices. Lofts were generally located in commercial districts, and any displacement, as Zukin argues, meant the further loss of industry and working-class jobs. Deindustrialization of industrial centers created the "preconditions for the residential redevelopment of loft space."[27] Therefore, although both types of gentrifiers were termed "pioneers," the "natives" were fundamentally different. In urban residential neighborhoods, the poor and minority residents represented the "natives." In urban manufacturing centers the "wilderness" is understood to be empty, as illustrated in guidebooks such as *Pioneering in the Urban Wilderness*. However, as depicted in the sixteenth-century illustration of Lower Manhattan, there were residents present before the Dutch discovered the land. Likewise, the displacement of the industrial economy (as symbolized by loft conversions) was inconsequential and invisible to the knowledge-cultural professionals, the front-runners of the postindustrial economy.

Design books and magazines extended the analogy of the open wilderness of the city center to the interior of loft space. Authors proclaimed that the size, lack of interior walls, and openness of loft spaces permitted almost limitless possibilities in terms of layout. Because loft spaces are not divided into a series of specialized rooms, architectural and interior design publications presented a variety of layouts for domestic use. However, because of the immense size of loft spaces, most designs displayed large open spaces. In most layouts the living and service zones occupied the same space, in contrast to the layout of the typical residential home. Some loft layouts also eliminated the boundary between the living and private zones of the home.

As loft conversions became more popular, architectural design guides featured spaces for families. The incorporation of family life reveals the contradictions in the loft space, and arguably changes in work more broadly. How does one achieve privacy and work-life balance in a space that is physically open and speaks directly to the market economy and the importance of work? In the space planning section of one guide, the authors advise potential loft dwellers to consider the need for privacy: "If you have children, you may very well want to build a totally soundproof room to get away from it all. In fact, it would probably be better to build a bedroom for them as well as one for yourself, because even in a 100-foot-long loft there is little privacy for most adults from the inquisitive eyes of children."[28] Another example, "Family Loft Living," designed by a husband and wife design team, features "flexible living space for a family of four" in 4,500 square feet of space.[29] The authors describe the design elements "devised to negotiate the demands for privacy with the desire for open space."[30]

Sliding doors, glass panels, and pivoting doors divide the loft into informal and formal spaces as in a traditional home. The Chathams' loft has a "children's zone" at one end of the space and the master bedroom at the other end. The loft also features a dedicated study and a studio space above the master bedroom. The layout addresses privacy while simultaneously emphasizing the necessity of work.

The layout for the bedroom-study area of "Family Loft Living" is especially interesting, as the study is positioned next to the bedroom, which places it within the "informal" spaces. On one side of the space, pivot doors separate the master bedroom from the study. This design is similar to *Playboy*'s configuration of the bachelor pad discussed in chapter 11. (See figure 11.1). The study is an extension of the bedroom in the bachelor pad; however, the loft bedroom is an extension of the study, as the loft in its entirety acts as a space of work and leisure. Therefore, easier transitions between work and leisure become the guiding principle in the loft space—more important than privacy and the family in traditional spaces of domesticity such as the suburban middle-class home. The openness of the loft means a loss of the privacy that individual family members have come to expect in domestic spaces. In its arrangement of the family room and bedrooms and its sheltered position from the street, the suburban home represents the valuation of the family as a unit. Traditional homes in the United States are constructed as private spaces, but the open design of loft spaces puts more emphasis on the public zones of the home. The presence of workspaces bolsters the importance of work over leisure in the loft.

As many early loft layouts were designed for artists and other cultural professionals, work and living spaces overlapped, implying "an easy transition from one activity to another."[31] The urban loft is essentially the bedroom-study realized in its entirety. As Zukin argues, these design choices "eliminate the hierarchy of functions that is typical of most household arrangements."[32] Labor activities—whether in service of the market or to maintain the domestic sphere—and leisure activities converge in the domestic space of the loft. One design guide featured a suggested layout for the "Live/Work Dualities Loft." The loft was smaller than average, 875 square feet. The author described the space as "adapted for living and working in the same space."[33] The design plan for the space was to create an "operable collage system of movable components."[34] The layout consisted of three primary spaces: workroom, bedroom, and bathroom. The workspace overlaps with the kitchen, and movable walls separate the bedroom from the workspace. Podmore argues that the loft "embodies a modernist concept of space because it offers the possibility of multipurpose spaces and a functional aesthetic."[35] I would argue that loft spaces also embody premodern concepts of domestic space even though the loft aesthetic is modern. Everyday practices in loft spaces are reminiscent of old multiuse spaces and old social practices in the premodern household-based economy as examined in chapter 1.

Zukin argues that factory space converted into domestic space is "dead as far as productive activity is concerned."[36] She continues: "Thus the most fundamental part of a mode of production—the space where products are actually produced—is shifted to another use. This new use refers to a purpose quite different from the reproduction of capital in industry. As housing, the former factory space provides for the reproduction of the labor force. Significantly, the workers who are housed here are professionals, academics, executives in private industry, government bureaucrats, other service-sector employees, and self-employed artists."[37] However, I would argue that Zukin's understanding of the loft conversion phenomenon is true under the socioeconomic conditions of the industrial economy. Yes, the former factory space acts as a space of reproduction, but loft spaces are inherently contradictory. Productive activity is not dead in the live-work space of the domestic loft under the conditions of the emerging postindustrial economy. The creative and knowledge workers depicted in representations of loft living, whether in sitcoms, books, or national newspapers, participate in a larger economic system, producing goods for a knowledge- and service-based economy often within the home. In the space of manufacturing, the knowledge-cultural professionals Zukin refers to replace the working class, which she refers to as the "classical industrial proletariat."[38] Therefore, the live-work space of the loft simultaneously represents three historical modes of production: the cottage industry, industrial manufacturing, and the knowledge-based economy. The incorporation of the private sphere in nineteenth-century manufacturing buildings is an inversion of the turn-of-the-century practice of home-based manufacturing in the domestic sphere.

CLOSING THOUGHTS

Although they represent a small segment of the population, loft dwellers are nonetheless socially significant, as they are emblematic of the broader incorporation of work and leisure within the home. Two themes emerge in the examination of public discourse on the live-work lifestyle and representations of workspaces in the home during the postindustrial period. First, although the myth of the home as a space outside the sphere of work persists in the construction of the domestic sphere, counterrepresentations, such as the loft, emerged regarding the nature of the home and the possibilities for market-based work. The 1980s represented the commencement of the shift to late capitalism by the upper middle class in the breakdown of traditional job demarcations, in this case the location of work. Consequently, it is crucial to recognize that since the 1980s the issue of access to work-life balance, represented by the live-work lifestyle of loft living, concealed changing conceptions of work in the new economy. Second, work, education, and leisure are increasingly organized around access to technology, as discussed at the beginning of this chapter. The live-work space of the new economy would not be possible without communication technologies. The personal computer and the Internet were marketed as business tools for knowledge-cultural workers to facilitate and embrace careerism within the home. The home office became a natural space to locate these new instruments of work and leisure. Computer companies recognized the opportunity to market to telecommuters and home-based businesses (in extra bedrooms) and started to advertise and market software for business use in the home. By the 1980s, computers offered a substitute for watching television and replaced the typewriter, and in the 1990s the telephone became linked to personal computing in many middle-class households. Computer advertisements during the 1980s and early 1990s conflated work and leisure. Therefore, unlike other domestic technologies, the computer represented the convergence of work and leisure in a single machine.

Working conditions and quality of life have dramatically improved for most Americans since the late nineteenth century. However, I would argue that middle-class professional families, or the "knowledge class," have benefited the most from advances in communication technology because of their ability to adopt flexible schedules and to work at home (for example, by converting extra bedrooms or other spaces into home offices). Flexibility and unalienated labor have emerged as immaterial forms of social capital conferred by job status, separating the working class and the service-oriented middle class from the professional class. This focus on the impact of new technologies illustrates Lynn Spigel's argument that "discourse on new technologies has essentially been aimed at the people who can buy them—most typically the propertied class—it has tended to deal mostly with the issues that concern these class interests."[39] Consumption, consumerism, and individual socioeconomic success through work—enduring and competing values in the idealization of upper-middle-class family life—are at the root of the failure to obtain an idealized work-life balance in pursuit of the good life.

Today, the workplace is always available when we access our portable devices. Communication technologies such as smartphones and video chat services, as well as the growth of residential Wi-Fi, have created new ways for employees to pursue professional goals and be flexible, giving employers the incentive to expect more productivity from workers. Technology allows for flexible workspaces and increased productivity in the private sphere. Work, education, and leisure are increasingly organized around access to and representations of the central role of technology within the domestic sphere. However, this is detrimental to individual well-being and family life. Professional middle-class family life is represented as an ideal in public discourse. People appear to benefit from work-life balance even though the institutions that shape and support family life have not changed for the better. The school day still ends before the workday, and high childcare costs, low wages for service workers, and the dismantling of unions reduce opportunities to monitor children, manage educational opportunities, and participate in extracurricular activities that reproduce class privilege. Historically, popular culture and public discourse have persuaded knowledge workers to forget that they are in solidarity with the working class. Thus, work-life balance as it is currently constructed is a myth that keeps workers from recognizing the exploitation of their labor and the dependence on service workers to support work-life balance. Knowledge-cultural professionals need to recognize that they are first and foremost workers, even though they love their jobs, claim to do interesting and fulfilling work, and are celebrated in the media. Working at home in your favorite T-shirt or pajamas is still labor.

ACKNOWLEDGMENTS

Most of the research done to write this book was based on archival sources. Therefore, I would like to thank the archival and curatorial staffs at the AT&T Archives and History Center, the Levittown Historical Society, and the Hagley Museum for their assistance in finding relevant archival material. Also, I would like to thank the librarians at the Library of Congress in Washington, D.C., for helping me find relevant manuscripts and periodicals from the postwar period. I especially want to thank Sheldon Hochheiser of the AT&T Archives and History Center for going the extra mile in not only helping me find materials for my project onsite, but also scanning and e-mailing images. Thank you to the Stanford University Department of Special Collections archival and curatorial staff for helping me navigate the vast Apple Computer, Inc. business records. Thank you, Wendy Shay, of the Smithsonian National Museum of American History, for taking the time to convert ¾ inch U-matic tapes to DVDs so that I could watch postwar commercials. Finally, I would like to thank the reading room staff of the Library of Congress Rare Book Collection for helping me access and navigate the *Playboy* magazine collection.

This book developed from my graduate studies and a number of conference papers presented at the National Communication Association, the Society for Cinema and Media Studies, and the PCA/ACA National Conference over the past eight years. Parts of chapters 5 and 6 were published in "Where Does Work Belong? Home(work) and Communication Technology within the Middle-Class American Postwar Home" in *Technology and Culture* in 2019. Also, parts of chapters 8 and 12 were published in *Home Sweat Home: Perspectives on Housework and Modern Domestic Relationships* (Elizabeth Patton and Mimi Choi, eds., 2014), and part of chapter 11 was published in "Transforming Work into Play within the Domestic Sphere" in *Media History* in 2015.

I am so grateful to Marita Sturken, my dissertation chair, and Nicholas Mirzoeff and Aurora Wallace, my committee members, for supporting my research and scholarship; your mentorship was outstanding during my graduate education at New York University. Thank you, Mara Mills, for steering me toward the AT&T Archives in Warren, New Jersey, which were invaluable. I would also like to thank Rebecca Adelman, Mimi White, and Jason Loviglio for their advice and willingness to read my work during the long process of writing and revising this book and related articles.

I have been fortunate to have exceptional support at the Rutgers University Press. Specifically, my editor, Lisa Banning, was amazing through every stage of the publishing process. Thank you to the anonymous readers for your thoughtful and detailed feedback and to everyone at Rutgers University Press who assisted in the production of this book.

I owe my deepest thanks to close friends and family. Thank you, Mom, Dad, Regina, Staci, Michael, Abby, and Gregory for your words of encouragement during this long process. Finally, I would like to thank my son Cian and my partner John for all their love and support—specifically, John for your support and hard work raising a child during this challenging but rewarding period in our lives, and Cian for letting me work on my laptop while playing in his room!

NOTES

INTRODUCTION

1. For contemporary discussions about work-life balance, see, for example, Stephen Marche, "Home Economics: The Link between Work-Life Balance and Income Equality," *The Atlantic*, July–August 2013, https://www.theatlantic.com/magazine/archive/2013/07/the-masculine-mystique/309401/; Sheryl Sandberg, *Lean In: Women, Work, and the Will to Lead* (London: W. H. Allen, 2015); Anne-Marie Slaughter, *Why Women Still Can't Have It All* (Richmond, VA: OneWorld, 2015); Laura Vanderkam, "Work/Life Integration Is the New Normal," *Fortune* 171, no. 4 (March 15, 2015): 139.
2. Dalton Conley, *Elsewhere, U.S.A.: How We Got from the Company Man, Family Dinners, and the Affluent Society to the Home Office, BlackBerry Moms, and Economic Anxiety* (New York: Vintage Books, 2010).
3. Ibid., 8.
4. See, for example, Lynn Spigel. "Designing the Smart House: Posthuman Domesticity and Conspicuous Production," *European Journal of Cultural Studies* 8, no. 4 (November 2005): 403–426.
5. Lynn Spigel, *Welcome to the Dreamhouse: Popular Media and Postwar Suburbs* (Durham, NC: Duke University Press, 2001), 89.
6. Raymond Williams, *Television: Technology and Cultural Form*, ed. Ederyn Williams (New York: Routledge, 2003).
7. Nancy Fraser, *Rethinking the Public Sphere: A Contribution to the Critique of Actually Existing Democracy* (Milwaukee: University of Wisconsin–Milwaukee Center for Twentieth Century Studies, 1990), 110.
8. Ibid.
9. See, for example, Andrew Ross, *No-Collar: The Humane Workplace and Its Hidden Costs* (Philadelphia: Temple University Press, 2004).
10. Roger Silverstone and Eric Hirsch, eds., *Consuming Technologies: Media and Information in Domestic Spaces* (London: Routledge, 2005).
11. In this book, I use the expressions "the public sphere" and "the private sphere" because they are commonly understood and are useful in conceptualizing the home as an ideological space.
12. Spigel, *Welcome to the Dreamhouse*, 91.
13. Susan Gal and Gail Kligman, *Politics of Gender after Socialism: A Comparative-Historical Essay* (Princeton, NJ: Princeton University Press, 2000), 41.

CHAPTER 1 THE HOME AND ITS FUNCTION

1. The English words "economy" and "economics" can be traced back to the Greek word *οἰκονόμος*, meaning "one who manages a household." The contemporary use of the word "economy" to mean "the economic system of a country" did not develop until the nineteenth century. *Oxford English Dictionary*, 2nd ed. (1989), s.v. "economy."
2. Letter from Abigail Adams to John Adams, 16 July 1775, *Adams Family Papers: An Electronic Archive*, Massachusetts Historical Society, http://www.masshist.org/digitaladams/aea/cfm/doc.cfm?id=L17750716aa.

3. Tamara Hareven, "The Home and the Family in Historical Perspective," *Social Research* 58, no. 1 (1991): 253–285.
4. Philippe Ariès and Georges Duby, *A History of Private Life* (Cambridge, MA: Harvard University Press, 1987); Elizabeth Cromley, "Sleeping Around: A History of American Beds and Bedrooms; The Second Banham Memorial Lecture," *Journal of Design History* 3, no. 1 (1990): 1–17.
5. Cromley, "Sleeping Around."
6. The wealthy did have separate sleep chambers with beds, but they also used these rooms to conduct business and greet guests.
7. Peter W. Ward, *A History of Domestic Space* (Vancouver: UBC Press, 1999).
8. Hareven, "The Home and the Family," 255.
9. John Claudius Loudon, *An Encyclopaedia of Cottage, Farm, and Villa Architecture and Furniture* (London: Longman, Brown, Green, and Longmans, 1846), iv.
10. Ibid., 1.
11. Sharon Zukin, *Loft Living: Culture and Capital in Urban Change* (New Brunswick, NJ: Rutgers University Press, 1982), 67.
12. Michel de Certeau, *The Practice of Everyday Life*, vol. 2, trans. Timothy J. Tomasik (Minneapolis: University of Minnesota Press, 1988).
13. Stuart Hall and Paul du Gay, eds., *Questions of Cultural Identity* (London: Sage, 1996).
14. Zukin, *Loft Living.*
15. Jürgen Habermas, *The Structural Transformation of the Public Sphere* (Cambridge, MA: MIT Press, 1989), 27.
16. Walter Benjamin, Michael William Jennings, Brigid Doherty, Thomas Y. Levin, and E.F.N. Jephcott, *The Work of Art in the Age of Its Technological Reproducibility, and Other Writings on Media* (Cambridge, MA: Harvard University Press, 2008), 103.
17. Hareven, "The Home and the Family."
18. Jeanne Boydston, *Home and Work: Housework, Wages, and the Ideology of Labor in the Early Republic* (New York: Oxford University Press, 1990), 99.
19. For further discussion of the ideology of the cult of domesticity, see Mary Louise Roberts, "True Womanhood Revisited," *Journal of Women's History* 14, no. 1 (2002): 150–155.
20. See, for example, "*Godey's Lady's Book* (Bookshelf)," Project Gutenberg, https://www.gutenberg.org/wiki/Godey%27s_Lady%27s_Book_(Bookshelf).
21. Clifford Clark Jr., "Domestic Architecture as an Index to Social History: The Romantic Revival and the Cult of Domesticity in America, 1840–1870," *Journal of Interdisciplinary History* 7, no. 1 (1976): 33–56.
22. John L. Vollmer, Pamela A. Schulze, and Janice M. Chebra, "The American Master Bedroom: Its Changing Location and Significance to the Family," *Journal of Interior Design* 31, no. 1 (2005): 1–13.
23. Richard Sennett, *The Conscience of the Eye: The Design and Social Life of Cities* (New York: Knopf, 1990), 27.
24. Clark, "Domestic Architecture."
25. Candace M. Volz, "The Modern Look of the Early Twentieth-Century House," in *American Home Life, 1880–1930: A Social History of Spaces and Services*, ed. Jessica H. Foy and Thomas J. Schlereth (Knoxville: University of Tennessee Press, 1992), 31.
26. In fact, according to Clifford Clark, businessmen often came home around 3 P.M. for dinner and remained in the home for the remainder of the day to work on their accounts in the library/study.
27. Volz, "The Modern Look."
28. Gwendolyn Wright, *Building the Dream* (Cambridge, MA: MIT Press, 1988).

29. John Tosh, *A Man's Place: Masculinity and the Middle-Class Home in Victorian England* (New Haven, CT: Yale University Press, 2007).
30. Ibid.; also see Picker's essay on housebound professionals' desire for a soundproof study to escape the street noise in Victorian London. John Picker, "The Soundproof Study Victorian Professionals, Work Space, and Urban Noise," *Victorian Studies* 42, no. 3 (1999/2000): 427–453.
31. Ibid.
32. Ibid., 60.
33. Jennifer Wilkinson, "From the Bedroom to the Streets; Intimacy and the New Public Order," *DisClosure* 15 (2006): 9–26.
34. Mark Wigley, "Untitled: The Housing of Gender," in *Sexuality and Space*, ed. Beatriz Colomina and Jennifer Bloomer (Princeton, NJ: Princeton Architectural Press, 1992), 327–390.
35. Jonathan Katz, *The Invention of Heterosexuality* (New York: Dutton, 1995).
36. Ibid., 41.

CHAPTER 2 INDUSTRY STAY OUT

1. Boydston, *Home and Work*, 159.
2. Ibid.
3. *Godey's Lady's Book* 42 (January 1851), https://www.gutenberg.org/ebooks/15080.
4. Eileen Boris, *Home to Work: Motherhood and the Politics of Industrial Homework in the United States* (Cambridge: Cambridge University Press, 1994), 93.
5. Jacob Riis, *How the Other Half Lives: Studies among the Tenements of New York* (New York: Dover, 1971), originally published 1890.
6. For an in-depth discussion about married working-class women, see Boris, *Home to Work*, 109.
7. Ibid.
8. U.S. Department of Labor, Children's Bureau, *Industrial Homework of Children*, Bureau Publication No. 100 (Washington, DC: Government Printing Office, 1922).
9. Boris, *Home to Work*, 118.
10. U.S. Department of Labor, *Industrial Homework of Children*.
11. U.S. Department of Labor, Women's Bureau, *The Commercialization of the Home through Industrial Home Work*, Bulletin No. 135 (Washington, DC: Government Printing Office, 1935).
12. Mark H. Leff, "Consensus for Reform: The Mothers'-Pension Movement in the Progressive Era," *Social Service Review* 47, no. 3 (1973): 397–417.
13. See, e.g., "Baby-Farming," *Baltimore Sun*, May 23, 1896, 12.
14. "A Victim of Baby-Farming," *Cincinnati Enquirer*, July 29, 1874, 1.
15. "Doctoring the Poor for 35 Years: Dr. Annie S. Daniel Tells of Her Long Service on East Side," *New York Times*, March 15, 1914, SM5.
16. National Child Labor Committee (U.S.) Records, Manuscript Division, box 26, Library of Congress, Washington, DC.
17. "Tenement Homework: Child Labor in Homes in New York, Massachusetts, and Rhode Island," Lewis Wickes Hine (1874–1940) Photographic Collection, Library of Congress Prints and Photographs Division, Washington, DC.
18. State of New York Factory Investigating Commission, *Preliminary Report of the Factory Investigating Commission* (Albany, NY: Argus, 1912).
19. Ibid., 94.
20. Ibid., 116.

21. National Child Labor Committee, *Child Labor Bulletin* 3, no. 1 (May 1914): 95.
22. Ibid., 97.

CHAPTER 3 THE TELEPHONE AND BETTER LIVING

1. See, for example, "Telephone Was Only a Scientific Toy," *Boston Daily Globe*, October 28, 1906.
2. "Girls' Bedroom Telephones," *Washington Post*, March 15, 1903.
3. Ibid.
4. Ibid.
5. Ibid.
6. Anthony Giddens, *The Consequences of Modernity* (Stanford, CA: Stanford University Press, 1990), 18–19.
7. Quoted in Claude S. Fischer, *America Calling: A Social History of the Telephone to 1940* (Berkeley: University of California Press, 1992), 62.
8. Ibid., 23.
9. Ibid.
10. Bell Telephone Company was founded by Alexander Graham Bell and associates in 1877. Over the next twenty years, Bell established several subsidiary companies. In 1885, American Telephone and Telegraph Company (AT&T) was established to develop a long-distance telephone network. By 1899, AT&T became the parent company of the Bell System. For more information see, *Encyclopaedia Britannica*. s.v. "AT&T Corporation," https://www.britannica.com/topic/ATandT-Corporation.
11. American Telephone and Telegraph Company, "The Telephone Unites the Nation," magazine advertisement, c. 1915, AT&T Archives, Warren, NJ (hereafter AT&T Archives).
12. Ibid.
13. Fischer, *America Calling*, 23.
14. A chamber has been historically defined as a room in a private house used primarily for sleeping. Eighteenth- and nineteenth-century floor plans for the main floor and private floors (second and third) often used the terms "bedroom" and "chamber" interchangeably and seem to imply extra rooms that could serve multiple purposes according to the needs of the household and how many children lived in the home.
15. Brian L. Ott and Robert L. Mack, *Critical Media Studies: An Introduction* (Malden, MA: John Wiley and Sons, 2009), 185.
16. Michèle Martin, *Hello, Central? Gender, Technology, and Culture in the Formation of Telephone Systems* (Montreal: McGill-Queen's University Press, 1991), 140.
17. Ibid., 9.
18. Sidney H. Aronson, "Bell's Electrical Toy: What's the Use? The Sociology of Early Telephone Usage," in *The Social Impact of the Telephone*, ed. Ithiel De Sola Pool (Cambridge, MA: MIT Press, 1977), 31.
19. Ibid., 27.
20. Referring to the telephone as a "toy" is significant. Because it was originally understood as a device for entertainment, its ability to potentially alter the sanctity of the ideal middle-class home may initially have seemed nonthreatening. See "The History and Development of the Telephone in Wisconsin," *Wisconsin Magazine of History* 10, no. 2 (December 1926), Wisconsin Historical Society, https://www.wisconsinhistory.org/libraryarchives/.
21. "First Telephone Put in Somerville in 1877," *Boston Daily Globe*, May 11, 1924.
22. *State Journal* (Lincoln, NB), September 5, 1879.

23. Department of Commerce Bureau of the Census, *Census of Electrical Industries: 1917, Telephones* (Washington, DC: Government Printing Office, 1920).
24. "Spread of the Telephone," *Boston Daily Globe*, May 6, 1907.
25. "The Telephone in England and America," *Saturday Review*, August 21, 1920.
26. Herbert N. Casson, *The History of the Telephone* (Chicago: A. C. McClurg, 1911), 204.
27. Ibid.
28. "Telephone Uses: Some Odd Ones That Will Soon Be Commonplace," *New York Tribune*, March 31, 1907.
29. "Neighborizing the Farmer," AT&T marketing materials, May 1915, AT&T Archives.
30. "The Telephone in England and America."
31. "Telephone Uses."
32. "The Telephone as an Alarm Clock," *New York Times*, May 20, 1895.
33. "Railroad Tickets at Your Home," *Wall Street Journal*, December 2, 1907.
34. Quoted in Fischer, *America Calling*, 67.
35. "Scientific Inquisitors," in *The Living Age*, vol. 208 (Boston: Little, 1896), 822.
36. "Send Your Voice," *Wall Street Journal*, August 29, 1910, 7.
37. Aronson, *The Social Impact of the Telephone*, 33.
38. *Morning Oregonian*, July 7, 1912, 11.
39. Ibid.

CHAPTER 4 PORTABLE TYPEWRITERS FOR HOME USE

1. Ruth Schwartz Cowan, "The 'Industrial Revolution' in the Home: Household Technology and Social Change in the 20th Century," *Technology and Culture* 17, no. 1 (1976): 1–23.
2. Christine Frederick, *The New Housekeeping: Efficiency Studies in Home Management* (Garden City, NY: Doubleday, Page, 1913), vii.
3. Laurel D. Graham, "Domesticating Efficiency: Lillian Gilbreth's Scientific Management of Homemakers, 1924–1930," *Signs* 24, no. 3 (1999): 633–675.
4. Frederick, *The New Housekeeping*, 101.
5. Clarence Wilbur Taber and S. Maria Elliott, *The Business of the Household* (Philadelphia: J. B. Lippincott, 1918).
6. Ibid., v.
7. Ibid., 269.
8. Edith Louise Allen, *Mechanical Devices in the Home* (Peoria, IL: Manual Arts Press, 1922), Home Economics Archive: Research, Tradition and History (HEARTH), Albert R. Mann Library, Cornell University, Ithaca, NY (hereafter HEARTH).
9. Ibid.
10. Marketing Brochures, Trade Catalogs, and Advertisements for the Education Division, box 5, folder 32, Remington Rand Division Records.
11. "60 Years Ago: Women Were Freed," Remington advertisement, 1933, box 1, folder 10, Sperry Rand Corporation, Remington Rand Division Records, Subgroup III, Advertising and Sales Promotion Department (Accession 1825.III), Hagley Museum and Library, Wilmington, DE (hereafter Remington Rand Division Records).
12. U.S. Bureau of Labor Statistics, Consumer Price Index Inflation Calculator, https://www.bls.gov/data/inflation_calculator.htm.
13. "Manual of Instructions for Remington Salesmen on the Sale of the Remington Portable," June 1, 1928, Marketing Brochures, Trade Catalogs, and Advertisements for the Education Division, box 5, folder 32, Remington Rand Division Records.

14. Products—Multiple Model Promotions, Sales Literature, 1928–c. 1948, box 5, folder 42, Remington Rand Division Records.
15. "At Home in Your Home," advertisement for the Royal Portable Typewriter, *Good Housekeeping*, November 1927, HEARTH.
16. "How the Typewriter Captured the Family," marketing brochure, 1924, Marketing Brochures, Trade Catalogs, and Advertisements for the Education Division, box 5, folder 32, Remington Rand Division Records.
17. Marketing brochure for portable typewriter, c. 1925, Marketing Brochures, Trade Catalogs, and Advertisements for the Education Division, box 5, folder 32, Remington Rand Division Records.
18. "Manual of Instructions for Remington Salesmen on the Sale of the Remington Portable," June 1, 1928.
19. Ibid., 4, emphasis added.
20. Ibid., emphasis added.
21. Margery W. Davies, *Woman's Place Is at the Typewriter: Office Work and Office Workers, 1870–1930* (Philadelphia: Temple University Press, 1982).
22. Ibid., 70.
23. "60 Years Ago."
24. Emmett Leroy Shannon, *Money for the Woman Who Wants It: A Practical Presentation of the Principles Underlying the Planning of Successful Enterprises and Spare Time Work for the Woman Who Wants to Earn* (Schenectady, NY: Woman's Progress Association, 1920).
25. University of Minnesota, *Vocations Open to College Women* (Minneapolis: University of Minnesota, 1913), Collection Development Department, Widener Library, Harvard University, Cambridge, MA.
26. Catherine Filene, *Careers for Women* (Boston: Houghton Mifflin, 1920); Shannon, *Money for the Woman Who Wants It.*
27. Shannon, *Money for the Woman Who Wants It*, 2.
28. Ibid., viii.

CHAPTER 5 THE QUEST FOR EASY LIVIN' IN THE SUBURBAN HOME

1. See, for example, Stephanie Coontz, *The Way We Never Were: American Families and the Nostalgia Trap* (New York: Basic Books, 2000); Jessica Weiss, *To Have and to Hold: Marriage, the Baby Boom, and Social Change* (Chicago: University of Chicago Press, 2000).
2. Ruth Schwartz Cowan, *More Work for Mother: The Ironies of Household Technology from the Open Hearth to the Microwave* (New York: Basic Books, 1985), 18.
3. Judith A. McGaw, "No Passive Victims, No Separate Spheres: A Feminist Perspective on Technology's History," in *In Context: History and the History of Technology*, ed. Stephen Cutliffe and Robert W. Post (Bethlehem, PA: Lehigh University Press, 1988), 172–191.
4. Carolyn Goldstein, "Home Economics: Mediators," in *Gender and Technology: A Reader*, ed. Nina E. Lerman, Ruth Oldenziel, and Arwen Mohun (Baltimore: Johns Hopkins University Press, 2003), 360.
5. Otis Wiese, "Live the Life of *McCall's*," *McCall's*, May 1954.
6. Pamela Robertson Wojcik, *The Apartment Plot: Urban Living in American Film and Popular Culture, 1945 to 1975* (Durham, NC: Duke University Press, 2010), 197–198.
7. For further discussion about the history of postwar leisure ideals and consumerism within the domestic sphere, see Rachel Maines, *Hedonizing Technologies: Paths to Pleasure in Hobbies and Leisure* (Baltimore: Johns Hopkins University Press, 2009); Lizabeth Cohen,

A Consumers' Republic: The Politics of Mass Consumption in Postwar America (New York: Vintage, 2003).

8. Of course, noncompensated work was always present in the home in the form of gendered invisible labor.

9. See Raymond Williams's discussion of the evolution of the country/city dichotomy in English literature in *The Country and the City* (New York: Vintage Classics, 2016).

10. L. B. Wheildon, "National Housing Emergency, 1946–1947," *Editorial Research Reports 1946*, vol. 2 (Washington, DC: CQ Press, 1946), 855–876, http://library.cqpress.com/cqresearcher/cqresrre1946121700.

11. Steven Mintz and Susan Kellogg, *Domestic Revolutions: A Social History of American Family Life* (New York: Free Press, 1989).

12. Simmons Company Records, 1900–1997, Archives Center, National Museum of American History, Washington, DC.

13. Frank Hobbs and Nicole Stoops, *Demographic Trends in the 20th Century.* U.S. Census Bureau, Census 2000 Special Reports, Series CENSR-4, Demographic Trends in the 20th Century (Washington, DC: Government Printing Office, 2002).

14. Ibid.

15. Cohen, *A Consumers' Republic*, 141.

16. John A. Schindler, *Woman's Guide to Better Living 52 Weeks a Year* (Englewood Cliffs, NJ: Prentice-Hall, 1957), 92–93.

17. Coontz, *The Way We Never Were*, 25.

18. See, for example, George Lardner Jr., "Happy Suburban Homeowners Agree Livin' Is Easy, Washington Not Missed," *Washington Post*, October 6, 1963.

19. Wojcik, *The Apartment Plot.*

20. Nina Leibman, *Living Room Lectures: The Fifties Family in Film and Television* (Austin: University of Texas Press, 1995).

21. See chapter 6 for further discussion of this film.

22. See, for example, Katherine Morrow Ford and Thomas H. Creighton, *The American House Today: 85 Notable Examples* (New York: Reinhold, 1951).

23. See, for example, John Callender, *Before You Buy a House* (New York: Crown, 1953).

24. See, for example, "House for Family Living," *Life*, July 10, 1950; "The US Needs More Livable Homes," *Life*, September 15, 1958.

25. Barbara M. Kelly, *Expanding the American Dream: Building and Rebuilding Levittown* (Albany: State University of New York Press, 1993), 53–57.

26. Cape Cod floor plan, display copy, c. 1952, Levittown Historical Society, 150 Abbey Ln, Levittown, NY 11756; The Blake, National Homes of Moderate Cost, 1949, Antique home.org.

27. The following are examples of established suburbs by the postwar period that were originally established in the late nineteenth century: Takoma Park, MD (Washington, DC); Oak Park, IL (Chicago); and Rye, NY (New York City).

28. See, for example, John Wallace, "House of the Week: Rancher Is Keyed to 3 National Polls," *Baltimore Sun*, October 20, 1957, A27.

29. Katherine Morrow Ford and Thomas Creighton, *Designs for Living: 175 Examples of Quality Home Interiors* (New York: Reinhold, 1955), 151.

30. Ibid.

31. Ibid.

32. See, for example, "Room for Study a Necessity in Today's Home," *Atlanta Daily World*, December 26, 1958; "'Apartness' Keynote of the New Home," *Sun* (Baltimore), October 22, 1961, C12.

33. “House of Ideas,” *House and Garden*, February 1962.
34. See, for example, Elmer H. Johnson, “Family Privacy in a Multi-unit Dwelling,” *Marriage and Family Living*, August 1952, 219–225; F. Stuart Chapin, “The Psychology of Housing,” *Social Forces*, Fall 1951, 11–15.
35. Ford and Creighton, *Designs for Living*, 136.
36. Ibid. See, for example, Stella Roach, “Happier Home Balance: Privacy Gaining on Togetherness,” *Los Angeles Times*, July 13, 1961, E3; Caroline Lewis, “Parents Can Escape Overdone Togetherness in This Home,” *Chicago Tribune*, September 21, 1963, W A4.
37. See, for example, Lewis, “Parents Can Escape Overdone Togetherness.”
38. *Saturday Evening Post*, January 10, 1959.
39. See, for example, “Special! 50 Page Home Section,” *Popular Mechanics*, October 1955; Kenneth MacDonald, “Home Office under Stairway,” *Popular Mechanics*, October 1955, 177.
40. Clipping from the *Saturday Evening Post*, January 10, 1959; Thomas W. Ennis, “Remodeling Bill Put at 15 Billion: Renovations Top New Starts . . . ,” *New York Times*, February 10, 1957.
41. Wallace, “House of the Week”; George O’Brien, “How to Live with Your Work,” *New York Times*, October 29, 1961, SM62.
42. “Room for Study a Necessity in Today’s Home.”
43. “‘Apartness’ New Trend in Homes,” *Chicago Tribune*, October 2, 1966.

CHAPTER 6 THE BIG BUSINESS OF HOMEMAKING

1. See, for example, Cynthia Kellogg, “Desk Space-At Home,” *New York Times*, April 20, 1958, SM:84; Caroline Lewis, “Home Office Furniture Glamorous,” *Chicago Tribune*, July 13, 1961, C9.
2. Lewis, “Home Office Furniture Glamorous.”
3. Betty Friedan, *The Feminine Mystique* (New York: W. W. Norton, 2001), 57.
4. See “Maid to Order” (S2:E17), “Samantha’s Super Maid” (S5:E14), and “Samantha’s Yoo Hoo Maid” (S6:E02).
5. Lynn Spigel and Michael Curtin, *The Revolution Wasn’t Televised: Sixties Television and Social Conflict* (New York: Routledge, 1997), 59.
6. Mimi Marinucci, “Television, Generation X, and Third Wave Feminism: A Contextual Analysis of *The Brady Bunch*,” *Journal of Popular Culture* 38, no. 3 (2005): 508.
7. Ibid., 515.
8. Mitra Toossi, “A Century of Change: The U.S. Labor Force, 1950–2050,” *Monthly Labor Review*, May 2002, https://www.bls.gov/opub/mlr/2002/05/art2full.pdf.
9. Barbara M. Kelly, *Expanding the American Dream: Building and Rebuilding Levittown* (Albany: State University of New York Press, 1993).
10. Ibid., 85.
11. Paula McFarland, “An ‘Office’ in Home Saves Time and Money,” *Chicago Daily Tribune*, February 8, 1959, E2.
12. Mary Ann Callan, “Mother Keeps a Home Office,” *Los Angeles Times*, January 22, 1960.
13. Home economics classes were widely promoted by educational professionals during the postwar period. A good example that argues that young women need to take home economics before they get married to successfully manage a household is a short film that was distributed to high school students in Kansas, made by the Centron Corporation under the supervision of the University of Kanas. See Margaret Travis (script) and Herk Harvey (dir.), “Why Study Home Economics,” Centron Corporation, 1955, http://www.archive.org/details/WhyStudy1955.

14. Lynn Spigel, *Make Room for TV: Television and the Family Ideal in Postwar America* (Chicago: University of Chicago Press, 1992), 74.
15. See, for example, McFarland, "An 'Office' in Home."
16. "You Can Have an Office at Home," *Chicago Daily Tribune*, July 4, 1958, B2.
17. Margery W. Davies, *Woman's Place Is at the Typewriter: Office Work and Office Workers, 1870–1930* (Philadelphia: Temple University Press, 1982).
18. "The American Family in Trouble," *Life*, July 26, 1948, 89.
19. Ibid.
20. Ibid.
21. "How Mrs. Littlejohn's Telephone Helps Her through Busy Days," Ad Study Report No. 65, 1954, Southwestern Telephone Company, AT&T Corporate Archives, Warren, NJ.
22. "How to Save Yourself 76 Miles of Walking Each Year," Bell Telephone, 1965, AT&T Corporate Archives.
23. "Where Do You Want Your Extension Telephones?," Ad Study Report No. 90, 1954, New York Telephone Company, AT&T Corporate Archives.
24. U.S. Census Bureau, *Statistical Abstract of the United States: 20th Century Statistics, 1999*, "No. 1428. Housing Units—Historical Trends for Selected Characteristics: 1940 to 1997," https://www.census.gov/prod/99pubs/99statab/sec31.pdf.
25. "There's Nothing Like a Bedroom Telephone," *195 Magazine* 29 (1956), Doc. 0002-000169, AT&T Corporate Archives.
26. "Where Do You Want Your Extension Telephones?," AT&T Corporate Archives.
27. "Home-Wide Telephone Convenience," Bell Telephone advertisement, c. 1950s, AT&T Corporate Archives.
28. "The Well-Telephoned Home," *195 Bulletin*, September 1954, pp. 4–7, Doc. 0001-000179, AT&T Corporate Archives.
29. Marketing brochures for Remington Portable, 1924–1927, box 3, folder 17, Remington Rand Papers: Advertising and Sales Promotion Department—Typewriter Division, Hagley Museum, Wilmington, DE.
30. Marketing brochures from 1944 to 1969, box 5, Remington Rand Papers: Advertising and Sales Promotion Department—Typewriter Division.
31. Television commercial for the Office Writer, Remington Rand, 1958, https://archive.org/details/1958CommercialsForRemingtonRandTypewriters.
32. "Incredible! Now You Can Add + Subtract—Multiply × Electrically at Home or Office," advertisement for Smith-Corona Figurematic, *Life* magazine, October 28, 1966.
33. See, for example, Alice Mulcahey, "Women at Work: Part-Time Job Bonanza," *Baltimore Sun*, February 9, 1964, WM8.
34. Isabel Stevens Webster, *How to Make Money at Home* (New York: McGraw, 1949), 40; Lansing Morse Paine and Isabel Stevens Webster, *Start Your Own Business on Less Than $1000* (New York: McGraw-Hill, 1950).
35. Webster, *How to Make Money at Home*, 39.
36. See, for example, classified ad no. 4, *Los Angeles Times*, December 30, 1956, M3.
37. Shirley Lowry, "Mothers Pay Bills with Old Office Skills," *Chicago Daily Tribune*, June 10, 1954, SA8.
38. "Ladies! Earn Cash by Typing at Home," *Kiplinger's Personal Finance*, February 1954, 27–28.
39. Boris, *Home to Work*, 311.
40. Ibid., 324.
41. Lowry, "Mothers Pay Bills."
42. Ibid.

43. Joan Beck, "She Earns $10,000 at Home by Typing: Housewife Solves Problem of Budget and Boredom," *Chicago Daily Tribune*, July 8, 1954.
44. Boris, *Home to Work*, 319.
45. Ibid., 314.

CHAPTER 7 JUNIOR-SIZED OFFICES

1. Sonia Livingstone, *Young People and New Media: Childhood and the Changing Media Environment* (New York: Sage Publications, 2002).
2. Ibid.
3. Leonard W. Besinger Jr., "Why Does a Family Buy a Home?," *Chicago Daily Tribune*, May 17, 1959.
4. Ibid.
5. See, for example, "Youth Needs Privacy, Sense of Possession," *Hartford Courant*, October 27, 1957.
6. Katherine Morrow Ford and Thomas Creighton, *Designs for Living: 175 Examples of Quality Home Interiors* (New York: Reinhold, 1955).
7. "Youth Needs Privacy, Sense of Possession."
8. See, for example, "Bedroom-Study Provides Teenagers with Privacy," *Newsday*, November 29, 1956; "Teen-Age Territory," *Christian Science Monitor*, September 8, 1950.
9. Ford and Creighton, *Designs for Living*, 161.
10. Ibid.
11. "Small Rooms and How They Grow," *Seventeen*, March 1950.
12. Ethan Allen advertisement, *Seventeen*, September 1959.
13. "Your Very Own Music Box," *Seventeen*, August 1951.
14. "You and Your Typewriter," *Seventeen*, August 1951.
15. See, for example, "Telephone Wiring Goes into Hiding," *Washington Post*, November 8, 1958.
16. Frances Story, "Should a Teenager Have a Private Phone?," *Newsday*, April 28, 1958.
17. However, in most of the shows I reviewed, the parents at some point were shown as having a phone in their bedroom.
18. See, for example, "Designers Strive for Privacy for Each Child," *Chicago Tribune*, June 22, 1963.
19. See, for example, "Students Need Proper Environment for Study," *Los Angeles Times*, August 25, 1957.
20. Brian P. Gill and Stephen L. Schlossman, "A Nation at Rest: The American Way of Homework," *Educational Evaluation and Policy Analysis* 25 (2003): 319–337.
21. Ibid.
22. Promotion brochures for student typewriter rentals, 1934–1940, box 1, folder 21, Advertising and Sales Promotion Department—Typewriter Division, Remington Rand Records.
23. Marketing brochures, trade catalogues, and advertisements for the Education Division, box 5, Advertising and Sales Promotion Department—Typewriter Division, Remington Rand Records.
24. Remington advertisement, *Popular Science*, September 1957.
25. Television commercial for the Quiet-riter, Remington Portable Typewriter Division, Sperry Rand Corporation, 1958, https://archive.org/details/1958CommercialsForRemington RandTypewriters.

26. Remington advertisement, *Popular Science*, September 1957.
27. "Put Your Child's Hand over This One," advertisement, Royal Typewriter Company, Silver-Seiko for Litton Industries, *Life*, October 27, 1967.
28. Remington Monarch portable typewriter advertisement, Remington Portable Typewriter Division, Sperry Rand Corporation, *Life*, April 28, 1961.
29. "I'm a Miss with a Mission," advertisement for Smith-Corona portable, LC Smith and Corona Typewriters, Inc., 1949, Advertising Archives, http://www.advertisingarchives.co.uk/en/page/show_home_page.html.
30. "You and Your Typewriter."
31. Carl Spielvogel, "Advertising: New Products, New Markets; Smith-Corona Aims at Widening Field with Two Models," *New York Times*, November 17, 1957, F10.
32. "Play-Office Sets for Ages 7–12 by Eberhard Faber," *Playthings*, April 1960, 87, Brian Sutton-Smith Library and Archives of Play, Strong National Museum of Play, Rochester, NY.
33. Ibid.
34. Lisa Jacobson. "Allowances and Spending Money," in *Girlhood in America: An Encyclopedia*, vol. 1, ed. Miriam Forman-Brunell (Santa Barbara, CA: ABC-CLIO, 2001), 34–38.
35. Ibid.
36. Grace Palladino, *Teenagers: An American History* (New York: Basic Books, 1996), 98.
37. "Teenage Market Now $11 Billion Annually," *New York Amsterdam News*, February 27, 1965.
38. This is not the case for poor and working-class children, as well as children that lived on farms, for example.
39. Viviana A. Zelizer, *Pricing the Priceless Child: The Changing Social Value of Children* (New York: Basic Books, 1985), 3, 6.
40. Ibid., 98.
41. Robert Wuthnow, *American Misfits and the Making of Middle-Class Respectability* (Princeton, NJ: Princeton University Press, 2017).
42. Ibid.

CHAPTER 8 AN OFFICE AWAY FROM THE OFFICE

1. John Beynon, *Masculinities and Culture* (Buckingham, UK: Open University Press, 2002), 100.
2. Weiss, *To Have and to Hold*.
3. Andrew Gorman-Murray, "Masculinity and the Home: A Critical Review and Conceptual Framework," *Australian Geographer* 39, no. 3 (2008): 369.
4. Weiss, *To Have and to Hold*.
5. James Gilbert, *Men in the Middle: Searching for Masculinity in the 1950s* (Chicago: University of Chicago Press, 2005), 54.
6. Ralph LaRossa, *The Modernization of Fatherhood: A Social and Political History* (Chicago: University of Chicago Press, 1997).
7. Ibid., 1.
8. Benjamin Spock, *The Common Sense Book of Baby and Child Care, with Illustrations by Dorothea Fox* (New York: Duell, Sloan, and Pearce, 1946).
9. Weiss, *To Have and to Hold*.
10. Robert Coughlan, "Changing Roles in Modern Marriage," *Life*, December 24, 1956, 115.
11. Wojcik, *The Apartment Plot*.
12. Philip Wylie, "The Womanization of America," *Playboy*, September 1958, 52, 77.

13. See, for example, *Popular Mechanics'* annual home section. The October 1956 issue featured convertible bedroom/den architectural plans and masculine interior design suggestions for the study/den.
14. Royal Wills, *Living on the Level: One Story-Houses* (Boston: Houghton Mifflin, 1955).
15. "Lady Stay 'Way from That Den," *Kiplinger Magazine*, September 1956, 45.
16. William H. Whyte, *The Organization Man* (New York: Simon and Schuster, 1956).
17. Ibid., 3; emphasis added.
18. Advertisement for the 1960 Underwood Home-Office Typewriter, Library of Congress Archives, Washington, DC.
19. Whyte, *The Organization Man*, 144.
20. Edmond J. Bartnett, "Office-at-Home Designer Helps the Overworked Business Man," *New York Times*, September 25, 1960.
21. Whyte, *The Organization Man*, 144–148.
22. Leibman, *Living Room Lectures*.

CHAPTER 9 REAL MEN LIVE IN THE CITY

1. Elizabeth Fraterrigo, *Playboy and the Making of the Good Life in Modern America* (Oxford: Oxford University Press, 2009).
2. Philip Wylie, "The Womanization of America," *Playboy*, October 1958, 52.
3. Wylie, "The Womanization of America," 52.
4. Robert Moskin, "Why Do Women Dominate Him?," in *The Decline of the American Male*, by the editors of *Look* (New York: Random House, 1958), 24.
5. Fraterrigo, *Playboy and the Making of the Good Life*.
6. Ibid.
7. Ibid., 95.
8. George Wagner, "The Lair of the Bachelor," in *Intimus: Interior Design Theory Reader*, ed. Mark Taylor (London: Wiley-Academy, 2006), 378.
9. Wojcik, *The Apartment Plot*, 15.
10. Jane Abrams, "Bachelor Pads Should Avoid the Extremes," *Chicago Tribune*, April 17, 1971, W:A33.
11. Enid Nemy, "When the Bachelor, Goes Home," *New York Times*, April 6, 1966, 38.
12. Carl Kramer, "Turning an Apartment into a Bachelor Pad: 'Scaled-Down Hugh Hefner,'" *Washington Post*, November 8, 1970, H1.
13. "Modern Living Playboy Plans a Duplex Penthouse," *Playboy*, January 1970, 151.
14. See for example, "Playboy on the town in Chicago," *Playboy*, August 1959.
15. Bill Osgerby, "The Bachelor Pad as Cultural Icon: Masculinity, Consumption and Interior Design in American Men's Magazines, 1930–65," *Journal of Design History* 18, no. 1 (2005): 100.
16. "A Playboy Pad: Manhattan Tower," *Playboy*, August 1965.
17. "*Playboy*'s Penthouse Apartment (Part I)," *Playboy*, September 1956, 53.
18. Shepherd Mead, "The Dream House and How to Avoid It," *Playboy*, July 1956, 53.
19. Wylie, "The Womanization of America," 77.
20. Ibid.
21. "*Playboy*'s Penthouse Apartment (Part II)," *Playboy*, October 1956, 63.
22. See, for example, *Playboy*, front cover art, June 1961.
23. Hugh Hefner, "Editorial: Inaugural Issue," *Playboy*, December 1953, 3.
24. Ibid.; as I examine in chapter 11, Hugh Hefner ended up following this assertion to the extreme, conducting his business and personal life almost entirely in his master bedroom suite.

25. Fraterrigo, *Playboy and the Making of the Good Life*, 85.
26. Osgerby, "The Bachelor Pad as Cultural Icon," 99.
27. Ibid., 100.
28. Ibid.
29. Wojcik, *The Apartment Plot*, 88.
30. Osgerby, "The Bachelor Pad as Cultural Icon," 110.

CHAPTER 10 PSEUDO-BOHEMIAN BACHELORETTES

1. Steven Seidman, *Romantic Longings: Love in America, 1830–1980* (New York: Routledge, 1991).
2. Ibid., 118.
3. Coontz, *The Way We Never Were*, 185.
4. Seidman, *Romantic Longings*, 122.
5. Elana Levine, *Wallowing in Sex: The New Sexual Culture of 1970s American Television* (Durham, NC: Duke University Press, 2007).
6. Ibid.
7. Coontz, *The Way We Never Were.*
8. Seidman, *Romantic Longings*, 125.
9. T. J. Jackson Lears, "From Salvation to Self-Realization," in *The Culture of Consumption: Critical Essays in American History, 1880–1980*, ed. Richard Wrightman Fox and T. J. Jackson Lears, 3–38 (New York: Pantheon, 1983).
10. Marita Sturken and Lisa Cartwright, *Practices of Looking: An Introduction to Visual Culture*, 2nd ed. (New York: Oxford University Press, 2009), 268.
11. Thomas Frank, *The Conquest of Cool: Business Culture, Counterculture, and the Rise of Hip Consumerism* (Chicago: University of Chicago Press, 1998), 9.
12. Coontz, *The Way We Never Were*, 175.
13. Katherine J. Lehman, *Those Girls: Single Women in Sixties and Seventies Popular Culture* (Lawrence: University Press of Kansas, 2011).
14. See, for example, Elizabeth Trotta, "Make Your Own Rules: Last of a Two-Part Series," *Newsday*, September 6, 1963; Diana Goldin, "New Towne House Has Room for the Single Girl," *Newsday*, September 14, 1967.
15. Lehman, *Those Girls.*
16. Ibid.
17. Ibid., 5, 155.
18. Ibid., 5.
19. Margaret A. Nash and Lisa S. Romero, "'Citizenship for the College Girl': Challenges and Opportunities in Higher Education for Women in the United States in the 1930s," *Teachers College Record* 114, no. 2 (2012): 1–35.
20. Ibid., 5.
21. Edith M. Stern, "Women Are Household Slaves," *American Mercury* (January 1949): 75–76.
22. Betty Friedan, *The Feminine Mystique* (1963. Reprint, New York: Norton, 2001), 92.
23. Ibid., 235, 309.
24. Lehman, *Those Girls*, 73.
25. Ibid.
26. Helen Gurley Brown, *The Cosmo Girl's Guide to the New Etiquette* (New York: Cosmopolitan Books, 1971), 119.
27. Helen Gurley Brown, *Sex and the Single Girl* (New York: Bernard Geis Associates, 1962).

28. Ibid., 6.
29. Ibid.
30. Ibid., 155.
31. Ibid., 154.
32. "Two Creative Pads That You Can Copy," *Cosmopolitan*, March 1967.
33. Ibid., 117.
34. Quoted in Yael Kohen, *We Killed: The Rise of Women in American Comedy* (New York: Sarah Crichton Books, 2012), 61.
35. See, for example, "Income Tax and the Working Girl," *Cosmopolitan*, March 1966.
36. Hughie Mackay and Gareth Gillespie, "Extending the Social Shaping of Technology Approach: Ideology and Appropriation," *Social Studies of Science* 22, no. 4 (1992): 690.
37. Wojcik, *The Apartment Plot*, 147.
38. See, for example, Harry Golden, "Only in America: Sex and the Apartment Dweller," *Chicago Daily Defender*, January 11, 1965; Albin Krebs, "If the Girl Next Door Is a Call Girl . . . ," *New York Times*, October 31, 1976.

CHAPTER 11 WORK WHERE YOU LIVE

1. Wojcik, *The Apartment Plot*, 14.
2. Wylie, "The Womanization of America."
3. The founding of *Playboy* is discussed in chapter 9.
4. Russell Miller, *Bunny: The Real Story of Playboy* (New York: Holt, Rinehart and Winston, 1984), 44.
5. Thomas Weyr, *Reaching for Paradise: The Playboy Vision of America* (New York: Times Books, 1978), 70.
6. Fraterrigo, *Playboy and the Making of the Good Life*, 79.
7. Ibid., 79.
8. Kenon Breazeale, "In Spite of Women: *Esquire* Magazine and the Construction of the Male Consumer," *Signs* 20, no. 1 (1994): 3, doi:10.1086/494952.
9. Fraterrigo, *Playboy and the Making of the Good Life*, 48, 58.
10. See David Ley, *The New Middle Class and the Remaking of the Central City* (Oxford: Oxford University Press, 1996); Dalton Conley, *Elsewhere, U.S.A.: How We Got from the Company Man, Family Dinners, and the Affluent Society to the Home Office, BlackBerry Moms, and Economic Anxiety* (New York: Random House, 2009); and Richard Florida, *The Rise of the Creative Class* (New York: Basic Books, 2003).
11. Michael Hardt and Antonio Negri, *Empire* (Cambridge, MA: Harvard University Press, 2000), 293.
12. See Ley, *The New Middle Class*, and Florida, *Rise of the Creative Class*.
13. See, for example, David Bell, *The Coming of Post-Industrial Society: A Venture in Social Forecasting* (New York: Basic Books), 1973; Manuel Castells, *The Rise of the Network Society: The Information Age: Economy, Society and Culture*, vol. 1 (Malden, MA: Blackwell, 1996); and Florida, *Rise of the Creative Class*.
14. See, for example, Saskia Sassen, *The Global City: New York, London, Tokyo* (Princeton, NJ: Princeton University Press, 2001); and Florida, *Rise of the Creative Class*.
15. For a detailed discussion, see Ley, *The New Middle Class*.
16. Quoted in ibid., 72.
17. Becky Conekin, "Fashioning the Playboy: Messages of Style and Masculinity in the Pages of *Playboy* Magazine, 1953–1963," *Fashion Theory* 4, no. 4 (2000): 456; Fraterrigo, *Playboy and the Making of the Good Life*, 79; Joanne Hollows, "The Bachelor Dinner: Masculinity,

Class and Cooking in *Playboy*, 1953–1961," *Continuum* 16, no. 2 (2002): 148, doi:10.1080/10304310220138732.

18. Hugh Hefner, "The *Playboy* Philosophy," *Playboy*, January 1964, 188.

19. Hugh Hefner, "The *Playboy* Philosophy," *Playboy*, January 1963, 41.

20. Pierre Bourdieu, *Distinction: A Social Critique of the Judgement of Taste* (Cambridge, MA: Harvard University Press, 1984), 325. In *Distinction*, Bourdieu uses the term "cultural intermediary" to describe the emergence of a new middle class of cultural or "symbolic" occupations in postwar France. Although his research observations were primarily focused on France, his use of the term is relevant to understanding the growth of consumer culture and class restructuring in other Western countries, specifically the United States.

21. See "Airy Aerie," *Playboy*, May 1964; "Manhattan Tower," *Playboy*, August 1965; "Palm Springs Oasis," *Playboy*, April 1966; and "New Haven Haven," *Playboy*, October 1969.

22. Carrie Pitzulo, *Bachelors and Bunnies: The Sexual Politics of Playboy* (Chicago: University of Chicago Press, 2011), 82; Weyr, *Reaching for Paradise*, 29–31.

23. Pitzulo, *Bachelors and Bunnies*, 82.

24. Miller, *Bunny*, 136.

25. U.S. Department of Commerce, Bureau of the Census, *Income in 1965 of Families and Persons in the United States* (Washington, DC: Bureau of the Census, Department of Commerce, 1967), 1–2.

26. Wylie, "The Womanization of America," 52.

27. "What Is a Playboy?," *Playboy*, April 1956, 73.

28. Frank, *The Conquest of Cool*, 22.

29. Ibid.

30. Wylie, "The Womanization of America," 52.

31. Bourdieu, *Distinction*, 367.

32. Ibid.

33. Ibid., 132.

34. Ibid., 283.

35. Steven Cohan, "So Functional for Its Purposes: The Bachelor Apartment in *Pillow Talk*," in *Stud: Architectures of Masculinity*, ed. J. Sanders (New York: Princeton Architectural Press, 1996), 28.

36. Wojcik, *The Apartment Plot*, 85.

37. Fraterrigo, *"Playboy and the Making of the Good Life*, 82.

38. "A Playboy Pad—Airy Aerie," *Playboy*, May 1964.

39. Ibid., 74.

40. Ibid.

41. "Playboy's Penthouse Apartment (Part II)," *Playboy*, October 1956, 65.

42. Cohan, "So Functional," 31.

43. Ibid., 32.

44. "Playboy's Penthouse Apartment (Part I)," *Playboy*, September 1956, 60; emphasis added.

45. Ibid.

46. Ibid., 67.

47. Ibid.

48. Ibid., 63.

49. Ibid., 67.

50. Spigel, *Welcome to the Dreamhouse*, 70.

51. "The Playboy Mansion," *Playboy*, January 1966, 105.

52. Ibid., 113.

53. Ibid.

54. "Modern Living: The Playboy Bed; Designed for Luxurious Lounging and Sleeping," *Playboy*, November 1959, 66.
55. Raymond Williams, *Television: Technology and Cultural Form*, ed. Ederyn Williams (New York: Routledge, 2003), 19.
56. Ibid.
57. Hugh Hefner, *The Playboy Philosophy* (Chicago: HMH, 1962).
58. "The Playboy Philosophy," *Playboy*, February 1963, 41.
59. Ibid., 45; emphasis added.
60. "The Playboy Mansion," *Playboy*, January 1966, 202.
61. See Wylie, "The Womanization of America."
62. "Playboy's Penthouse Apartment (Part II)."
63. Bill Osgerby, "The Bachelor Pad as Cultural Icon: Masculinity, Consumption and Interior Design in American Men's Magazines, 1930–65," *Journal of Design History*, 18, no. 1 (2005): 108–109.
64. Tom Wolfe, "Hugh Hefner, Chicago Recluse—King of the Status Drop-Outs," *Sunday Herald Tribune Magazine*, November 7, 1965, republished in Tom Wolfe, *The Pump House Gang* (New York: Farrar, Straus and Giroux, 1999), 75.
65. Ibid.
66. Ibid., 72.
67. For a detailed discussion, see Neil Smith, *The New Urban Frontier: Gentrification and the Revanchist City* (London: Routledge, 1996), and Bruce Schulman, *The Seventies: The Great Shift in American Culture, Society, and Politics* (New York: Free Press, 2001).
68. Smith, *New Urban Frontier*, 30–31.
69. Ley, *The New Middle Class*, 24.
70. See, for example, ibid.; Sassen, *Global City*; and Smith, *New Urban Frontier*.
71. Mike Featherstone, *Consumer Culture and Postmodernism* (Thousand Oaks, CA: Sage Publications, 2007), 88.
72. Ibid., 84.

CHAPTER 12 THE ELECTRONIC COTTAGE

1. Apple Computer, Inc. Records, M1007, Dept. of Special Collections, Stanford University Libraries, Stanford, CA (hereafter Apple Computer Records, M1007, Dept. of Special Collections).
2. IBM Archives, "IBM Highlights 1970–1984," March 2003, http://www-03.ibm.com/ibm/history/documents/pdf/1970-1984.pdf.
3. For an in-depth discussion of the placement of televisions in the postwar home, see Spigel, *Make Room for TV*.
4. William Dutton, Everett M. Rogers, and Suk-Ho Jun, "Diffusion and Social Impacts of Personal Computers," *Communication Research* 14, no. 2 (1987): 231.
5. Edna Mitchell, "Fathers and Home-Video Game Play," in *Personal Computers and the Family*, ed. Marvin B. Sussman (New York: Haworth Press, 1985), 127.
6. Everett M. Rogers, "The Diffusion of Home Computers among Households in Silicon Valley," *Marriage and Family Review* 8 (1985): 89–100; Nicholas P. Vitalari, Alladi Venkatesh, and Kjell Gronhaug, "Computing in the Home: Shifts in the Time Allocation Patterns of Households," *Communications of the Association for Computing Machinery (ACM)* 28 (1985): 512–522; W. D. Danko and J. M. MacLachlan, "Research to Accelerate the Diffusion of a New Invention," *Journal of Advertising Research* 23 (1983): 39–43.

7. "Apple President Addresses Wall Street Analysts—New Organization Is Working," *Apple Street Journal* 1, no. 1 (November 4, 1985), Series 2: Communications/newsletters (internal), box 1, folder 17, Apple Computer Records, M1007, Dept. of Special Collections.
8. Peter Schuyten, "New Breed Emerges in Home Computers," *New York Times*, quoted in "On the Market—News from Apple," *Appletter* 5 (July 1980), Series 2: Communications/newsletters (internal), box 1, folder 12, Apple Computer Records, M1007, Dept. of Special Collections.
9. "Apple's New Focus on Business," *Business Week*, quoted in "On the Market—News from Apple," *Appletter* 5 (July 1980), Series 2: Communications/newsletters (internal), box 1, folder 12, Apple Computer Records, M1007, Dept. of Special Collections.
10. Schuyten, "New Breed Emerges in Home Computers."
11. "Apple President Addresses Wall Street Analysts—New Organization Is Working," *Apple Street Journal* 1, no. 1 (November 4, 1985).
12. Ibid.
13. "Home Market Computer Owner Profile," *Apple II News: An Information Source for Apple II Developers* 1, no. 2 (April 1985), Series 7: Marketing and sales newsletters, box 1, folder 12, Apple Computer Records, M1007, Dept. of Special Collections.
14. Advertising Co-op Binder: Target Market and PR Tips, 1983, Series 7: Dealer and Customer Financing, box 8, folder 20, Apple Computer Records, M1007, Dept. of Special Collections.
15. U.S. Department of Commerce, Bureau of the Census, *Home Computers and Internet Use in the United States: August 2000*, Current Population Reports: Special Studies, September 2001 (Washington, DC: U.S. Department of Commerce, Bureau of the Census).
16. Dutton, Rogers, and Jun, "Diffusion and Social Impacts of Personal Computers."
17. Robert Kominski, *Computer Use in the United States: 1989*, Current Population Reports: Special Studies, Series P-23, February 1991 (Washington, DC: U.S. Department of Commerce, Bureau of the Census), 23–171.
18. Ibid.
19. U.S. Department of Commerce, Bureau of the Census, *Home Computers and Internet Use in the United States: August 2000*, 6.
20. Danko and MacLachlan, "Research to Accelerate the Diffusion of a New Invention," 42.
21. Scott Donaton and Joe Mandese, "'Home Office Computing' Surges," *Advertising Age*, January 18, 1993, 39.
22. Apple IIe marketing booklet promoting home use to manage the household, circa early 1985, Marketing & Sales, Series 7: General Product Marketing, box 10, folder 2, Apple Computer Records, M1007, Dept. of Special Collections; *It Goes with You. It Grows for You*, Apple IIc brochure, 1984, Marketing & Sales, Series 7: Brochures, box 9, folder 9, Apple Computer Records, M1007, Dept. of Special Collections.
23. Dutton, Rogers, and Jun. "Diffusion and Social Impacts of Personal Computers," 239.
24. Kominski, *Computer Use in the United States: 1989*, 23–171.
25. U.S. Department of Commerce, Bureau of the Census, *Home Computers and Internet Use in the United States: August 2000*.
26. *It Goes with You. It Grows for You.*
27. Texas Instruments advertisement, *Scientific American*, May 1980.
28. Apple IIe marketing booklet, circa early 1985.
29. Apple advertisement, circa 1982, Series 7: Brochures, box 9, folder 4, Apple Computer Records, M1007, Dept. of Special Collections.
30. IBM PCjr advertisement, *Popular Science*, June 1984.
31. Marsha F. Cassidy, "Cyberspace Meets Domestic Space: Personal Computers, Women's Work, and the Gendered Territories of the Family Home," *Critical Studies in Media Communication* 18, no. 1 (2001): 48.

32. Apple IIc Software Sampler catalog, Summer 1984, Series 7: Catalogs, box 6, folder 12, Apple Computer Records, M1007, Dept. of Special Collections.
33. Ibid.
34. See, e.g., Georgia Dullea, "Sleeping Is in Line for Priority in Bedroom," *Chicago Tribune*, November 30, 1980.
35. Cassidy, "Cyberspace Meets Domestic Space," 55.
36. "Transforming Homes into Centers for Work, Video Entertainment," *Los Angeles Times*, April 20, 1986, SE6.
37. Lisa Foderaro, "Working Women Speak Out on Home Design," *New York Times*, August 21, 1986, C1.
38. See, e.g., Steven Morris, "It's Easy to Put Extra Bedrooms to Work," *Chicago Tribune*, August 15, 1987, B1; "Dual-Career Couples Going for Larger Homes," *Chicago Tribune*, July 26, 1986, A17.
39. U.S. Department of Commerce, Census Bureau, American Housing Survey, 1996. https://www.census.gov/programs-surveys/ahs/.
40. Conley, *Elsewhere, U.S.A.*, 54.
41. Lana F. Rakow, "Gendered Technology, Gendered Practice," *Critical Studies in Media Communication* 5, no. 1 (1988): 60.
42. Lizabeth Cohen, *A Consumers' Republic*, 270.
43. Roger Silverstone, Eric Hirsch, and David Morley. "Information and Communication Technologies and the Moral Economy of the Household," in *Consuming Technologies: Media and Information in Domestic Spaces*, ed. Roger Silverstone and Eric Hirsch (London: Routledge, 1992), 16.
44. See Conley, *Elsewhere U.S.A.*; Fiona Allon, "An Ontology of Everyday Control: Space, Media Flows and 'Smart' Living in the Absolute Present," in *Media Space: Place, Scale and Culture in a Media Age*, ed. Nick Couldry and Anna McCarthy (London: Routledge, 2004), 253–274.
45. AOL commercial, 1995, Archive.org, https://archive.org/details/EarlyAOLCommercial1995.
46. David Harvey, *A Brief History of Neoliberalism* (Oxford: Oxford University Press, 2011), 3.
47. Ibid., 2.
48. Ibid.
49. David Harvey, *The Condition of Postmodernity: An Enquiry into the Origins of Cultural Change* (Blackwell, 1991).
50. Richard Florida, *Rise of the Creative Class*, 13.
51. For more details about the new middle class, see Ley, *The New Middle Class*; for a discussion of the no-collar workplace, see Andrew Ross, *No-Collar: The Humane Workplace and Its Hidden Costs* (New York: Basic Books, 2002); for a discussion of the creative class and knowledge professionals, see Conley, *Elsewhere, U.S.A.*, and Florida, *Rise of the Creative Class*.
52. Florida, *Rise of the Creative Class*.
53. See Mark Andrejevic, "Little Brother Is Watching: The Webcam Subculture and the Digital Enclosure," in *MediaSpace: Place, Scale, and Culture in a Media Age*, ed. N. Couldry and Anna McCarthy (London: Routledge, 2004), 109–124.
54. Donna Haraway, "The Cyborg Manifesto," in *The Cultural Studies Reader*, ed. Simon During (New York: Routledge, 1999), 286.
55. David A. Warren, "A Master Craftsman Builds His Own Home Office," *Popular Mechanics*, April 1981, 135–141.
56. *It Goes with You. It Grows for You.*
57. Ibid.

58. “The Move to Mobile Computing: Tomorrow’s Too Late! Date: 10/10/95,” slide show presentation to promote mobile computing (laptops), Marketing, Series 3: Research & Development Standards, box 11, folder 10, Apple Computer Records, M1007, Dept. of Special Collections.
59. Ibid.
60. Harvey, *Brief History of Neoliberalism*, 33.

CHAPTER 13 ADAPTABLE PARENTS, FLEXIBLE JOBS, AND ADAPTIVE HOMES

1. Alvin Toffler, *The Third Wave* (New York: Bantam Books, 1980).
2. Carol Kleiman, “Work May Get Closer to Home,” *Chicago Tribune*, December 31, 1989.
3. Toffler, *Third Wave*, 210.
4. Carol Krucoff, “Families: The Revolution upon Us,” *Washington Post*, November 30, 1979, B5.
5. Alvin Toffler, “Braving the Newest World: The Family of the Future; Many Varied Forms,” *Chicago Tribune*, April 27, 1980, A1.
6. Francis W. Horvath, “Work at Home: New Findings from the Current Population Survey,” *Monthly Labor Review*, November 1986 (Washington, DC: Division of Data Development and Users’ Services, Office of Employment and Unemployment Statistics, Bureau of Labor Statistics).
7. “For Millions of ‘Telecommuters,’ Workplace Is Always at Hand,” *Los Angeles Times*, December 27, 1988, 8.
8. Ibid.
9. U.S. Department of Transportation, Federal Highway Administration, National Household Travel Survey, NHTS Data Series, July 2008.
10. Andrejevic, “Little Brother Is Watching,” 197.
11. Bill Torpy, “Mr. Speaker: The Academic from Willing Pupil to Bold Professor; Gingrich Used the Classroom to Launch His Political Career,” *Atlanta Journal-Constitution*, January 7, 1995.
12. Andrejevic, “Little Brother Is Watching,” 198, 201.
13. Stuart Loory, “Computer Hookup to Home Foreseen,” *New York Times*, December 5, 1966, 47.
14. C. Christian Beels, “The Family: The Case of the Vanishing Mommy,” *New York Times*, July 4, 1976, SM8.
15. Ibid.
16. Ibid.
17. See, e.g., Kleiman, “Work May Get Closer to Home.”
18. Deborah Blumenthal, “At Work They Are at Home,” *New York Times*, July 15, 1979, R1.
19. Eileen Boris and Cynthia R. Daniels, introduction to *Homework: Historical and Contemporary Perspectives on Paid Labor at Home* (Urbana: University of Illinois Press, 1989), 6–7.
20. Cassidy, “Cyberspace Meets Domestic Space,” 59.
21. Spigel, *Make Room for TV.*
22. Cassidy, “Cyberspace Meets Domestic Space,” 51.
23. Boris, *Home to Work*, 305.
24. See, e.g., Kathleen Christensen, “The New Era of Home-Based Work,” *Chicago Tribune*, August 20, 1986, 19; Kenneth B. Noble, “Commuting by Computer Remains Largely in the Future,” *New York Times*, May 11, 1986, E22.
25. Weiss, *To Have and to Hold*, 113.

26. Andrew Singleton and JaneMaree Maher, "The 'New Man' Is in the House: Young Men, Social Change, and Housework," *Journal of Men's Studies* 12, no. 3 (2004): 227–240.
27. Irene Backalenick, "He's at Home to Make a Living—and She to Make It a Home," *New York Times*, May 27, 1972.
28. Theodore Pettus, "Home Is Where the Office Is," *New York* magazine, April 12, 1982, 28–34.
29. Ibid.
30. Ibid.
31. See, e.g., Blumenthal, "At Work They Are at Home"; Georgia Dullea, "An Office Makes Room for Baby," *New York Times*, June 3, 1982.
32. For an in-depth discussion of how family sitcoms during the 1980s incorporated workplace issues, specifically childcare, see Alice Leppert, "Solving the Day-Care Crisis, One Episode at a Time: Family Sitcoms and Privatized Child Care in the 1980s," *Cinema Journal* 56, no. 2 (2017): 67–90.
33. Mary Douglas Vavrus, "Domesticating Patriarchy: Hegemonic Masculinity and Television's 'Mr. Mom,'" *Critical Studies in Media Communication* 19, no. 3 (2002): 352.
34. Ibid., 355.
35. Coontz, *The Way We Never Were*, 94.
36. James D. Hunter, *Culture Wars: The Struggle to Control the Family, Art, Education, Law, and Politics in America* (New York: Basic Books, 1992), 299.
37. A fourth child was introduced in 1988 keeping with the traditional image of the large nuclear family as opposed to the reality of smaller families in the 1980s. In fact, the opening credits featured historical images of families from ancient times to the postwar period, creating a sense of the assured continuity and permanence of the nuclear family.
38. Andrew Gorman-Murray, "Masculinity and the Home: A Critical Review and Conceptual Framework," *Australian Geographer* 39, no. 3 (2008): 371.
39. I grew up watching *The Cosby Show* in the 1980s. As a child, I did not recognize the problematic representations of race, gender, and class it depicted. The show channeled a myth of economic success and black middle-class identity through the promotion of education and hard work, ignoring the barriers of structural racism. Although I did not understand the concept of work-life balance at the time, I imagined a life where I could be with my family and have a successful career working from my home office. My nostalgia for *The Cosby Show* was tempered by Bill Cosby's "pull yourself up by your bootstraps" lectures to black youth in the early 2000s and shattered by the revelation that he sexually assaulted women. Still, my experience viewing the show as a child introduced me to the intersectional politics that would later inform my research interests.
40. Lawrence Christon, "The World according to the COS," *Los Angeles Times*, December 10, 1989.
41. Ibid., 42.
42. Bambi L. Haggins, "There's No Place Like Home: The American Dream, African-American Identity, and the Situation Comedy," *Velvet Light Trap* 43 (1999): 31.
43. Ibid.
44. Vavrus, "Domesticating Patriarchy," 365.

CHAPTER 14 URBAN PROFESSIONAL LIFESTYLES

1. Ley, *The New Middle Class*.
2. Lance Freeman, *There Goes the 'Hood: Views of Gentrification from the Ground Up* (Philadelphia: Temple University Press, 2006).

3. Wolf von Eckhardt, "Suburban Sprawl Reversing," *Los Angeles Times*, November 1, 1980, B6.
4. Ruth Glass, *London: Aspects of Change* (London: MacGibbon and Kee, 1964).
5. Smith, *The New Urban Frontier*, 30–31.
6. See, e.g., Ley, *The New Middle Class*; Sassen, *The Global City*; Smith, *The New Urban Frontier*.
7. Steve Lohr, "The Internet as an Influence on Urbanization," *New York Times*, September 16, 1996, D1.
8. Ley, *The New Middle Class*, 24.
9. Florida, *Rise of the Creative Class*.
10. Ley, *The New Middle Class*, 15.
11. "Is Gentrification a Dirty Word?," display ad 16, *New York Times*, December 23, 1985, A17.
12. George Bush, "Address before a Joint Session of the Congress on the State of the Union," January 28, 1992, The American Presidency Project by Gerhard Peters and John T. Woolley, https://www.presidency.ucsb.edu/node/266921.
13. Sassen, *The Global City*.
14. Andrew Ross, "Dot.com Urbanism," in *MediaSpace: Place, Scale, and Culture in a Media Age*, ed. Nick Couldry and Anna McCarthy (London: Routledge, 2004), 154.
15. In the pilot episode we learn that Nicole's mother had an affair with both men in the summer of 1974. Michael and Joey are awarded joint custody after her death. For the entire series the audience never learns if Michael or Joey is her biological father.
16. Carol Vogel, "A Cottage Industry in a New York City Loft," *New York Times*, May 15, 1986, C6.
17. City Planning Commission. "Amendments of the Zoning Resolution, pursuant to Section 200 of the The New York City Charter, relating to various sections concerning artists living and working quarters in manufacturing districts." CP-21256A. January 20, 1971. https://www1.nyc.gov/assets/planning/download/pdf/about/cpc/CP21256a.pdf.
18. Trish Hall, "Gray is showing in SoHo's punk look." *New York Times*, November 23, 1989, B1.
19. Julie Podmore, "(Re)Reading the 'Loft Living' Habitus in Montreal's Inner City," *International Journal of Urban and Regional Research* 22, no. 2 (1998): 284.
20. Ibid., 287.
21. James R. Hudson, *The Unanticipated City: Loft Conversions in Lower Manhattan* (Amherst: University of Massachusetts Press, 1987), 64.
22. "SoHo: The Most Exciting Place to Live in the City," *New York* magazine, May 20, 1974, 52–54.
23. Hudson, *The Unanticipated City*, 5; Zukin, *Loft Living*.
24. Peter Jackson, "Neighbourhood Change in New York: The Loft Conversion Process," *Tijdschrift voor Econ. En Soc. Geografie* 76, no. 3 (1985): 202–215.
25. Ross, "Dot.com Urbanism," 155.
26. Jim Stratton, *Pioneering in the Urban Wilderness* (New York: Urizen Books), 1977.
27. Zukin, *Loft Living*, 18.
28. Kingsley C. Fairbridge and Harvey-Jane Kowel, *Loft Living: Recycling Warehouse Space for Residential Use* (New York: Saturday Review Press / E. P. Dutton, 1976), 38.
29. Felicia Eisenberg Molnar, *Lofts: New Designs for Urban Living* (Gloucester, MA: Rockport, 1999), 76.
30. Ibid.
31. Zukin, *Loft Living*, 69.
32. Ibid., 68.

33. Molnar, *Lofts*, 32.
34. Ibid., 76.
35. Podmore, "(Re)Reading the 'Loft Living' Habitus," 290.
36. Zukin, *Loft Living*, 19.
37. Ibid.
38. Ibid.
39. Spigel, *Welcome to the Dreamhouse*, 95.

SELECTED BIBLIOGRAPHY

Adams, Annmarie. *Architecture in the Family Way: Doctors, Houses and Women, 1870–1900.* Montreal: McGill-Queen's Press, 1996.

Allon, Fiona. "An Ontology of Everyday Control: Space, Media Flows and 'Smart' Living in the Absolute Present." In *Media Space: Place, Scale and Culture in a Media Age,* edited by Nick Couldry and Anna McCarthy, 253–274. London: Routledge, 2004.

Andrejevic, Mark. "Little Brother Is Watching: The Webcam Subculture and the Digital Enclosure." In *MediaSpace: Place, Scale, and Culture in a Media Age,* edited by Nick Couldry and Anna McCarthy, 109–124. London: Routledge, 2004.

Ariès, Philippe, and Georges Duby. *A History of Private Life.* Cambridge, MA: Belknap Press of Harvard University Press, 1987.

Aronson, Sidney H. "Bell's Electrical Toy: What's the Use? The Sociology of Early Telephone Usage." In *The Social Impact of the Telephone,* edited by Ithiel De Sola Pool, 15–39. Cambridge, MA: MIT Press, 1977.

Bell, David. *The Coming of Post-Industrial Society: A Venture in Social Forecasting.* New York: Basic Books, 1973.

Beynon, John. *Masculinities and Culture.* Buckingham, UK: Open University Press, 2002.

Boris, Eileen. *Home to Work: Motherhood and the Politics of Industrial Homework in the United States.* Cambridge: Cambridge University Press, 1994.

Boris, Eileen and Cynthia R. Daniels. "Introduction." In *Homework: Historical and Contemporary Perspectives on Paid Labor at Home.* Urbana: University of Illinois Press, 1989.

Bourdieu, Pierre. *Distinction: A Social Critique of the Judgement of Taste.* Cambridge, MA: Harvard University Press, 1984.

Boydston, Jeanne. *Home and Work: Housework, Wages, and the Ideology of Labor in the Early Republic.* New York: Oxford University Press, 1990.

Breazeale, Kenon. "In Spite of Women: *Esquire* Magazine and the Construction of the Male Consumer." *Signs* 20, no. 1 (1994): 1–22. doi:10.1086/494952.

Cassidy, Marsha F. "Cyberspace Meets Domestic Space: Personal Computers, Women's Work, and the Gendered Territories of the Family Home." *Critical Studies in Media Communication* 18, no. 1 (2001): 44–64.

Casson, Herbert N. *The History of the Telephone.* Chicago: A. C. McClurg, 1911.

Castells, Manuel. *The Information Age: Economy, Society and Culture.* Vol. 1, *The Rise of the Network Society.* Malden, MA: Blackwell, 1996.

Clark, Clifford, Jr. "Domestic Architecture as an Index to Social History: The Romantic Revival and the Cult of Domesticity in America, 1840–1870." *Journal of Interdisciplinary History* 7, no. 1 (1976): 33–56.

Cohan, Steven. "So Functional for Its Purposes: The Bachelor Apartment in *Pillow Talk.*" In *Stud: Architectures of Masculinity,* edited by J. Sanders. New York: Princeton Architectural Press, 1996.

Cohen, Lizabeth. *A Consumers' Republic: The Politics of Mass Consumption in Postwar America.* New York: Vintage, 2003.

Conekin, Becky. "Fashioning the Playboy: Messages of Style and Masculinity in the Pages of *Playboy* Magazine, 1953–1963." *Fashion Theory* 4, no. 4 (2000): 447–466.

Conley, Dalton. *Elsewhere, U.S.A.: How We Got from the Company Man, Family Dinners, and the Affluent Society to the Home Office, BlackBerry Moms, and Economic Anxiety*. New York: Random House, 2009.

Coontz, Stephanie. *The Way We Never Were: American Families and the Nostalgia Trap*. New York: Basic Books, 2000.

Couldry, Nick, and Anna McCarthy, eds. *Media Space: Place, Scale and Culture in a Media Age*. London: Routledge, 2004.

Cowan, Ruth Schwartz. "The 'Industrial Revolution' in the Home: Household Technology and Social Change in the 20th Century." *Technology and Culture* 17, no. 1 (1976): 1–23.

Cromley, Elizabeth C. *Alone Together: A History of New York's Early Apartments*. Ithaca, NY: Cornell University Press, 1990.

———. "A History of American Beds and Bedrooms, 1890–1930." In *American Home Life, 1880–1930: A Social History of Spaces and Services*, edited by Jessica Foy and Thomas Schlereth, 120–143. Knoxville: University of Tennessee Press, 1992.

———. "Sleeping Around: A History of American Beds and Bedrooms; The Second Banham Memorial Lecture." *Journal of Design History* 3, no. 1 (1990): 1–17.

Danko, W. D. and J. M. MacLachlan. "Research to Accelerate the Diffusion of a New Invention." *Journal of Advertising Research* 23 (1983): 39–43.

Davies, Margery W. *Woman's Place Is at the Typewriter: Office Work and Office Workers, 1870–1930*. Philadelphia: Temple University Press, 1982.

De Certeau, Michel. *The Practice of Everyday Life*. Vol. 2. Translated by Timothy J. Tomasik. Minneapolis: University of Minnesota Press, 1998.

———. "Practices of Space." In *On Signs*, edited by Marshall Blonsky, 122–145. Baltimore: Johns Hopkins University Press, 1985.

Dutton, William, Everett M. Rogers, and Suk-Ho Jun. "Diffusion and Social Impacts of Personal Computers." *Communication Research* 14, no. 2 (1987): 219–250.

Featherstone, Mike. *Consumer Culture and Postmodernism*. Thousand Oaks, CA: Sage Publications, 2007.

Fischer, Claude S. *America Calling: A Social History of the Telephone to 1940*. Berkeley: University of California Press, 1992.

Florida, Richard. *The Rise of the Creative Class*. New York: Basic Books, 2003.

Frank, Thomas. *The Conquest of Cool: Business Culture, Counterculture, and the Rise of Hip Consumerism*. Chicago: University of Chicago Press, 1998.

Fraterrigo, Elizabeth. *Playboy and the Making of the Good Life in Modern America*. Oxford: Oxford University Press, 2009.

Freeman, Lance. *There Goes the 'Hood: Views of Gentrification from the Ground Up*. Philadelphia: Temple University Press, 2006.

Friedman, Avi, and David Krawitz. *Peeking through the Keyhole: The Evolution of North American Homes*. Montreal: McGill-Queen's University Press, 2001.

Giddens, Anthony. *The Consequences of Modernity*. Stanford, CA: Stanford University Press, 1990.

Gilbert, James. *Men in the Middle: Searching for Masculinity in the 1950s*. Chicago: University of Chicago Press, 2005.

Gill, Brian P., and Steven L. Schlossman. "A Nation at Rest: The American Way of Homework." *Educational Evaluation and Policy Analysis* 25, no. 3 (2003): 319–337.

Glass, Ruth. *London: Aspects of Change*. London: MacGibbon and Kee, 1964.

Gorman-Murray, Andrew. "Masculinity and the Home: A Critical Review and Conceptual Framework." *Australian Geographer* 39, no. 3 (2008): 367–369.

Graham, Laurel D. "Domesticating Efficiency: Lillian Gilbreth's Scientific Management of Homemakers, 1924–1930." *Signs* 24, no. 3 (1999): 633–675.

Habermas, Jürgen. *The Structural Transformation of the Public Sphere*. Cambridge, MA: MIT Press, 1989.

Haggins, Bambi L. "There's No Place Like Home: The American Dream, African-American Identity, and the Situation Comedy." *Velvet Light Trap* 43 (1999): 23–37.

Hall, Stuart, and Paul du Gay, eds. *Questions of Cultural Identity*. London: Sage Publications, 1996.

Haraway, Donna. "The Cyborg Manifesto." In *The Cultural Studies Reader*, edited by Simon During, 271–291. New York: Routledge, 1999.

Hardt, Michael, and Antonio Negri. *Empire*. Cambridge, MA: Harvard University Press, 2000.

Hareven, Tamara. "The Home and the Family in Historical Perspective." *Social Research* 58, no. 1 (1991): 253–285.

Harvey, David. *A Brief History of Neoliberalism*. Oxford: Oxford University Press, 2011.

———. *The Condition of Postmodernity: An Enquiry into the Origins of Cultural Change*. Oxford: Blackwell, 1991.

Hayden, Dolores. *Building Suburbia: Green Fields and Urban Growth, 1820–2000*. New York: Vintage, 2004.

Hobbs, Frank, and Nicole Stoops. *Demographic Trends in the 20th Century*. Census 2000 Special Reports, Series CENSR-4, U.S. Census Bureau. Washington, DC: U.S. Department of Commerce, 2002.

Hollows, Joanne. "The Bachelor Dinner: Masculinity, Class and Cooking in *Playboy*, 1953–1961." *Continuum* 16, no. 2 (2002): 143–155. doi:10.1080/10304310220138732.

Hudson, James R. *The Unanticipated City: Loft Conversions in Lower Manhattan*. Amherst: University of Massachusetts Press, 1987.

Hunter, James D. *Culture Wars: The Struggle to Control the Family, Art, Education, Law, and Politics in America*. New York: Basic Books, 1992.

Jackson, Kenneth T. *Crabgrass Frontier: The Suburbanization of the United States*. New York: Oxford University Press, 1985.

Jacobson, Lisa. "Allowances and Spending Money." In *Girlhood in America: An Encyclopedia*, vol. 1, edited by Miriam Forman-Brunell, 34–38. Santa Barbara, CA: ABC-CLIO, 2001.

Katz, Jonathan. *The Invention of Heterosexuality*. New York: Dutton, 1995.

Kelly, Barbara M. *Expanding the American Dream: Building and Rebuilding Levittown*. Albany: State University of New York Press, 1993.

Kohen, Yael. *We Killed: The Rise of Women in American Comedy*. New York: Sarah Crichton Books, 2012.

LaRossa, Ralph. *The Modernization of Fatherhood: A Social and Political History*. Chicago: University of Chicago Press, 1997.

Lears, T. J. Jackson. "From Salvation to Self-Realization." In *The Culture of Consumption: Critical Essays in American History, 1880–1980*, edited by Richard Wrightman Fox and T. J. Jackson Lears, 3–38. New York: Pantheon, 1983.

Lefebvre, H. *Critique of Everyday Life*. New York: Verso, 1991.

Lehman, Katherine J. *Those Girls: Single Women in Sixties and Seventies Popular Culture*. Lawrence: University Press of Kansas, 2011.

Leibman, Nina. *Living Room Lectures: The Fifties Family in Film and Television*. Austin: University of Texas Press, 1995.

Leppert, Alice. "Solving the Day-Care Crisis, One Episode at a Time: Family Sitcoms and Privatized Child Care in the 1980s." *Cinema Journal* 56, no. 2 (2017): 67–90.

Levine, Elana. *Wallowing in Sex: The New Sexual Culture of 1970s American Television*. Durham, NC: Duke University Press, 2007.

Ley, David. *The New Middle Class and the Remaking of the Central City*. Oxford: Oxford University Press, 1996.

Livingstone, Sonia. *Young People and New Media: Childhood and the Changing Media Environment*. New York: Sage Publications, 2002.

Mackay, Hughie, and Gareth Gillespie. "Extending the Social Shaping of Technology Approach: Ideology and Appropriation." *Social Studies of Science* 22, no. 4 (1992): 685–716.

Maines, Rachel. *Hedonizing Technologies: Paths to Pleasure in Hobbies and Leisure*. Baltimore: Johns Hopkins University Press, 2009.

Marinucci, Mimi. "Television, Generation X, and Third Wave Feminism: A Contextual Analysis of *The Brady Bunch*." *Journal of Popular Culture* 38, no. 3 (2005): 505–524.

Martin, Michèle. *Hello, Central? Gender, Technology, and Culture in the Formation of Telephone Systems*. Montreal: McGill-Queen's University Press, 1991.

May, Elaine Tyler. *Homeward Bound: American Families in the Cold War Era*. New York: Basic Books, 1999.

Miller, Russell. *Bunny: The Real Story of "Playboy."* New York: Holt, Rinehart and Winston, 1984.

Mintz, Steven, and Susan Kellogg. *Domestic Revolutions: A Social History of American Family Life*. New York: Free Press, 1989.

Mitchell, Edna. "Fathers and Home-Video Game Play." In *Personal Computers and the Family*, edited by Marvin B. Sussman, 127–128. New York: Haworth Press, 1985.

Moores, S. "The Doubling of Place: Electronic Media, Time-Space Arrangements and Social Relationships." In *Media Space: Place, Scale and Culture in a Media Age*, edited by Nick Couldry and Anna McCarthy, 21–36. London: Routledge, 2004.

Nash, Margaret A., and Lisa S. Romero. "'Citizenship for the College Girl': Challenges and Opportunities in Higher Education for Women in the United States in the 1930s." *Teachers College Record* 114, no. 2 (2012): 1–35.

Osgerby, Bill. "The Bachelor Pad as Cultural Icon: Masculinity, Consumption and Interior Design in American Men's Magazines, 1930–65." *Journal of Design History* 18, no. 1 (2005): 99–113.

Palladino, Grace. *Teenagers: An American History*. New York: Basic Books, 1996.

Picker, John. "The Soundproof Study Victorian Professionals, Work Space, and Urban Noise." *Victorian Studies* 42, no. 3 (1999/2000): 427–453.

Pitzulo, Carrie. *Bachelors and Bunnies: The Sexual Politics of "Playboy."* Chicago: University of Chicago Press, 2011.

Podmore, Julie. "(Re)Reading the 'Loft Living' Habitus in Montreal's Inner City." *International Journal of Urban and Regional Research* 22, no. 2 (1998): 283–302.

Pool, Ithiel S. *Forecasting the Telephone: A Retrospective Technology Assessment*. Norwood, NJ: Ablex, 1982.

Rakow, Lana F. "Gendered Technology, Gendered Practice." *Critical Studies in Media Communication* 5, no. 1 (1988): 57–70.

Rogers, Everett M. "The Diffusion of Home Computers among Households in Silicon Valley." *Marriage and Family Review* 8 (1985): 89–100.

Ross, Andrew. "Dot.com Urbanism." In *MediaSpace: Place, Scale, and Culture in a Media Age*, edited by Nick Couldry and Anna McCarthy, 145–162. London: Routledge, 2004.

———. *No-Collar: The Humane Workplace and Its Hidden Costs*. New York: Basic Books, 2002.

Sassen, Saskia. *The Global City: New York, London, Tokyo*. Princeton, NJ: Princeton University Press, 2001.

Schlereth, Thomas J. "Conduits and Conducts." In *American Home Life, 1880–1930: A Social History of Spaces and Services*, edited by Jessica H. Foy and Thomas J. Schlereth, 225–241. Knoxville: University of Tennessee Press, 1992.

Schulman, Bruce J. *The Seventies: The Great Shift in American Culture, Society, and Politics*. New York: Free Press, 2001.

Seidman, Steven. *Romantic Longings: Love in America, 1830–1980*. New York: Routledge, 1991.

Sennett, Richard. *The Conscience of the Eye: The Design and Social Life of Cities*. New York: Knopf, 1990.

Silverstone, Roger, Eric Hirsch, and David Morley. "Information and Communication Technologies and the Moral Economy of the Household." In *Consuming Technologies: Media and Information in Domestic Spaces*, edited by Roger Silverstone and Eric Hirsch, 9–17. London: Routledge, 1992.

Smith, Neil. *The New Urban Frontier: Gentrification and the Revanchist City*. London: Routledge, 1996.

Spigel, Lynn. *Make Room for TV: Television and the Family Ideal in Postwar America*. Chicago: University of Chicago Press, 1992.

———. *Welcome to the Dreamhouse: Popular Media and Postwar Suburbs*. Durham, NC: Duke University Press, 2001.

Spigel, Lynn, and Michael Curtin. *The Revolution Wasn't Televised: Sixties Television and Social Conflict*. New York: Routledge, 1997.

Sturken, Marita, and Lisa Cartwright. *Practices of Looking: An Introduction to Visual Culture*. 2nd ed. New York: Oxford University Press, 2009.

Tosh, John. *A Man's Place: Masculinity and the Middle-Class Home in Victorian England*. New Haven, CT: Yale University Press, 2007.

Vavrus, Mary Douglas. "Domesticating Patriarchy: Hegemonic Masculinity and Television's 'Mr. Mom.'" *Critical Studies in Media Communication* 19, no. 3 (2002): 352.

Vitalari, Nicholas P., Alladi Venkatesh, and Kjell Gronhaug. "Computing in the Home: Shifts in the Time Allocation Patterns of Households." *Communications of the Association for Computing Machinery (ACM)* 28 (1985): 512–522.

Vollmer, John L., Pamela A. Schulze, and Janice M. Chebra. "The American Master Bedroom: Its Changing Location and Significance to the Family." *Journal of Interior Design* 31, no. 1 (2005): 1–13.

Volz, Candace M. "The Modern Look of the Early Twentieth-Century House." In *American Home Life, 1880–1930: A Social History of Spaces and Services*, edited by Jessica H. Foy and Thomas J. Schlereth, 25–48. Knoxville: University of Tennessee Press, 1992.

Wagner, George. "The Lair of the Bachelor." In *Intimus: Interior Design Theory Reader*, edited by Mark Taylor, 375–379. London: Wiley-Academy, 2006.

Ward, Peter W. *A History of Domestic Space*. Vancouver: UBC Press, 1999.

Wasser, Frederick. *Veni, Vidi, Video: The Hollywood Empire and the VCR*. Austin: University of Texas Press, 2001.

Weiss, Jessica. *To Have and to Hold: Marriage, the Baby Boom, and Social Change*. Chicago: University of Chicago Press, 2000.

Wigley, Mark. "Untitled: The Housing of Gender." In *Sexuality and Space*, edited by Beatriz Colomina and Jennifer Bloomer, 327–379. Princeton, NJ: Princeton Architectural Press, 1992.

Wilkinson, Jennifer. "From the Bedroom to the Streets; Intimacy and the New Public Order." *DisClosure* 15, no. 1 (2006): 9–2.

Williams, Raymond. *Television: Technology and Cultural Form*, ed. Ederyn Williams. New York: Routledge, 2003.

———. *The Country and the City*. New York: Vintage Classics, 2016.

Wojcik, Pamela R. *The Apartment Plot: Urban Living in American Film and Popular Culture, 1945 to 1975*. Durham, NC: Duke University Press, 2010.

Wolfe, Tom. *The Pump House Gang*. New York: Farrar, Straus and Giroux, 1999.

Wright, Gwendolyn. *Building the Dream*. Cambridge, MA: MIT Press, 1988.

Wuthnow, Robert. *American Misfits and the Making of Middle-Class Respectability*. Princeton, NJ: Princeton University Press, 2017.

Zelizer, Viviana A. *Pricing the Priceless Child: The Changing Social Value of Children*. New York: Basic Books, 1985.

Zukin, Sharon. *Loft Living: Culture and Capital in Urban Change*. New Brunswick, NJ: Rutgers University Press, 1982.

INDEX

Page numbers in *italics* indicate a figure.

ABOUT THE AUTHOR

ELIZABETH A. PATTON is an assistant professor of media and communication studies at the University of Maryland, Baltimore County. Her research interests include media history, representations of urbanism and suburbanism in popular culture, and the impact of communication technologies on space. Her research can be found in the journals *Media History*, *Technology and Culture*, and the *New Review of Film and Television Studies*.